Enhancing Social Work Management

University of Connecticut

Enhancing Social Work Management

Theory and Best Practice from the UK and USA

Edited by Jane Aldgate, Lynne Healy,
Barris Malcolm, Barbara Pine,
Wendy Rose and Janet Seden

Jessica Kingsley Publishers
London and Philadelphia

First published in 2007
by Jessica Kingsley Publishers
116 Pentonville Road
London N1 9JB, UK
and
400 Market Street, Suite 400
Philadelphia, PA 19106, USA

www.jkp.com

Library of Congress Cataloging in Publication Data
Enhancing social work management : theory and best practice from the UK and USA / edited by Jane
Aldgate ... [et al.].
    p. cm.
Includes bibliographical references and index.
ISBN 978-1-84310-515-2 (alk. paper)
    1. Human services--Great Britain--Management. 2. Human services--United States--Management. 3.
Social work administration--Great Britain. 4. Social work administration--United States. 5. Great
Britain--Social policy--1979- 6. United States--Social policy--1993- I. Aldgate, Jane, 1945-
    HV245.E55 2007
    361.3068--dc22
                                          2006039572

British Library Cataloguing in Publication Data
A CIP catalogue record for this book is available from the British Library

ISBN 978 1 84310 515 2

Printed and bound in Great Britain by
Athenaeum Press, Gateshead, Tyne and Wear

Contents

List of Figures

List of Tables

List of Boxes

Acknowledgements

We are grateful to many people who helped us with this book. Special thanks go to Kay Davidson, Dean of the University of Connecticut School of Social Work and Lesley-Anne Cull, Dean of the Faculty of Health and Social Care at The Open University, for supporting the concordat between our two institutions that led to this book and providing continuing support and encouragement. We would also like to thank others from The Open University: Mick Jones and Gill Gowans who helped us in the production process to publication and Anne Bullman who helped us in the earlier stages of production. We could not have progressed without her support. We want to express our gratitude to Richard Whipp from the University of Wales, Cardiff, whose outstanding paper on issues in social work management inspired us in the early stages of the book's formation. We also would like to thank the social work students we have taught over the years, who have shared case examples and enhanced our understanding of management practice. The same goes for the many practitioners and managers from whom we have learnt so much. We are grateful to Stephen Jones from Jessica Kingsley Publishers, who was immensely encouraging and helpful throughout.

The Editors

Introduction

Jane Aldgate and Barbara A. Pine

Sometimes books come about by serendipity. The idea for this book derived from a visit to the School of Social Work, University of Connecticut, by one of the UK editors, Jane Aldgate. During that visit, in conversations with Dean Kay Davidson, Barbara Pine, Lynne Healy and Myron Weiner, the idea was conceived of developing a formal concordat between the School of Social Work at the University of Connecticut and the School of Health and Social Welfare at The Open University (now Faculty of Health and Social Care) in recognition of the common ground between the two institutions. The aim was to ferment exchanges of ideas and look for opportunities to work together on projects. The concordat was formally endorsed by the Deans of both Schools in 2002.

At that time, five of the Open University (OU) contributors to the book, Jill Reynolds (as Chair), Janet Seden (Chair in presentation), Jane Aldgate, Wendy Rose and Vivien Martin were engaged in the development of an OU distance learning course, Managing Care (K303). Sheila Peace contributed to the course materials and Trish Ross provided practice examples. John Harris has been external examiner for K303 from 2003 to the present. Wendy Rose had worked closely with Julie Barnes on a number of projects for the government in England. Barbara Pine, Lynne Healy and Myron Weiner held an international reputation for their work on human services management. Barbara Pine was heading the Administration concentration in the Master's program at the School of Social Work in Connecticut and, along with Lynne Healy and Myron

Weiner, the teaching team included Barris Malcolm. The School's academic team had connections with senior academics who were experts in human services management in other universities in the US, including Mark Ezell and Robert Madden, and with Peter Petrella, a member of the School of Social Work who is also a practising manager. And so this book was conceived as the first formal exemplar of the concordat between our two schools. Though long in its gestation, it has come together at a time when social work management in both countries has never been more important to the standards of the profession.

During the period of writing the book, there have been significant changes in the administration of the UK through devolution. Although Northern Ireland is, at the time of writing, administered from Westminster, Scotland and Wales now have their own national legislative assemblies. The Scottish Parliament, re-established in 1999 after 300 years of administration from Westminster, has responsibility for governance on most matters through the Scottish Executive, except for issues such as taxation, immigration and the security of the realm. Scotland develops its own policies on all health and social issues. Though Wales still works closely with England, cultural differences are being asserted through publication of all formal documents bilingually in Welsh and the Welsh Assembly Government, established in 2000, is increasingly developing its own statutory instruments specifically for implementation in Wales. These changes have affected the presentation of material in this book from the UK perspective and we have been careful to identify where policies are discrete to different countries. Inevitably, because of the location of the authors, there is a bias towards developments in England, although we have endeavoured to include comparative material from the other countries.

There is always a tension in international collaborations about the use of language. There is a well-known saying sometimes attributed to G.B. Shaw, that 'England and America are two nations separated by a common language.' We have endeavoured to address this by respecting each other's use of the English language and terms of reference, adding explanations where necessary. So throughout the book, we alternate between human services management, social work and social care management. Each country's authors have retained their country's spelling and grammar but where there are common international usages of spelling we have adopted the US versions.

There are one or two significant differences in the organization of social work in the two countries, to which we would like to draw attention. In the US, social work is divided between public social work services and not-for-profit and private agencies. The most important difference in the UK is that public social work services are offered within organizations called local authorities. Not only are these local government umbrella organizations responsible for social work but for a whole range of local government services, from education to the maintenance of roads, and other services affecting the infrastructure of local living such as policing. Local authorities work closely with National Health Service Trusts. Recently the law has been changed so that social work can also be offered within primary local health care provision. There are also not-for-profit (voluntary) agencies and some private agencies but local authority social services are the dominant partner.

In spite of local differences, what has emerged in the life of producing the book are common themes and values in social work management on both sides of the Atlantic, such as leadership, ethics, participation and diversity. Responding to change and demands for accountability and 'results-oriented management' are other shared themes. There are also pockets of originality in research that have produced new takes on old themes, such as the importance of the management of space, the tracking of policy implementation and development of expertise in managing finance and developing technology. What we have done, therefore, is to draw together the themes into an anthology of chapters. Some emphasize the academic and research developments in social work and social care management; others emphasize innovations or developments in policy and practice. In short, the chapters as a whole attempt to balance theory and practice as the title promises.

Mindful that the book is likely to be read by students of management and practising managers, most of the 12 chapters in the book contain real-life case examples that serve to illustrate their main themes or points. While there are many similarities in the provision of social services in the UK and the US, the legal and organizational contexts are quite different. The reader will notice that case material the authors have used reflects these differences. Where possible and relevant, case material from one context has been added to chapters whose main focus is on the other. Moreover, while the book focuses on the US and the UK, we hope the material is of interest to social work and social care managers in other places as the trends discussed are related to globalization and its impacts everywhere.

The book begins with a chapter by John Harris in which he explores the concept of 'new public management' with its increased emphasis on more economic, efficient and effective services. This overarching force affecting social services has taken different routes in the US and the UK but with similar outcomes in both including: increased competition, contracting out for services, increased attention to consumerism (involving service-users), increased scrutiny and accountability, requirements for measurable and sometimes pre-set outcomes, increased productivity (higher workloads) and more rationing of resources. These trends and changes have produced new challenges and opportunities for social work/social care managers, accompanied by greater complexity of their roles. Thus Harris sets the stage for the remainder of the book, whose chapters reflect these challenges and opportunities and suggest strategies for managing them successfully.

In Chapter 2 Barbara Pine and Lynne Healy discuss leadership theory and practice as it has evolved over the past century. Then they focus on more current forms of leadership, namely transformational leadership, its relevance for social work and social care managers and the roles they play in involving other agency stakeholders in a wide range of managerial activities. Case examples illustrate leadership in activities that engage staff, board members, clients, volunteers and others in program design and evaluation, continuous quality improvement and strategic planning.

In Chapter 3 Julie Barnes focuses on one of the trends Harris identifies – increased scrutiny – to describe new performance assessment processes, called star ratings, for public services in the UK and their impact on managers. After reviewing a wide range of empirical data on performance success and failure, Barnes presents and illustrates an agency-wide organization development intervention called Appreciative Inquiry as a solution to turning around an agency given a low 'star rating'. A unique feature of Appreciative Inquiry, as an action research and feedback organizational development strategy, is its focus on maximizing and expanding what works in the organization: in short, maximizing the positive.

Chapter 4, by Lynne Healy and Barbara Pine, features an often overlooked yet essential topic in management texts: ethics and the importance of ethical management practice. The increasing complexity of management and leadership roles means that social work and social care managers often face competing obligations and must be able to weigh multiple options in making moral choices. In addition to ethical decision-making, moral managers must also set a climate in which others can make ethical decisions and ensure that there is congruence between the code of ethics and their agency's practices. The chapter describes a number of tools that managers can use to increase their ability to engage in ethical reflection and judgement.

Vivien Martin, in Chapter 5, explores the growing demand for interagency collaboration and partnerships that offer 'wraparound' or more seamless services to people in need as one strategy for improved service quality. In looking at some of the obstacles to service integration, Martin draws a set of principles and values from a national charter in the UK on interagency working, in particular client involvement in planning and evaluating services, to illustrate this new trend and its implications for managers.

In Chapter 6 Barris Malcolm presents the challenges and the moral mandate of creating and managing a diverse workforce in the increasingly diverse social contexts of the UK and the US. He begins with a review of many of the theoretical underpinnings of racism, social exclusion, diversity and multiculturalism, and past approaches to dealing with diversity, mainly with regard to social agency staff. He then discusses the notion of diversity competence as it applies to individual staff members and the organization as a whole.

Robert Madden, in Chapter 7, stresses the need for social work and social care managers to become legally competent, calling this as important a management competence as, say, diversity or cultural competence. Following a discussion of how the human services are shaped by legal principles, Madden delineates the requisite knowledge and skills of legal competence. A related theme in this chapter is safety. The chapter also provides guidelines for the creation and management of a safe, risk-free environment for clients and staff.

Chapter 8, by Jill Reynolds and Sheila Peace, broadens the discussion of environment positing that the environment in care settings (e.g. care homes) is bounded within space, place, time and behaviour. The topic of the environment of a social agency is rarely present in management texts and in training curricula. Yet the physical environment is an important factor in the wellbeing of both clients and staff. Reynolds and Peace discuss such issues as privacy and territorial ownership and provide several case examples of management intervention into space issues.

In Chapter 9 Janet Seden and Trish Ross relate the new push for accountability – more scrutiny according to Harris – to greater involvement of clients and consumers of services in their design and management. They provide case examples to show the challenges and rewards of involving parents in family support and child care programs and lay out a set of principles for greater client involvement.

The wide-ranging impact of new technology on social services is the topic of Chapter 10, by Myron Weiner and Peter Petrella. In it they discuss the possibilities and opportunities available to social work and social care managers to put technology to work in their human services organizations. The authors present guidelines for considering and planning for the agency's technology needs and for implementing systems that work to strengthen all aspects and dimensions of its services. They stress that managing information through technology is as important as managing money or people when it comes to achieving the agency's mission.

Mark Ezell, in Chapter 11, focuses on managing money, which in the new funding and policy context of human services means diverse sources of funds. Greater diversity of funding sources creates more complex accounting practices and adherence to a wider range of requirements. After reviewing some of the funding sources and strategies and their limitations, Ezell presents a set of guidelines and management practices designed to help social work and social care managers to stay on mission and out of financial trouble.

In reviewing the lessons learned from the results of their extensive case study of policy implementation in a local authority, Wendy Rose, Jane Aldgate and Julie Barnes in Chapter 12, the book's final chapter, tie together a number of themes addressed by contributors to this book. Their case study examined local implementation of the national Assessment Framework for Children in Need and their Families, introduced in England in 2000 and Wales a year later. They found that success depended upon ethical practice, having good information technology and other systems in place, collaboration with other agencies and having strong, involved, staff-oriented leaders able to effectively implement change.

We hope this book draws attention to the need to prepare social workers for management roles in social services everywhere. Such specialist training is essential if the social work profession is to maintain, and in some cases regain, its leadership of services designed to meet human needs. Social work leadership can ensure that these services are consistent with social work values and are delivered by organizations using modern management techniques such as those presented in the following chapters.

Chapter 1

Looking Backward, Looking Forward: Current Trends in Human Services Management

John Harris

Introduction

The suggestion that there are 'trends' in human services management implies movement, not only towards somewhere but also away from somewhere; it suggests processes of destabilization, as well as possibilities of reform. What has been destabilized is a view of the management of public and voluntary or not-for-profit agencies as being essentially administrative. There has been a move away from seeing management as a form of custodianship or stewardship, aimed at keeping going what was already there. The traditional distinction between administration of social services and private business management rested on the assumption that the ethos of social services was very different to that of private business and the management of those services had to be grounded in an understanding of their specific purposes, conditions and tasks. This administrative approach to the management of social services was founded on respect for professionalism: its knowledge base and its identification of what was considered to be professionally correct practice. Administrative management was superimposed on professionalism through structures that were hierarchical and through rules and procedures within and through which professionalism operated. Within this administrative framework, professional staff were accorded areas of discretion within their practice. This view of management required managers to take on a number of responsibilities: for themselves, individual staff, groups of staff, training, resources and relationships with people outside and in other parts of the organization (Harris and Kelly 1992).

From the 1980s onwards, there have been pressures for change away from this administrative approach to management. In many countries this has stemmed from stressing the need for national competitiveness in response to economic globalization (Flynn and Strehl 1996), resulting in increased attention being given to ideas derived from the market, appeals to the superiority of the private sector (Flynn 2000) and the lessons it might teach to other sectors. In these national contexts, public expenditure has usually been depicted as a burden that needs to be at least contained and preferably reduced (Flynn 2000; Milner and Joyce 2005).

In parallel to concerns about costs, publicly provided services have been criticized for inflexibility and inefficiency and voluntary agencies have been regarded as more likely to provide services that are responsive. In addition, it has been claimed that a more discerning public has emerged that experiences high levels of service in the market and demands correspondingly high levels of service from public and voluntary agencies (see Flynn and Strehl 1996, pp.17–18), rather than the mass processing identified by Lipsky (1980). In the US, privatization of social services has extended to increased use of for-profit, proprietary firms for service delivery as a result of the philosophy that the business sector is particularly efficient (Karger and Stoesz 2006). Such arguments have led to an overall trend away from administrative approaches to managing (Minogue, Polidano and Hulme 1998) and call for a transformation of social services management.

This chapter explores the form of management that has emerged, usually referred to as 'new public management'. It then considers the development of new public management in an international context and explores specific aspects of developments in the US and the UK.

New public management

In the transformational discourse that often accompanies new public management – with injunctions to managers to shift from conformance to performance, for example – it is often forgotten that management is about continuity as well as change. Managers, as we shall see, may be urged by new public management to do things differently, but they also still have to keep things running. The coverage of a recent book of over 500 pages on managing public services makes this combination of old and new, of continuity and change, very clear in the topics it adopts. These include:

- managing in the changing context
- managing resistance to change
- managing strategy and change
- managing the market
- managing quality
- managing groups and leading teams
- managing leadership and motivation
- managing individuals
- managing budgets
- managing resources
- managing audit, accountability and performance
- managing information and communication
- managing learning
- managing personal development. (Doherty and Horne 2005)

Despite the need for continuity in management, 'new public management' is a term that has been used predominantly to describe changes that have either taken place or are seen as necessary in public (and increasingly in voluntary) social services (and other services) in many parts of the world. New public management arose from extensive expectations being placed on what 'management' had to offer to social services, as part of a wider assumption that better management would 'prove an effective solvent for a wide range of economic and social ills' (Pollitt 1993, p.1). The search for better management for the public and voluntary sectors focused on the world of private business in the belief that a generic model of management, which minimized the differences between managing private businesses and delivering social services, would hold the key to improving the performance of the latter. There is an alternative view, expressed in much of the social work management literature in the US, that 'social welfare management is a distinctive variant of general management' and requires special knowledge and skills (Patti 2000, p.7). Nonetheless, the urge to learn from the private sector led to the language of the private sector increasingly being found in the public and voluntary sectors. For example, the much-publicized reductions in crime achieved by the New York Police Department were referred to by William Bratton, the Police Commissioner, as 'the public sector equivalent of profit' (Milner and Joyce 2005, p.48). Although it has been argued in both the US (Moore 2002) and the UK (Leach, Stewart and Walsh 1994; Pollitt 2003) that the contexts and purposes of private businesses are very different from those of other sectors, the enthusiasm for a generic model of management has been widespread. A widely expressed view about the public sector, for example, has been that it has lagged behind and needs to catch up with the private sector (see Milner and Joyce 2005, p.1).

The impact of private management ideas on public social services

As far as social services are concerned, the relevant dimensions of new public management are its emphasis on contracting out service delivery from the public sector to the private and voluntary sectors and applying ideas drawn from private business management that focus on securing more economic, efficient and effective services (Hood 1991; Karger and Stoesz 2006). Underpinning these dimensions is new public management's privileging of managers, rather than professionals, and an insistence on managers' 'right to manage' in order to improve performance and bring about change, with 'a high degree of prominence placed upon the achievement of targets, the attainment of pre-ordained

service levels and a high degree of emphasis placed upon efficiency'
(Milner and Joyce 2005, p.49).

In an early and very influential formulation, Osborne and Gaebler
(1992) argued for public sector managers to be set free to achieve the
goals set for them by politicians on behalf of the people who had elected
them. Such managers were no longer meant to operate as custodians of
the work of professionals but rather were proactively to seek the achievement of managerial goals, pushing down priorities from the top of the
organization (Flynn 1999; Kirkpatrick, Ackroyd and Walker 2005) by
separating strategic from operational management (see Harris 2003,
pp.64–65).

The promise of private sector approaches was that strategic proactive
management, combined with competition amongst suppliers of services
such as voluntary agencies, would result in increased productivity, as a
consequence of holding down resource allocation and maintaining or
improving the quality of services (Pollitt 1993; Flynn and Strehl 1996).
Increasingly, the means adopted to pursue greater productivity was contracting, with high levels of accountability for contract compliance.
Contracts have been part of a wider emphasis on performance management, including the setting of targets and auditing whether they have
been reached. Overall, nothing less than a wholesale shift in culture was
seen as the imperative towards which management should be steering
organizations.

Service-users as customers

A key dimension in achieving radical culture change is the belief that
responsiveness to consumer preferences is central to improving the experience of services and increasing organizational effectiveness. Users of
services are seen more as customers: individuals whose relationship to
services is based on the extent of their satisfaction with the services they
receive. A typical example of this belief is provided by an influential
report from Al Gore, when he was the vice president in the Clinton era.
The report emphasized 'putting customers first' and envisioned a system
where customers have 'a voice and a choice', the latter being delivered
through service organizations competing on the basis of market mechanisms. The report called for services to respond to their users' preferences

in a way that satisfied them (quoted in Aberbach and Christensen 2005, p.235). There are echoes of Gore's report in a recent speech by a British government minister, indicating the similarity and longevity of such rhetoric:

> Empowering public service users themselves is…essential…that is why the Government must now focus on customer satisfaction as a key driving force in public service improvement… The Cabinet Office is exploring the possibility of developing a new standard measurement system that can identify and then track how satisfied customers are with the public services they get…this will be a powerful force for change from the ground up – showing which areas of public services are leading the way in providing a good service to customers and which need to improve. (Hutton 2005)

Trends that have had an impact on managers

The cumulative effect of new public management has been to produce a number of trends that have impacted on managers.

Competition

As we have seen, there is a belief that competition between (public, commercial and voluntary) social services providers results in more economical, efficient and effective services. Managers of provider agencies have to position their services in the competitive framework provided by (quasi-)markets. Other managers act as purchasers of services.

Contracting

Managers are often in working relationships characterized by a purchaser-provider split, in which, in the last instance, control resides with the purchaser. This clear separation in the roles of purchaser and provider is implemented through the use of contracts. The use of contracts ensures that the purchasing manager has the power to require the provider to deliver the contracted services to specified standards of quality, quantity and price. The provider manager has to comply with the contract.

Consumerism

Managers have to pay attention to feedback from users of their services and to involve them as much as possible in their choice of service and the manner in which it is delivered.

Performance indicators

Managers have been increasingly compelled to be preoccupied with measurable standards and pre-set output measures in the monitoring of social services' performance, either as part of contracts or as part of wider accountability to government or other funders.

More work

The underlying message, rarely explicitly articulated in the UK, is that managers have to deliver more for less by getting more work out of people and working harder themselves. Similarly, more-for-less is the new mantra in American workplaces, both public and private.

Increased scrutiny

Information technology systems allow detailed specification of social services tasks and checks on their completion, as Myron Weiner and Peter Petrella discuss in Chapter 10. Managers may be involved in monitoring the use of manuals, directions and guidelines that limit professional discretion and set up standardized and repetitive systems, with tightly defined criteria for eligibility to services, standardized assessment tools, interventions which are often determined in advance from a limited list, minimization of contact time and pressure for throughput.

Gate-keeping and rationing

Managers have been increasingly charged with these functions and with getting other workers to see themselves as micro-managers of resources who carefully control access to and ration the distribution of services.

The impact of 'Best Value' policies

In the UK, 'Best Value' has played a prominent role in the intensification of management in social (and other) services. Managers have been required to deliver continuous improvements in quality and cost since 1 April 2000 'by the most effective, economic and efficient means possible' (Local Government Act 1999, Annex A). (Addressing financial issues is explored further in Chapter 11 by Mark Ezell). The four principles set out as underpinning 'Best Value' encapsulate the key dimensions of new public management that have engaged managers' attention, to varying degrees, around the world:

- challenge (why and how a service is provided)
- compare (with others' performance, including the use of performance indicators in benchmarking exercises)
- consult (local taxpayers, service-users and the business community in setting performance targets)
- competition (as the means to efficient and effective services). (Department of the Environment, Transport and the Regions 1998)

The international context

New public management's ideas and the practices that stem from them have received widespread international attention, usually as an aspect of a political rationale concerning the pressure on nation states to reform their welfare systems in response to the demands for competitiveness in the global economy. This rationale is used to subordinate social services to the creation of economic and political conditions that will ensure international competitiveness and is linked to maintaining the conditions necessary for profitability in order to avert capital flight and to attract new investment from multinational corporations and international finance capital. Globalization is often represented as an uncontradictory, uncontrollable, unitary phenomenon to which nation states must adapt in ways required by private business. The academic accounts of geographical regions and individual countries that have been engaged in reform are staggering in their scope, for example:

Europe (Cousins 2005); Scandinavia, Continental Europe, Australia, New Zealand, Canada, the US, Latin America, East Asia and Central and Eastern Europe (Esping-Andersen 1998); Australia, Canada, Finland, France, Germany, the Netherlands, New Zealand, Sweden, the UK and the US (Pollitt and Bouckaert 2000). Within the overall scope of such studies, there has been sustained interest in some of the anglophone countries, as they are considered to have moved more decisively in the direction of new public management, initially under the influence of 'free market' policies. Taylor and his contributors, for example, considered the social effects of 1980s free market policies on the UK, Australia, the US and New Zealand (Taylor 1990), the four countries usually cited as the standard bearers for new public management.

The globalization of changes

Although the origins of new public management lay predominantly in these anglophone countries, its effects eddied out across the world:

> The radical public sector reform programmes of the 1980s that began in the UK, the USA, Australia and New Zealand have fostered a wave of reform in developed, developing and transitional countries. (Minogue et al. 1998, p.xv)

International organizations like the World Bank, the International Monetary Fund (IMF) and the Organization for Economic Cooperation and Development (OECD) have played a crucial role in this wave of reform by representing the demands for management changes as stemming from a global ideological consensus around a universal model of efficient and effective management (Deacon, Hulse and Stubbs 1997; Common 1998). Countries with widely divergent economic and political systems appeared to be swept into the wave of reform, including: Ghana, Uganda, Vietnam (Minogue et al. 1998); Mexico, Argentina, India, Senegal (Ferguson, Lavalette and Whitmore 2005). However, in developing countries, implementation has been at best patchy (Minogue 1998; Polidano, Hulme and Minogue 1998; Manning 2001; McCourt and Minogue 2001). The early confidence of some writers, such as Osborne and Gaebler (1992), in a convergence process, through which there would be an inevitable and global movement towards a single model of new public management, was quickly reconsidered (Dunleavy and Hood 1994).

Diverse policies and practices

Most writers no longer regard new public management as a unified body of ideas, policies and practices but as a broader process of change, pursued by different countries for different reasons and along different routes:

> There should, therefore, be a measure of doubt as to whether the adoption of these practices represents a universal trend to some homogeneous private and public style of management that is being forced on all states by the economic and social consequences of globalisation. (Chandler 2000, p.255)

As indicators of variation, Pollitt points out that, in New Zealand and the UK, management reform followed economic crises, whereas the government of Finland introduced reforms when the Finnish economy was doing well and Clinton's National Performance Review in the US, partly inspired by his advisers Osborne and Gaebler, took place during a period of sustained economic boom (see Pollitt 2003, p.36). Ferlie *et al.* (1996) also noted variations in the practice of new public management, observing that whilst there was an increasing role for managers in services in many parts of the world, the nature of the role varied with local history, culture and politics and was not related to one political ideology. For example, although new public management is often though of as a creature of the political Right, in New Zealand it was adopted by the Labour Party.

Pollitt and Bouckaert, with a particular focus on the quality agenda in new public management, found a trend away from administrative approaches to management but also registered the existence of diversity (1995). In an in-depth study of seven European countries (the UK, the Netherlands, Sweden, France, Germany, Austria and Switzerland), Flynn and Strehl (1996) found management trends towards decentralized services, performance targets and measurement, consumerism and cost reduction but differences concerning politics and culture that resulted in different patterns of management.

The accrued evidence suggests that although new public management represents a broad trend that has had a wide influence on reforms in many countries, 'the interpretation and implementation...have been far patchier, messier, diverse and reversible...' (Pollitt 2003, p.38). Some writers suggest that in order to make sense of this messiness, it is crucially important to pay attention to the significance of local conditions and national institutions (see Esping-Andersen 1998, p.6; Flynn 2000, pp.36–38). In any event:

> The new PM...is a rather chameleon-like and paradoxical creature – something that springs up for different reasons in different places; that is 'edited', 'translated' or 'customised' for each different context in which it is introduced...that simultaneously promises managers more freedom, politicians more control and public service users more choice. (Pollitt 2003, p.26)

Whilst there has been this emphasis on 'path dependency' in the development of new public management in particular countries, with governance regimes and institutional arrangements figuring strongly in determining different outcomes in different national contexts (Harris and McDonald 2000; McDonald, Harris and Wintersteen 2003), two countries whose paths have overlapped more than most have been the UK and the US, with Esping-Andersen bracketing the US and UK together as examples of the liberal welfare regime in his classificatory scheme (Esping-Andersen 1990), Pollitt noting a 'striking uniformity' in management trends in the two countries (Pollitt 1993, p.21) and other authors seeing new public management as an Anglo-American phenomenon (Flynn and Strehl 1996, p.6; Kirkpatrick *et al.* 2005, p.13; Mishra 1999). The overlapping management agendas could be seen as part of a wider affinity between the two countries, symbolized by a succession of political pairings: Reagan–Thatcher (the originators of neo-liberal market economics and the politics of the New Right), Clinton–Blair (proponents of the 'Third Way') and Bush–Blair.

The US

Human services in the US were constructed within its particular regime of welfare, reflecting the valorization of particular personal dispositions such as individualism and self-reliance. A large voluntary sector has coexisted with public services since the early days of social work. Developments in the American version of new public management have not destabilized this underlying regime. Rather, they have exposed and cemented the core orientation. The configuration of social services found in the US emerged from a set of normative values that reflected the immigrant history of the country and the accompanying mythology that continues to influence their development (Jansson 2001). The people who went to the US did so in search of self-advancement and/or protection from oppressive political regimes. They assumed that they would have to work independently to succeed and assumed that others would do so as well. Independence and self-reliance were, and remain, much celebrated.

In contrast to the somewhat culturally marginalized position of public social services, the US has played the lead role in the production of management ideas and practices and their dispersal around the world (Grey and Antonacopoulou 2004; Chandler 2000). This leadership role is illustrated by the sub-title of a book concerned with organization and innovation: *Guru Schemes and American Dreams* (Knights and McCabe 2003). It extends to the social services sector as reflected in books such as *Total Quality Management in Human Service Organizations* (Martin 1993).

It could be argued that it should come as no surprise that management ideas have emerged from a country in which 'the great majority of citizens accept the values of a free economy with limited state intervention' (see Chandler 2000, pp.201–202 and Taylor 1990, p.299) and which has been the 'home base' for the neo-liberal politics (Clarke 2004, p.103) that led initially to new public management. In many parts of the world, the language of new public management is American-English, with its terminology often not translated into local languages (Flynn and Strehl 1996). Although the US has played the leading role in the deployment of new public management, it has done so in an overall national context of services that have been patchy, limited and (relatively) underfunded (Clarke 2004). In addition, service provision is complex, with 'myriad functions, layers and different types of organisations competing for resources' (Fabricant and Burghardt 1992, p.116).

In chapter 4 of his book *Managerialism and the Public Services* Pollitt (1993) provides a history of the development of public management in the US. He sees the failures of Planning, Programing and Budgeting Systems (extended by Johnson from the Department of Defense to the rest of the federal government in 1965), and what he claims as the failures of the War on Poverty and the Great Society programs of the 1960s as crucial in providing fuel for the right's arguments in favour of a new approach to management. (The successes of the anti-poverty programs such as Head Start are overlooked in the arguments against services provided by government.) Jimmy Carter criticized federal waste in his 1976 campaign and began to undertake reforms following his election. In the aftermath of the OPEC crisis in the mid-1970s, the economic drain of the Vietnam war and the rise in global competition, economic growth, corporate profits and manufacturing fell in almost every Western industrialized country (see Fabricant and Fisher 2002, p.65). These developments gave added impetus to Reagan in his 1980 campaign, following a similar pattern to Carter by criticizing federal waste. When in power, Reagan set up the 'Grace Commission' (1982–1984) to seek ways of improving management and reducing costs. Through the Commission, more than 2000 business men and women were invited into the federal government to improve its management. The message was clear: best management practice was in the private sector and was transferable to the public sector. As Pollitt (1993, p.181) points out, Thatcher and Reagan had broadly similar ideologies and wanted to introduce more business-derived practices into services that were seen as inefficient. One of the differences in the situations they confronted was that managerial approaches already occupied a more prominent and accepted place in US life.

By the early 1990s 'state and city governments everywhere confront[ed] the fiscal and political consequences of recession and federal abandonment…despite claims about "a thousand points of light", community resources are flickering' (Epstein 1992, p.ix). This was a reference to suggestions that charity and altruism could supplant public financing. In the mid-1990s, the 'Contract with America', initiated by Republicans in Congress, endorsed further cuts in social services, leaving many voluntary agencies 'with the triple threat of reduced funding from every level of government – city, state and federal' (Fabricant and Fisher 2002, p.8). The funding that remained was (and remains to the present day) largely dispensed through purchase of service contracts (ibid., p.81). In the early 1990s, Smith and Lipsky (1993) showed how voluntary agencies were being affected by heightened demand and decreasing resources, emphasizing that it was not that voluntary agencies were experiencing a simple redefinition of performance measures; they were being expected to do more with less (and see Fabricant and Fisher 2002, p.5), coupled with heightened and time-consuming demands for accountability (ibid., p.82).

Ginsberg (2001) added to the debate by referring to a 'revolution in accountability' in describing the shift to outcome-focused programs in the human services. However, this has been a 'protracted revolution, as pressures for increased accountability have been building for several decades' (Pine, Healy and Maluccio 2002, p.86). The impact of managed care approaches to health and mental health services have further increased the emphasis on measurable service outcomes and time-limited service. For almost 20 years, results and outcomes have been dominant themes in the literature of social work/human service management in the US and have spawned new approaches such as the logic model (see, for example, Hudson 1988; Wahl 1993; Mika 1996; Kettner, Moroney and Martin 1999; Alter and Egan 1997; Mullen and Magnabosco 1997).

The major trends affecting the management of social services in the US, then, are the recurrent mantra concerning the need to curb 'big government' by reining in spending, and the rigours of purchase of service contracts. This presents a challenging context for social services managers.

The UK

Whilst the US experienced substantial continuity in the trend towards new public management, in the UK its arrival represented a substantial break with the past. The central principle underpinning the establishment of Britain's post-war welfare state was that citizens had collective obligations for each other's welfare through the agency of the state (Marshall 1963). The tension between market-generated inequality and the democratic political system was to be managed by the state through the provision of social rights to health, education, housing, income maintenance and social services. One representation of this regime is that it produced 'client-citizens' (Roche 1987, p.369), with the state as the 'caretaker' of their social existence (Keane 1988, p.4). There was a heavy reliance on professionalism as the vehicle for service delivery. The state was considered to be a guarantor of provision that would be professional and managed administratively, subject to democratic political control, as central government legislation was implemented through local government structures and policies.

The introduction of new public management in the UK emerged in the aftermath of the OPEC crisis and the 'Winter of Discontent' from a direct ideological attack by the Thatcher government on the post-war settlement, with an 'emphasis on achieving revolutionary change [and] dismantling existing structures' (Kirkpatrick et al. 2005, p.15). This attack was aimed at discrediting the social democratic approach to social services provision through local government agencies. The strengthening of central government (vis-à-vis local government) and changes in the mechanics of funding and delivery were therefore inseparable from the rejection of the social democratic welfare state and the promotion of a form of new public management in which, preferably, state provision was to be avoided. In England, local government social services became metaphors for the ills of the welfare state and a radical legislative program led to the implementation of a market-oriented strategy built upon the use of contracting and an enhanced role for voluntary agencies. The utilization of 'management' was a political choice that involved a claim to management's possession of distinctive and valuable expertise. That claim to expertise was used to dictate the direction social services should take.

Given that the origins of new public management lay in the agenda of the Conservative governments from the early 1980s onwards, when New Labour came into office in 1997 it inherited social services in which new public management was firmly entrenched. In response, New Labour positioned itself as the 'Third Way', which was presented as a depoliticized position within which objective choices could be made. On taking power, this enabled the New Labour government to take over the 'objective' language and practices of new public management from the New Right and to continue to support its key ideas, such as the setting of explicit targets for services, performance monitoring and the use of market or market-type mechanisms. However, the Labour government also developed its own distinctive twists to new public management, involving the use of more sophisticated performance measures, greater emphasis on partnership (Glendenning *et al.* 2002), longer planning cycles linked to longer-term goals and targets, a greater emphasis on using management to achieve policy goals, rather than as an end in itself, and the use of concepts derived from business practice such as 'stakeholders' (Cutler and Waine 2000; Newman 2005).

New Labour's preferred discourse is 'modernization'. A belief in management is a key aspect of this discourse, particularly in its identification of the need for 'continual improvement' (see 'Best Value' above) and the imperative for public and voluntary agencies to become more managerially attuned to the private, profit-making sector. The pursuit of continual improvement involves strict regulation of social services and re-visioning government as the guardian (but not the direct implementer) of the social interest (Freeden 1999, p.49). Accordingly, standards are set for social services and the results of performance against them are publicized, with the threat of direct intervention from central government in the event of failure. The top-down policing of professional performance powerfully reinforces the message New Labour inherited from the Conservative government that professionals cannot be trusted. The regulation regime that is a core component of New Labour's new public management has four drivers:

- It addresses public anxiety about the availability and quality of public services.

- It enables a fragmented system to be managed at arm's length.

- It attempts to take politics out of policy and practice.

- It demonstrates that service provision is being taken seriously. (Clarke 2004, pp.133–134)

As with their US counterparts, UK managers are likely to be affected by contracting but, perhaps, to a more limited extent. However, they find themselves caught up in the panoply of performance management, constantly having to be mindful of how their agencies will fare when their performance is publicized in league tables and star ratings. (The issue of performance indicators is explored further in Chapter 3 of this book).

Conclusion

New public management has unleashed a multitude of management trends around the world. The US and the UK have been at its forefront, as it has become embedded into the shaping of each country's social services arrangements. Managers on both sides of the Atlantic have taken on greater significance under new public management. They have been charged with wider responsibilities. They are expected to be imaginative, purposeful, enterprising and calculating strategists, not just technicians (Moore 2002, p.20 and p.293). They are seen as the key people in delivering improvements in social services and they are more directly accountable for providing or purchasing services. The greater complexity of managerial roles found in new public management means that managers are faced with a range of considerations and interests (White and Harris 2001, 2004), which can be experienced as inconsistent and contradictory. The remainder of the book explores these considerations and interests and reflects upon the problems and possibilities encountered by managers in the current context. The next chapter begins the exploration by looking at the role of leadership in human services management.

Chapter 2

New Leadership for the Human Services: Involving and Empowering Staff through Participatory Management

Barbara A. Pine and Lynne M. Healy

Management in social work/social care has changed dramatically in the past 25 to 30 years. As pointed out elsewhere in this volume, today's leaders in social work and social care must effectively create and manage a diverse work force, solid inter-organizational relationships and strategic alliances, diverse funding streams, the solid support of competent volunteers, current and workable technological and operating systems, and an ethically based, mission-driven organization. They also must creatively foster and manage agency change, organizational improvement, and environmental safety and risk. All of this takes place in a highly competitive and increasingly conservative environment, with limited and even shrinking resources for human services.

Vaill has used the metaphor of "permanent whitewater" to describe the turbulent and rapidly changing environment of opportunity mixed with danger constantly confronting today's leaders of organizations. He defines permanent whitewater as "a continual disorderly procession of surprising, novel, ill-structured events that demand a leader's learning, with high costs of inattention or misinterpretation" (Vaill 1997, p.72). Anyone familiar with the kinds of events facing social care and social work leaders in services that, for example, protect children and elderly people, provide health care, treat people with mental health problems, and empower the dispossessed will certainly agree to the aptness of Vaill's metaphor.

There has been great attention to leadership in the UK, deriving in large part from the government's modernization agenda (Hartley and Allison 2000; Rogers and Reynolds 2003a). In the US, whole sections of bookstores are now devoted to leadership and seminars on developing one's leadership style and skills are ubiquitous.

Leadership has been defined in terms of its role in achieving goals: "the process of influencing others toward attainment of organizational goals" (Yukl 1989, p.251); "an attempt at interpersonal influence, directed through the communication process, toward the attainment of some goal or goals" (Fleishman 1973, p.3); "the process of social influence in which one person is able to enlist the aid and support of others in the accomplishment of a common task" (Chemers 1997, p.3). Leadership has also been defined in terms of human relations: "leaders don't lead as much as they build, sustain, and direct the commitment, skills, and attention of followers and collaborators" (Rubin 2002, p.14); new leadership approaches represent a "shift to a 'bring out the best in people' leadership style" (Robson and Gomph 1994, p.27); leadership is "orchestration of human elements into a whole…[to] encourage communication… [to]form cooperative problem-solving groups" (Lewis *et al.* 2001).

Leadership has also been defined in terms of the roles managers must play in order for their organizations to be successful. Some authors have pointed to the difference between management and leadership, noting that organizations need to be both well managed and well led, but not always by the same person (Knauft, Berger and Gray 1991). Others have identified technical competence as a requisite for organizational efficiency and leadership competence as a requisite for organizational effectiveness (Lewis *et al.* 2001). Chemers (1997) posits a dichotomous approach, citing the responsibility leaders have to balance the competing demands for order and stability in the internal maintenance of the organization with those demanding external adaptability and change. The most comprehensive approach sets out four dimensions of leadership on two axes: internal vs. external and control vs. flexibility. This competing values framework, developed by Quinn (1984) has been used to assess organizational effectiveness and leadership skills (Edwards and Austin 1991; Austin 2002). Austin delineates the skills needed to function well in all four dimensions including mentoring, facilitating, monitoring, coordinating, innovating, brokering, producing, and directing, and suggests that the leaders must pay attention to both the whole of the organization and its parts (Austin 2002). Finally, in their recent assessment of texts and casebooks used for teaching social service management, Austin and Kruzich (2004) identify 11 key management roles in 3 major types. Leadership roles include boundary spanner, innovator, organizer, and team builder. Interactional roles include communicator, advocate, supervisor, and facilitator. Analytic roles include resource manager, evaluator, and policy practitioner.

So what is needed to be a successful leader and manager in social care/social work? In this chapter we begin with a brief discussion of leadership theory and practice as it has evolved over the past century. Then we focus on the "fifth generation" of leadership theory, discussing the definition and attributes associated with transformational leadership. An important aspect of this leadership style, also called "SuperLeader" (Sims and Lorenzi 1992), distributed leadership (Rogers and Reynolds 2003a), pluralistic management (Nixon and Spearmon 1991), and participatory management (Van Vlissingen 1993) is the extent to which these leaders involve others in the work at hand. Thus, we then turn to the what and why of participatory management as a dominant theme in leading today's human services workplaces where professional social work staff are empowered to make decisions about the job, on the job. This is done through their involvement in such key activities as program evaluation, strategic planning, total quality improvement projects, and problem-solving teams and task forces. We provide brief examples of some of these participatory management strategies and discuss the rewards and leadership requisites for successfully carrying them off, even in large, bureaucratic social care/social work agencies.

Leadership theories

Trait theory

In the past century, leadership theory has evolved through several stages. Trait theories of leadership reflected early twentieth-century attempts to measure individual differences in all things, for example, intelligence. In early trait theory, leadership was seen as the province of those with special features and capabilities (Chemers 1997). These could include physical and/or personality characteristics or abilities (Northouse 2001). Northouse (2001) reports findings from five integrative studies of leadership traits conducted between 1948 and 1991 which show the breadth of leadership characteristics these studies have identified, and draws out five traits common to all five studies: intelligence, self-confidence, determination, integrity, and sociability. Whereas early ideas about leadership traits saw them as innate, later work posited that they could be learned. Moreover, current ideas about leadership, for example transformational leadership as we will discuss below, focus much on the *traits* of a good transformative leader.

Behavior theory

Later theory development looked at what good leaders do and sought to explain leadership behavior or styles of leadership. Blake and Mouton's (1964) work, which is the best known in this area, identified two dimensions of leadership behavior: one in which the leader shows concern for the organizational tasks that must be accomplished, and the other focusing on concern for the people within the organization. The Management Grid they developed could be used to plot a leader's style simultaneously on these two dimensions. So, for example, a 9.9 leader would be high on attention to both task and people, whereas a 1.1 represents a leader in name only, one who is uninvolved and indifferent (Northouse 2001). Style theory also manifested a continuum of leadership behaviors from, on the one side, leader-dominated, rule-centered, autocratic and authoritarian, to the other which was group-dominated, people-centered, consultative, and democratic (Chemers 1997). It communicated the idea of an optimal style.

Situational theory

A later stage of leadership theory sought to explain both characteristics (traits) and behavior depending upon the situation. It moved away from the idea of an optional style, recognizing that what is optional depends on the situation. Hersey and Blanchard's (1983, 1988) work in situational leadership is the best known. In this, the leader adapts his or her style to the subordinate's need for either direction or support. A four-part grid shows four styles: high supportive, low directive; high directive, high supportive; low supportive, low directive; and high directive, low supportive. As the level of maturity of staff increases, there is less need for direction and support. Mature, committed staff would enjoy relative independence to take responsibility for their own work with consultation from the leader (Hersey and Blanchard 1983). A number of training curricula and leadership assessment tools use the situational leadership approach (Northouse 2001; Casey Family Services 2005).

Transactional leadership theory

Transactional leadership explains leadership as a series of exchanges between leaders and followers. Leaders use variations of the "carrot-stick" approach to achieve the goals of the organization. Leaders set goals and offer incentives to workers who carry out the work to achieve the goals. Transactional leadership theory explains that transactions are the most common form of leadership behavior (Sims and Lorenzi 1992).

Transformational leadership theory

Transformational leadership, what we are calling fifth-generation leadership theory, has been the focus of attention since the 1980s. It builds, however, on much earlier work by experts such as Kurt Lewin and Douglas MacGregor. The latter, a former president of Antioch College, is best known for his seminal 1960 book *The Human Side of Enterprise*, in which he describes a new view of leader/follower relationships and sets forth his well-known *Theory Y*. Under *Theory Y*, which builds on Maslow's (1943) work on the hierarchy of human needs, leaders would see their workers as capable of commitment to the work and self-control, as compared to external control, in achieving organizational goals; workers are also capable of, and creative at, solving organizational problems, given the right work conditions and opportunities (Weisbord 1991). Ouchi's *Theory Z*, which followed MacGregor, is a people-centered approach to management where leaders serve as models and facilitators in an informal structure of active involvement and participation (Reisman 1986). The work of Rensis Likert also provided an important foundation for participative management styles, identifying management behavior in a model comprised of four systems which he then translated into a set of diagnostic tools for use with organizations (Weisbord 1991). Likert's System 4 management is synonymous with participatory management in that workers are intimately involved in program planning, a matrix approach uses cross-functional groups to organize the work, and management systems are viewed as helpful, rather than oppressive (Murphy and Pardeck 1986). In summary, it is easy to see the work of these earlier theorists/practitioners in more current thinking about transformational leadership.

Northouse (2001) defines transformational leaders as those who "set out to empower followers and nurture them in change. They attempt to raise the consciousness in individuals and to get them to transcend their own self interests for the sake of others" (p.142). Others have defined it as: "engagement with purpose and vision" (Rogers and Reynolds 2003a, p.70). As is evident in these definitions, transformational leadership integrates traits, behaviors, situations, and transactions with employees and other stakeholders to achieve the organization's mission. Central to these definitions is empowerment, which Sims and Lorenzi (1992) note is the "new paradigm for organizations" (p.304).

Bass (1985, 1990) is largely credited with distinguishing between transactional and transformational leadership and with identifying four factors that characterize the latter. These characteristics are both traits and behaviors and include charisma, inspiration, intellectual stimulation, and individual consideration. The charisma factor means that the transformational leader is a strong role model for others, creating a vision for the organization and a sense of the mission. She or he gains the respect and trust of others and instills pride in the work. This factor is also referred to as idealized influence. The inspiration factor means that the leader communicates high expectations and the important purposes of the organization to others in simple ways, motivating them to commit to and be a part of the team effort. The third factor, intellectual stimulation, describes the leader's encouragement of others to question basic assumptions, consider problems from new and unique perspectives, and to be creative and innovative in finding organizational solutions. In a recent study, Mary (2005) found that a transformational leadership style is related to positive leadership outcomes. The final factor, individual consideration, describes the leader's approach to others, giving personal attention and providing a supportive environment in which each person can grow and thrive. In transformational leadership, the focus is on empowering people to find meaning in their lives, at work and beyond (Bass 1990; Martin and Henderson 2001b; Northouse 2001; Manning 2003). Thus, Martin and Henderson (2001b), citing Alimo-Metcalfe (1998), describe transformational leaders as having:

> fundamental personal dispositions. These include empathy, openness to criticism and the ideas of others, a degree of selflessness, and some judicious risk-taking in empowering others…also…enthusiasm, articulating a clear vision and showing determination to achieve it, and involving others so they take on ownership of the vision. Transformational leaders are perceived as individuals of high integrity and self-confidence…maintain a close relationship with and accessibility to staff…are highly skilled in both internal organizational politics…and external politics…have the intellectual capacity to think broadly… (p.42).

The transformational leadership style is consistent with feminist leadership style, which is seen as promoting collaboration, sharing power (the notion of *power to* rather than *power over*) and decision-making, and focusing on both process and outcomes (Healy, Havens and Pine 1995). Transformational leadership also is very much like SuperLeadership described by Sims and Lorenzi (1992), which attempts to build followers who become self-leaders with initiative and creativity emphasizing a team-building approach. Rogers and Reynolds (2003a) use the term "distributed leadership" to describe a style that encourages the leadership of others through a variety of consultative and participatory practices.

In the following section, we define and describe participatory leadership approaches and provide a rationale for their use by today's social work/social care managers. We also want to stress at this point that our references to leadership are not solely to those typically seen as leaders: top administrators in the organization. Instead, we view leadership as a set of roles, attributes, values, and actions that can occur at all levels in the organization, from the executive director to the front-line worker who might be, for example, responsible for organizing and leading an inter-agency task force aimed at improving services.

Transformational leadership and participation

The old adage that the top thinks while the bottom acts has given way to participation as the dominant theme in the both the public and private sectors today. In a recent speech, Jack Welch, former CEO of General Electric, noted that "You're only as good as the reflected glory you get from the work of your people. Management isn't you doing it. Management is exciting others to do it better than you ever could have done it" (Bauman 2005, p.3). Effective leaders in human services organizations also count their employees as their most valuable resource (Cohen and Cohen 2000). Indeed staff, not equipment or machines, are the outcome producing resources of social agencies.

Participatory management is a commitment to carrying out a set of strategies that involve workers in organizational decisions. Participation means that staff members have a role in solving problems, making decisions about policies and operations, evaluating and improving programs and services, and developing inter-organizational relations (Pine, Warsh and Maluccio 1998). Participation takes a wide variety of forms including team meetings, case conferences, and ad hoc task forces and committees whose aim is to encourage and facilitate interaction around organizational issues (Manning 2003). Staff may also be involved in structured organizational development activities, such as quality circles, quality of work life and work redesign, and force field analysis, as well as other diagnostic activities (French and Bell 1999).

Participation also is an ethical imperative (Weisbord 1991). In the human services, this is especially true for a number of reasons. First, working with people is, as Manning notes, "moral work" (2003, p.23). Indeed, social workers in these organizations have power over the important life needs of their clients. Operating with guidance from their professional code of ethics, they guard client rights to informed consent, confidentiality, freedom from harms, and social justice. Moreover, a central function of social work interventions is client empowerment; this will not work if staff are not empowered as professionals (Hegar and Hunzeker 1988; Shera 1995). Social work leaders must serve as role models whose practices embody the values of the profession (Mary 2005). Thus, participatory management is highly congruent with social work values of empowerment as well as those of self-determination and human dignity (Katan and Prager 1986; Edwards and Gummer 1988; Malka 1989).

Additionally, all staff, from managers to front-line workers, share the ethical responsibilities of contributing to the public good by achieving the organization's mission, thus fulfilling its moral contract with society (Manning 2003). When stakeholders participate in designing organizational processes and structures, the agency is more likely to be in moral alignment, meaning that there is congruency between its mission and the ways in which it operates (Manning 2003). Lynne Healy and Barbara Pine provide examples of moral alignment in the discussion of this concept in chapter 4 of this book. Finally, social work in human service organizations is complicated and uncertain, making the values of dignity, meaning, and community, which are at the heart of participatory organizations and leadership, increasingly important (Weisbord 1991).

Benefits of participation

People who have low control over their work and work environment are hurt physically and emotionally according to Weisbord (1991). In contrast, participation can lead to increased staff satisfaction, and reduced burnout and turnover. Vinokur-Kaplan, Jayaratne, and Chess, in a study of child welfare staff (1994) found that social workers who perceived that their agencies offered job challenges and opportunities for promotion were more satisfied and less likely to seek other jobs. The rapidly changing environment of human service agencies requires flexibility and change. As Malcolm notes elsewhere in this volume, demographic shifts and increasingly diverse clients and staff have underscored the need to value diversity and use differences to improve both workplace climate and services. Increased accountability in the human services, and the emphasis on evidence-based practice result in pressures that demand the involvement of knowledgeable people, including clients, to ensure that there is a "larger portfolio of ideas" (Kanter 1989, p.xii) available for planning and problem-solving. Participation also increases the likelihood that staff will accept and adhere to policies or practices they have a hand in developing (Katan and Prager 1986; Weisbord 1991). Given the high stress of some social work jobs and the alienating qualities of some social agencies, participation can build consensus on the organization's values and goals, and increase feelings of achievement and satisfaction with the work, both of which are essential to high staff morale (Wodarski and Palmer 1985; Healy *et al.* 1995; Manning 2003).

Inter and intra-agency task forces and committees encourage relationship building across and within agency boundaries; new relationships can foster community-building and improved productivity (Katan and Prager 1986). Finally, participatory approaches provide opportunities for staff at all levels to develop new knowledge and skills. These may be substantive, such as an increased understanding of a particular program, intervention, or collaborative effort. The learning is also likely to focus on process skills, including negotiation, team-building, idea-sharing, and managing conflict (Pine *et al.* 1998). Learning and change to keep the organization adaptive and vital are consistent with the concept of the learning organization put forth by Senge (1990) in his seminal book entitled *The Fifth Discipline* (Lewis *et al.* 2001). Engaging in continuous learning has become the "primary survival strategy for organizations in the 1990s" (Cohen and Austin 1997, p.42).

What is participation?

There are many participatory strategies that may be used by leaders. These range from strategies that aim to manipulate participants to those that truly share power and decision-making. In an often-cited article on citizen participation, Arnstein (1969) defined an eight-step *ladder of participation* (see below). At the bottom of the ladder is manipulation, when participants are put onto committees whose only function is to approve decisions that have already been made. Rungs 3, 4, and 5 on the ladder are informing, consultation, and placation. Arnstein labels these as participation tokenism. Ranging from the one-way communication of informing, to requests for advice with no accountability or guarantees that advice will be used, to placation, the leader-controlled acceptance of inconsequential preferences of participants, these strategies may provide temporary illusions of participation, but often result in frustration and alienation.

True participation occurs higher up the ladder of participation through partnership, delegation, and citizen control. While leaders in human service organizations must retain ultimate control, there are many decisions that can be delegated and a partnership model can be effectively used. Even lower levels of participation can be useful if applied openly and honestly. A leader who consults with staff or clients for ideas, making it clear where ultimate decision authority lies and regularly and honestly reporting back to the participants on decisions reached, will usually retain the good will of the participants.

8 Citizen Control	
7 Delegated Power	Citizen Power
6 Partnership	

5 Placation	
4 Consultation	Tokenism
3 Informing	

| 2 Therapy | Non-participation |
| 1 Manipulation | |

(adapted from Arnstein's *Ladder of Participation* (1969))

Limits of participation

Participatory approaches are not appropriate in all situations; they may not always work. Hierarchical agency structures may make participation a challenge in some settings (Henderson and Seden 2004; Seden 2003). Representation is not the same as participation (Weisbord 1991). Moreover, not all managers have the requisite skills and knowledge to carry out these strategies for involving staff. Training and consultation, as well as other supports, may be needed. Staff who get involved need to trust that managers sanction their involvement and that their participation will affect outcomes (Manning 2003; Pine *et al.* 1998). At the same time, constraints on participation need to be clarified at the outset, as do the manager's continuing areas of responsibility (Vandervelde 1979).

Examples of participation

The following are actual examples of participatory approaches undertaken in human services organizations. They illustrate the benefits of staff and volunteer participation in program design and evaluation, improving agency programs, and in difficult program and policy decisions.

Problem-solving

Participatory management does not suggest a single style or approach. As the following example demonstrates, managers may have quite different understandings of the meaning of participation; some will seek participation by only a few trusted advisors, while others will engage the entire staff.

In a study on the impact of gender on leadership style, the following scenario was posed to equal numbers of male and female appointed department heads and deputy heads in state government in one state in the US:

> The governor directs the department to submit a plan within a month to cut its budget by 3 percent. In your department, describe how you would proceed, including who would be involved by position, what structure you would use, what decision-making pattern would be used, what role you would play, and how the final decision would be communicated to those who participated in the process. (Havens and Healy 1991, p.66)

The interview subjects explained that the scenario was not hypothetical, but that they had just recently had to prepare such budget cuts.

Therefore, they were describing their actual behaviors. Of the male managers, 77 percent indicated that they would involve a small group of two or three top staff to assist. Women managers were more likely to involve larger groups in their decision making process, including line staff (73%). Another interesting difference was that some leaders saw the goal of the participatory process as reaching consensus on a decision while others viewed the purpose of engaging others as primarily information-seeking. Thus close to half of the female leaders indicated that the staff would be involved in making the final decision, while all of the males said they would inform the staff of their decision after making the decision themselves.

This example demonstrates how leaders may use participation for a variety of purposes, ranging from informing to consultation to partnership and delegation by varying the scope and inclusiveness of participation, as was discussed earlier in the presentation of Arnstein's ladder.

Program design

As part of the growing mandate for accountability in the human services, social workers are increasingly being guided by outcome research and program evaluation in designing interventions. Evidence-based practice is the term now used to describe this emphasis on empirical knowledge (O'Hare 2005). In designing programs, social workers make every effort to select and use interventions that have been shown to be effective in outcome research. They also must develop written designs that incorporate guidelines for monitoring and evaluating their programs. Such designs quantify program inputs (for example, clients, staff, other resources), outputs, or what will be produced (for example, number of hours of clinical therapy or parent training), and program outcomes in the form of measurable process and outcome objectives (Pine *et al.* 2002). The following example illustrates the essential roles that direct service staff can and should play in designing programs. It also is a good example of agency structures and processes to ensure that program evaluation is participatory and integral to the program being evaluated.

A large, non-profit child welfare agency had been operating a specialty program for some time in partnership with its state child protection agency. The latter referred parents to the program, whose staff worked intensively with them to resolve the problems that had brought them to the attention of the state child welfare authorities. There was occasional consultation with the state agency staff, particularly when it was thought that families had stabilized and their cases could be closed. Program staff were frustrated, however, because they felt that the state agency was referring their most challenging cases and progress with these families was slow and often non-existent. The success rate was very low and staff were disappointed when their extensive efforts did not pay off. Their relationship with their state agency partners was often strained and another source of frustration.

Hearing their dissatisfaction, agency managers organized a committee comprised of the team leader in the program and the direct service staff, as well as representatives from the referring state agency. They appointed the team leader as chair of the committee, charging her and the committee to evaluate the current program and to design a new one that addressed the concerns and needs that had been identified. A consultant from the non-profit agency's central office was identified to serve on the committee. Working over the summer months, under the leadership of the chair, who wisely invited a member of the state agency staff to act as a co-leader, the group designed a new, model program. A key feature of the model was a very close, collaborative relationship between the program staff and their state agency partners when it was determined that both groups were very frustrated by their limited contact and failure to work in partnership on behalf of families referred to the program. The group also redefined eligibility for the program, limiting it to families who had not been known to the state agency before. In other words, referred families were likely to be younger and have problems more amenable to intervention. They were families with the best hope to be helped, not the last hope as those in the prior program had been.

Meetings were very interactive, and sometimes tension-filled as people from both agencies discussed their sometimes competing priorities and values for the service. In the end, however, the committee developed a model that satisfied all of its members, and the program was launched the following fall.

It is important to note that in this agency, supervisory staff, and even direct service staff are encouraged and supported in taking leadership roles. Moreover, worker participation in organizational improvement is formally sanctioned and is a part of the structure of the agency, an important feature of a participatory organization as defined by Cohen and Austin (1997). Time is set aside for committee meetings such as these, and management builds in opportunities to hear results and develop plans accordingly.

One response from management was to engage a team of external evaluators to evaluate the new model program, beginning with a process evaluation of its implementation. Staying with their overall participatory approach, the agency also organized a research advisory committee to work with the evaluation team. Because the staff were accustomed to being involved in decision-making, the evaluation team found it relatively easy to engage them in the selection of "clinical" and "normed" instruments for use in the outcome evaluation. This was especially important for two reasons: staff would be doing much of the data collection for the study using the instruments, and the instruments selected would be part of the assessment and evaluation of family progress well beyond the evaluation.

The evaluation team conducted a comprehensive case study using the program as its unit of analysis (Spath and Pine 2004). Then, with the resulting findings, the team worked with the program staff to develop a program design with measurable process and outcome objectives as a tool for all to use in monitoring progress and measuring outcomes. In this case, the evaluators also served in a teaching role, helping staff to learn effectiveness-based program planning and how to develop a solid, written program design.

The agency's structured continuous quality improvement process includes regular meetings, at least twice per year, involving all staff of each specialty program with top administrators to assess the program and plan improvements. In this case, the program "workgroup" meetings focused on recommendations made by the evaluation team for strengthening the program model. In this way, changes could be and were made immediately.

Program evaluation and the learning organization

The following case example illustrates the use of what Cohen and Austin (1997) have termed collaborative action research to evaluate an agency program. It also illustrates the use of teams and the kinds of agency supports that are needed for large-scale evaluation and restructuring projects, particularly in large, bureaucratic organizations. Finally, it is an example of effective leadership provided by a front-line supervisor to a major agency initiative.

A large, state child welfare agency was about to redouble its efforts to reunify families that had been separated by a child's placement in foster care. The deputy commissioner had learned about an assessment model that had been developed by an academic team at a nearby university and contracted with them to help the agency use the model to study its current family reunification program. As a first step, staff and others were asked to volunteer for the effort; a team of volunteers was convened, made up of the full range of staff involved in reunification, including attorneys, court personnel, front-line staff, supervisors, foster parents, and collateral providers. A "kick off" meeting led by the deputy commissioner and several other top managers explained the reasons for undertaking the project, clarified expectations, and outlined the process to be followed, including an all-day reporting out conference at the end.

During five full-day meetings a month apart the team examined every aspect of the agency's family reunification program, following a model consisting of best practices in each of 25 program components developed by the academics, who sat in on each meeting to provide clarification and guidance (see Pine *et al.* 1998). The academics also provided support to the team's facilitator and helped her to plan for each subsequent meeting.

Because "buy in" at all levels is critical, especially in large, hierarchical organizations, the deputy commissioner also convened a leadership group consisting of middle managers who met regularly throughout the five months to learn about the team's progress and results.

> The team's efforts produced a set of 65 recommendations for improvement in policy, program, training, and other resources in family reunification. The ideas were wide-ranging and explicit. They were shared with the agency's top level management and other staff at an all-day conference chaired by the commissioner. Work began immediately to implement some of the recommended changes. As one of the top managers noted: "Taking this approach is an opportunity to convey our trust in staff. If we trust people enough to decide that a child is safe to return home, we should also trust them to come up with useful policy recommendations." (Pine *et al.* 1998, p.26)

The above case example illustrates a number of key features of participatory approaches. The first is careful structure. The second is leadership of both the overall effort and the team project. The third is good communication within the team and at other levels in the organization. The fourth is encouraging people to be involved and to value their contributions. A member of the team said, "There seemed to be a special closeness of people gathered for a common purpose—to create a better system to help families. It was refreshing to have my input valued. I believe real good will come from this effort" (Pine *et al.* 1998, p.26; Warsh, Pine and Maluccio 1996). Finally, the contributions of staff to these major undertakings needs to be recognized and rewarded (Kanter 1989).

Making tough decisions by consensus

As noted earlier, participation can involve tokenism, consultation, or higher levels of delegated decision-making. Participation is relevant to all levels or domains of social service organizations from service providing to management to policy domains (Kouzes and Mico 1979). In not-for-profit organizations in the US, it is the voluntary board of directors that has ultimate decision authority on agency policy. When boards function well, information flows are regular and complete, and board members participate in serious discussion and strive to involve all members in important decisions. Decisions are often made by majority vote but, at other times, consensus models are used. The following case illustrates use of participatory strategies and consensus building to resolve conflicts over policy in a voluntary board of directors. The example shows the positive impact participatory strategies can have on healing conflict and team-building.

In the late 1980s, during the apartheid era in South Africa, a local YWCA in a US city considered a proposal to divest all agency funds from South African investments (the agency was indeed fortunate to have a significant endowment at that time of several million dollars). Two board members introduced the proposal to divest, assuming that this would be an easy decision. After all, the YWCA's mission was to follow what was called its one imperative: "to eliminate racism wherever it is found and by any means necessary." "Any means" surely would include divestiture from companies benefiting the apartheid regime. The two members introduced the proposal, provided some background information, and suggested that the board vote on the proposal at its next meeting.

The issue generated considerable debate on this all-female board. Some members were passionate about divestiture and perhaps a bit arrogant in presenting this as an imperative for the agency. Other women, especially those with backgrounds in financial affairs, questioned the fiscal impact of divestiture and argued that the decision might violate the fiduciary responsibilities of the board. Issues of race and racism, however, became the main source of heated conflict.

Some—especially those from social service agencies—accused the business-oriented members of being more concerned about the bottom line than about racism. Some of the African-American women on the board spoke about their feelings that the white members seemed much more concerned about racism in South Africa than racism at home. As the discussion proceeded, tensions rose and relationships became openly strained.

The Executive Director did not express her opinion on the issue. She did, however, suggest a consultation with other YWCAs that had considered the issue. After lengthy debate, the board decided to delay a decision and to undertake a process of board education and consultation so that all could be fully informed. Particularly helpful were consultations with two YWCAs. One had decided the issue by majority vote. This board suffered long term damage to board relations, as some members felt their views were not heard or not respected. A number of members left the board. The other YWCA had decided to take time to fully consider all views and to attempt to make a decision by consensus.

After six months of education, deliberation and team building exercises, the board of the local YWCA decided by consensus to divest its holdings from South African companies. It is particularly significant that early in the process, this board decided not to take a vote on divestiture, although the pro-divestiture members probably could have won a narrow majority. By using participation and consensus, relationships among board members and between the Executive and the board were strengthened, especially the levels of mutual respect and preparation for future decisions.

The Executive Director played a facilitating role in the process, although she initially opposed divestiture. As written in an earlier analysis: "seeing the threat posed by the conflict outlined above, she modified her role to that of quiet facilitator of the educational process. Although this might have been viewed through a traditional management lens as ineffective management, it represents higher-level self assurance and confidence in the board. The Executive then proceeded to replicate the educational process with staff, enhancing agency cohesion around this important policy issue. For issues of this importance, all agreed that consensus decision making is worth the investment of time and relationship building." (Healy et al. 1995, p.144)

As the four case examples above illustrate, there are many opportunities for, and benefits from active participation in agency processes. Other examples might include engaging a representative group of staff to conduct an ethics audit, a review of the agency's ethical policies and practices, as suggested by Healy and Pine in Chapter 4. The audit could be guided by one of two audit instruments they cite (Colorado

Association of Nonprofit Organizations (CANPO) 1994; Reamer 2001). Staff also could be involved in conducting a comprehensive, agency-wide cultural competence assessment as part of an agency's diversity plan discussed by Malcolm in Chapter 6. An instrument to guide such an assessment is available (Child Welfare League of America 1993). And, of course, strategic planning or future search efforts depend in large measure on the inclusion of key stakeholders throughout the process to ensure success.[1]

Conclusion

This chapter has emphasized two themes: the nature and importance of leadership to the human services and a focus on participatory models of leadership as particularly appropriate and effective in the social field. Participation is a model that fits with social work values and often improves service outcomes. However, it is important to acknowledge that there are forces in the current environment that may impede successful participation strategies and make it difficult to promote them in organizations. The globalization era management paradigm has encouraged privatization, contract employment and employment at will in the social services. These undermine managerial commitment to participation models and employee willingness to participate, as agency loyalty to workers and worker loyalty to agency diminishes. Contract employees—those paid only for actual sessions held or services rendered—are unlikely to be present to participate in agency deliberations. Employment-at-will is a phenomenon growing in the US; this means that employment contracts specify that staff can be terminated at any time and without reason. Surely this provision weakens worker commitment to the agency and, therefore, participation.

The current paradigm places heavy emphasis on efficiency, a theme taken up by John Harris in Chapter 1 of this book. Participation strategies do not appear on the surface to enhance efficiency and do not fit with a short-term results orientation. However, it is never efficient to reach a decision that no one will implement or commit to due to lack of involvement. Thus, viewed even with a medium-range perspective on efficiency, participation often strengthens program implementation and successful service outcomes.

In a recent book, Coulshed and Mullender (2001) provide an extensive list of the qualities of the "best" leaders. Their list focuses on what good leaders and managers do, emphasizing the need to act decisively on work-related problems, yet giving considerable attention to participatory skills and strategies, reflecting our emphasis in this chapter on participatory models. The best leaders, they say, keep everyone informed, enable teams to do their work, and have good interactional skills, building confidence, inspiring their colleagues, and settling conflicts when they arise. These are skills and behaviors that can be learned and modeled by competent staff at all levels of an organization and are, we believe, essential for good leadership in the social care/human services sector. Good leaders can blend individuals into self-directed, synergistic teams whose contribution to the organization exceeds the sum of their individual contributions (Douglas 2005). Navigating in white water conditions, as anyone who has done it knows, requires a team of mates who paddle together, in synchrony, "holding" or "digging" until the raft is successfully through the rapids.

Note

1 Future search is one approach to strategic planning in which a large group of stakeholders in the organization meet together in a specially planned conference, and with the help of a specially trained facilitator, assess the organization and its context and develop a plan for future direction.

Chapter 3

Improving Performance in Social Work through Positive Approaches to Managing Change

Julie Barnes

Introduction

In the opening chapter of this book, John Harris explored some of the issues relating to the demand for greater accountability from social service agencies from both private and government funders in both the UK and the US. Two major forces which have driven these developments have been *increased need* and *diminished resources*. Inevitably, trying to operate under these twin competing constraints, some agencies have had difficulties in meeting the newly constructed performance targets, as John Harris suggested. Such difficulties have been translated by government into the notion of *failing* organizations, terminology which has now entered the language of social care.

For agencies identified as 'failing to meet targets' or underperforming in some aspects of their functions, being given the designation of 'failing' becomes a self-fulfilling prophecy. Such agencies are publicly criticized and their reputations are damaged. Consequently, they begin to experience difficulties in the recruitment and retention of good staff. Morale plummets further and pressures on the organization become even greater.

Agencies and government have increasingly been seeking strategies which can turn the downward spiral into an upwards curve to increase effective performance. In 2003, the Department of Health in England commissioned a review of the literature (Department of Health 2003b) to identify effective factors for achieving successful change and improved performance in 'failing' local authority social services departments. Social services are local agencies administered by local government in the UK who provide statutory social work and social care services. These departments are assessed periodically by government inspectors to see if they are meeting the required standards of performance. If departments do not meet these standards they are deemed to be 'failing'.

The Department of Health review incorporated a wide range of academic, business, commercial, government and public sector sources to explore what is effective in improving poor performance and achieving sustainable change. Drawing on public and private sector sources, the review examined the nature of failure, the characteristics of success, the complexities of moving from one to the other and some common themes for working with organizations in crisis. It included public and private sector experiences in all types of service and organization. The review revealed an enormous academic, business and popular literature relating to organizational development, change and turnaround. This includes writing on organizational development, human resources, change management, private sector experience of management turnaround, public sector management, systems thinking, organizational learning and newly developing appreciative approaches to managing change positively (see Department of Health 2003b).

In recognition of the impact the review has had on government thinking, this chapter draws on some of the key messages from that commissioned work (Department of Health 2003b). It incorporates further thinking by Barnes, first published in a journal article in *Research, Policy and Planning* (Barnes 2004). Most importantly, the chapter focuses on organizational 'turnaround' in poorly performing organizations. It explores some of the latest thinking that has informed government in England about tackling poor performance. The chapter concludes that innovation may be the most effective way to achieve sustainable improvement. It considers how an approach called Appreciative Inquiry might be useful in social services and other public sector settings (Appreciative Inquiry 2006). Appreciative Inquiry is one of a developing menu of strategies aimed at organizational improvement. This intervention has been gaining increasing interest from government policy makers in the UK.

Although the chapter focuses on factors intended to improve service delivery in the UK, social work managers in the US face equal scrutiny from funding sources. For example, the federal government regularly evaluates state agencies' performance through the Department of Health and Human Services' child welfare reviews. In addition, private social services organizations face regular reviews from funders and accrediting bodies. Social work managers in the US are also interested in pursuing a strengths-focused approach to organization improvement, such as that contained in Appreciative Inquiry, which is described and illustrated here.

The contemporary context for measuring performance in human services in the UK

The introduction of the National Comprehensive Performance Assessment Framework for local authorities with responsibility for social services in England has led to a greater preoccupation with their overall performance than ever before. The Audit Commission introduced Comprehensive Performance Assessment (CPA) in 2002. Writing about the framework in 2005, the Audit Commission explained:

> CPA measures how well councils are delivering services for local people and communities while reducing the overall regulatory burden on them. It distils a complex set of judgements on local government bodies and the services that they provide into one simply understood rating. The strength of CPA is that it looks at performance from various perspectives which provide a more complete picture and a better understanding of where to focus activities to secure improvement. From the start CPA has evolved in response to changes in the operational and regulatory

environment, rising public expectations, and the performance of local government itself. And we continue to refine CPA.

Over the last three years, council services have improved significantly, and CPA is acknowledged to be one of the catalysts for this. CPA has also been a lever for reducing inspection and regulation in better performing councils and focusing support for others. (Audit Commission 2005, p.2)

CPA applies to every part of the local authority. In relation to social work and social care, it works as follows. Each year, every local authority social services department in England is 'star-rated', by the independent Commission for Social Care Inspection (CSCI). This body is deliberately set at arm's length from the relevant government department (the Department of Health) to give it more autonomy. The location of this function is set to change again in 2008, when social care services for adults and children are formally separated. The current method of assessing and reporting performance is also under review by the Commission itself at the time of writing, although the process is likely to be broadly similar to that undertaken for the last three years.

Evidence gathered from inspections, routine monitoring activities and quantitative performance indicators is collated and assessed against two dimensions: the quality of services provided over the past year and the likely 'capacity to improve' in the coming year. Star ratings are awarded, moderated across the country, and published in the autumn. These ratings feed the CPA.

Star ratings range from three (excellent) to zero (unacceptable). Three-star departments benefit from a 'lighter touch' inspection and monitoring regime and are applauded as 'high' performers. Those with a zero-star rating experience *special measures* from the Commission for Social Care Inspection, including closer monitoring and scrutiny, more frequent inspections and, in cases of greatest concern, a requirement to engage with external Performance Action Teams which work with the local authorities to improve their performance. A zero rating is regarded a serious event, with potentially far-reaching implications for service-users, staff morale, staff retention and recruitment and the overall reputation of the council, councillors and officers.

In a letter to local authorities in November 2002, the Social Services Inspectorate's Chief Inspector indicated that star ratings were a product of a wider performance assessment, including evidence from inspections and reviews, monitoring and performance indicators to form a picture over time across the criteria which included national priorities and strategic objectives; cost and efficiency; effectiveness of service delivery and outcomes; quality of services for users and carers and fair access to services (Chief Inspector Letter and Guidance 2002).

The awarding and announcement of the star ratings has raised the stakes by increasing public visibility, making new links to government, flexibilities and freedoms for high performers, and introducing sanctions for failure. This reflects the increasing centralization and control of the management and delivery of public services in the UK over the last eight years, with greater emphasis on public accountability, and statutory intervention or engagement when local improvements are not achieved.

The nature of failure

Accounts of failures from public and private sector sources have yielded evidence about the nature of failure, the characteristics of success, the complexities of moving from one to the other and some common themes for improving organizations in crisis. Lessons from the commercial world cannot be transferred directly to the public sector because of fundamental differences in the way the latter is organized and managed, its relationship to central government, local political controls, competing interests and its very different objectives and value base. Issues raised in the private sector, therefore, need to be understood and translated cautiously into a public sector context.

In the public sector, there is far less to draw on in the UK and much can be learned from the experience of the US. There are exceptions, such as in cases of child deaths. In some states in the US, Connecticut for example, when a child dies in the care of a public child welfare agency, a complete study of the case is commissioned by the State Child Advocate's Office. A task force is convened, the case is researched and a child fatality report is issued documenting and highlighting the oversights and failures that resulted in the tragedy. These reports are used as the basis for agency improvement plans. Similar investigations occur in the

UK, where a report may be commissioned by government to investigate the circumstances of a child's death and make recommendations for improvements in practice both locally and nationally. One such case, which has been influential in changing practices in relation to inter-agency collaboration was the murder of Victoria Climbié by her aunt, with whom she was privately fostered. Though several departments saw Victoria, information about her failed to be shared (Cmnd 5730 2003).

Though it is easy to identify failures in specific cases, a major prob-lem facing the government in England has been to define what is meant by failure in relation to assessing the overall performance of social ser-vices. It is always difficult to define terms, especially when they include value judgements. A key issue in trying to define 'failing' social services for the Department of Health has been the recognition that a *failing* authority is a value-laden term, and could be construed by those inter-ested in social construction as unhelpfully 'labelling' an organization caught up in particular circumstances (Department of Health 2003b).

In spite of this, the Department of Health has arrived at a definition of failure as: failing to provide safe, consistent and reliable services, fail-ing to meet statutory responsibilities and to manage resources effectively to reach those in need. In all cases, the consequences of failure for the people who use the services are given high priority (see Department of Health 2003b).

What is failure within the performance assessment framework?

The UK has developed certain procedures that take place after failure has been identified. When a council providing social services fails, it is placed on *special measures*. This means that the council is given a specific description of the elements in which it is failing. This description forms part of the action plan for improvement. So, in most cases, it is recog-nized that failure relates to specific aspects of service or performance rather than wholesale failure; interventions are then targeted at these aspects.

One of the main causes of failure is thought to be poor leadership and management in agencies. In *A Force for Change*, the Audit Commis-sion (2002a) concludes that 'serious and sustained service failure is often a failure of leadership by senior councillors and top managers'. Poor leadership includes lack of commitment to the service; lack of ambition; lack of awareness of poor performance; failure to take, and stick to, tough decisions and having unclear lines of accountability for performance.

The Audit Commission believes that poor leadership leads to poor systems and culture. These include poor strategic planning, targets not set or monitored and inadequate financial, personnel and information systems. There is also a focus on providers, not service-users, and a culture that doesn't support improvements. Collectively these factors lead to serious and sustained service failure such as children at risk and unallocated social work cases (Audit Commission 2002a, p.17).

The consequences of these failures in the public sector are very different from those in the private sector. In the private sector, failure is linked largely to economic measures such as market share, financial viability, loss of income or profit and, ultimately, company survival. By its nature, the experience of 'decline' in the public sector is different. Skelcher (2003, p.5) indicates that local authorities are 'affected by changes in the external environment, but seldom face problems of organizational survival because of the cushioning provided by their statutory and resource base'.

Responding to failure

In social services responses to a zero-star rating vary from relief (for those who recognize the need to improve) to shock, disbelief and fury for others (Barnes and Gurney 2004). How this is handled will affect the way that the organization subsequently moves forward. Likened by Owen (2000) to the stages of grieving following bereavement in a health process, failure is acknowledged, accepted and worked through. Organizations that deny or refuse to accept the judgement will take the longest time to 'recover'.

Successful turnaround will be affected by the way the 'failing' organization perceives and responds to this assessment. Edwards *et al.* (undated) noted that managers in the zero-starred hospital trusts were often surprised by their poor rating, even if it came as no surprise to external stakeholders. The authors speculate that either the performance management system was not acting as an efficient early warning system, or the failings were known about and action was not taken quickly enough, possibly because of a lack of systems to mobilize support or an absence of knowledge about what to do. Failure to achieve goals may be chronic and determined by structural factors (see Meyer and Zucker 1989).

Drawing on the work of Gardner (1965), Bibeault (1982) reports that: 'most ailing organizations have developed a functional blindness to their own defects. They are not suffering because they cannot solve their problems, but because they cannot see their problems.' It is noted that steadily poor performance seems to be tolerated as long as it does not develop into a crisis (see Bibeault 1982, p.74).

Bibeault (1982) identifies as crucial the 'moment of truth' when organizations finally admit the problem, 'for what they do and how they do it' will determine whether they survive. Early recognition is crucial as is accepting the need for change – 'when this acceptance ceases in any company, a hardening of the arteries starts to set in' (p.76).

Similarly, the way that a recovery team thinks and acts will be affected by its perception of the local authority and the task ahead. First actions will have a direct impact on the speed and nature of the recovery. Flynn observes that 'the response to scandals and events is usually a tightening of rules, procedures and scrutiny, and reduction in the discretion of front-line staff' (2002, p.272). The tendency to tighten central control of organizations after such an assessment can be counter-productive, by stifling the very innovation and creativity that may help to turn them around. Barker and Mone observed that 'performance declines may increase organizational rigidity and decrease the likelihood of innovative change' (1998, p.128), thereby lessening an organization's ability to improve.

The characteristics of success

In contrast with failing organizations, a feature of successful organizations is the engagement and empowerment of staff at all levels; staff have no chance to make their contribution if an organization is too tightly controlled from the centre. While success is also associated with strong leadership, clear vision and strategic approach, the literature suggests that a careful balance is needed. Successful organizations are generally characterized by strong visionary leadership with a clear strategy linked to explicit, measurable objectives and outcomes and sound working practices to engage and value staff at all levels (Department of Health 2003b; Barnes and Gurney 2004).

Wheatley and Kellner-Rogers also characterize success as the ability to respond to the unexpected:

> Organizations that learn to work together, that trust one another, and that become more expansive and inclusive, develop the capacity to deal with whatever happens. They have created a capacity for working and thinking together that enables them to respond quickly and intelligently to surprise and distress. (1998, p.19)

As noted by Barbara Pine and Lynne Healy in Chapter 2, these organizations are usually led by transformational leaders who know why and how to engage staff and negotiate the 'permanent white water' conditions in which social services must operate.

High performing work practices

Many commentators have written on the essential ingredients of high performing work practices (see Boyett and Boyett 1998, pp.133–138). Ashton and Sung describe high performance working practices as those which demonstrate 'the importance of workplace learning as a means of enhancing both work performance and the quality of working life'. The practices, i.e. job rotation, performance-related pay and self-directed work teams, 360 degree appraisal and personal development plans, are not new but what is different, they say, is 'the way in which these practices have been combined to create a working environment which not only provides the potential for developing the personality of the work, but also raises the productivity of the organisation' (2002, pp.1–2).

Evidence has been steadily accumulating over the last decade, across a number of countries, on the link between the use of high performance practices and organizational performance. Chapter 2 in this book provided some examples of innovative practices that involved employees and other stakeholders in improving services. Studies by Guest (1999) and Wood, de Menezes and Lasaosa (2001) indicate that 'employees respond to these practices by developing higher levels of commitment to the organisation, higher levels of motivation and by using their tacit knowledge to introduce continuous improvements, thereby increasing productivity and other organizational outcomes' (Ashton and Sung 2002, p.121).

Learning organizations

The literature on learning organizations is extensive, reflecting current interest in responding to the demands of successful management of change and innovation, and corporate renewal (see, for example, Pedlar *et al.* 1998; Senge 1990; Garvin 1993; Barrett 1995; Cummings and Worley 1997; Ashton and Sung 2002). Current thinking recognizes that change is inevitable and that organizations that are open to developing the knowledge and skills of their staff will be best placed to respond flexibly and nimbly to the demands they face. This has implications for working practices, systems and structure, culture and environment, and challenges the very basis on which power in organizations is distributed and used. A strong client focus; a focus on people rather than procedures; visible, achievable and explicit mission statements and a participatory approach to management all contribute to success in public agencies.

Success in the public sector

These indicators of success resonate with the results of the first CPAs of local authorities in England. In 2002, the Audit Commission (2002b) reported that local councils with high levels of performance are able to harness their capacity (people, internal and external resources, systems) to match high levels of ambition and vision. A clear focus on priorities, managing performance and building partnerships is emphasized. In its Annual Report in 2001/2, the Audit Commission's and Social Services Inspectorate's Joint Review Team summarized a total of 16 critical success factors of well-performing social services councils, grouped under three areas of leadership, strategy and involvement/empowerment.

Turnaround

Identifying what makes for successful organizations is only the beginning. Agencies that wish to escape from failure need to understand how their failings can be turned into success. This issue of turnaround is

Table 3.1: Critical success factors from joint reviews of councils with social services responsibilities

Leadership	Strategy	Involvement/Empowerment
Vision and ambition	Clear focus on priorities	Ownership of problems
Visibility of leaders	Strong and consistent performance management	Commitment to user participation
Putting basics right first	Having a best value orientation	Engaging staff
Good political leadership	Resourcing the changes	Cultural change
Leadership style		Communication
Corporate support		Developing strong partnerships

Adapted from: *Joint Review Team 2002.*

increasingly entering the literature along with examples of methodologies that can help achieve change in a positive way. Collaborative practices are seen as influential in these approaches (Fletcher 1999; Natiello 2001). Fletcher states:

> The organization of the future, we are being told, will need to move from hierarchical systems of prediction and control to more team-based structure and reward systems...where information is shared freely and openly across divisions and functional barriers. These organizations will need a new kind of worker, one that is a continuous learner as well as a continuous teacher, who is willing to enable others, to take responsibility for problems and work collaboratively with others to solve them. (1999, p.2)

The literature on turnaround in the private and public sector emphasizes the need to stabilize the organization and deal with the crisis. Balgobin and Pandit (2001) suggest that immediate responses may require different tactics and skills to those required for long-term, sustainable improvement and high performance. Different management teams may be needed for each phase. There is still much debate about balancing the appointment of temporary managers to rescue and lead a recovery, with engaging the resources of those who will be managing and working in the service in the longer term. In a recent review for the Department of Health into the effectiveness of Performance Action Teams (Barnes and Gurney 2004), one of the keys to success cited by participants was commitment and continuity from leaders.

Throughout the turnabout literature, (see, for example, Department of Health 2003b; Barnes and Gurney 2004), certain factors are emphasized. These include the quality of leadership by politicians and senior officers; the ability to develop and implement strategy on a number of fronts; engaging staff, service-users and other stakeholders, and communicating clearly with everyone. Crucially, priorities are linked to objectives and desired outcomes, are resourced by finance and people, and implemented and monitored appropriately. Learning organizations and those which promote high performance working practices are generally regarded as those most likely to be effective and to sustain improvement.

Flynn calls on people working in the public sector to find their own solutions and methods that recognize the context in which they are to be implemented:

> The development of improved management in the public sector requires that people learn from experience. It is not good enough to start each innovation or initiative as if nothing positive has gone before, nor is it good enough to rebrand old initiatives under new names. (2002, p.276)

Government approaches to tackling poor performance in England

In *People Need People*, the Joint Review Team highlighted four key areas for securing improvement in people management and therefore in services for users:

1. Becoming a learning organisation that delivers results.

2. Planning longer term to attract the right people.

3. Using qualifications and training to retain good people.

4. Implementing good practice consistently to drive up quality. (2000, p.1)

Further, in the Joint Review Annual Report (2002), the team reported that directors of social services 'saw changing the culture of their organisation as more important than changing the structure, and were perhaps more concerned with people than with systems and processes' (p.28). They focus on communicating priorities; aiming for consensus by managing people and relationships; leading by example; using self-appraisal; being transparent, honest, and willing to accept change (Joint Review Team 2002, p.28). Three phases of intervention have been identified in bringing about change: overcoming denial, taking action and having an exit strategy from failure (Audit Commission 2002b).

New approaches to improving performance

There are rapidly emerging ideas about the importance of working with complex organizations as whole systems, rather than focusing on isolated problems. Some authors (Chapman 2002; Dawson 2003) are critical of traditional, linear and mechanistic approaches to managing change, which fail to acknowledge and respond to the 'murky processes of change' (Dawson 2003, p.1), 'characterised by contradictions, ambiguities and untidiness' (Dawson 2003, p. 167). It is suggested that there are no solutions that are simple and universal as context is everything and interventions must reflect this.

To improve performance in complex systems, Chapman (2002) advocates taking a range of actions, evaluating the results and learning what works best. This evolutionary approach to learning requires both innovation (variety of actions) and effective feedback on the results of previous actions. Chapman concludes that the implications of working in this way are that:

- The interventions will introduce learning processes rather than specifying outcomes or targets.

- The emphasis will be on improving general system effectiveness as judged by the clients or users of the system, rather than quantitative performance indicators.

- The process of designing, formulating and implementing policies will be based more on facilitation of improvements than on control of the organisation or system. Innovative, complex behaviours can emerge through minimum specifications, clear direction, boundaries that must not be crossed, resources and permissions.

- Engaging with agents and stakeholders in policy will be based on listening and co-researching rather than telling and instructing.

- Implementation will include deliberate strategies for innovation, evaluation, learning and reflection. (2002, p.71)

Chapman (2002) also identifies the process of policy implementation as being not linear but circular, involving continuous learning, adaptation and improvement, with policy changing in response to implementation as well as vice versa. A good example of the complex process of implementation is outlined by Wendy Rose, Jane Aldgate and Julie Barnes in Chapter 12 of this book.

Systems approaches treat public services as complex adaptive systems – they are holistic and deal with complexity. The difference between this and a mechanistic, linear approach to policy is graphically illustrated by Pslek and Greenhalgh (2001), who compare the results of throwing a rock and a live bird. Mechanical linear models are excellent for understanding where the rock will land, but useless for predicting the trajectory of a bird.

Plsek and Greenhalgh's analogy is extended further with the idea of tying the bird's wings, weighting it with a rock and then throwing it. This will make the trajectory as predictable (nearly) as that of the stone, but in the process, the capability of the bird is completely destroyed. He says that this is more or less what policy makers try to do when using a scientific management (mechanical) approach, to try to control the behaviours of complex systems for which they are devising policy. It may be more successful to put a bird feeder at the destination and take account of the possible routes and behaviours of the bird's journey.

Wheatley and Kellner-Rogers add to the debate by addressing the issues of what should happen when complex systems failures occur. They assert that:

> complex-system failures cannot be solved alone. They require collaboration, participation, openness, and inclusion. These new problems force us to dissolve our past practices of hierarchies, boundaries, secrecy, and competition. In a systems crisis, the more we cling to these past practices, the more we deepen the crisis and prevent solutions. (1998, p.17)

They recommend that when complex systems fail it is best to engage with the whole system, asking 'who else should be involved?' Enough information should be created which is circulated through existing and new channels. An emphasis is placed on developing quality relationships with trust as the greatest asset. Collaboration should be supported and competition destroyed. Openness and focusing on new sustainable systems are essential (see Wheatley and Kellner-Rogers 1998, p.18)

The problem with problem-solving

There is a growing literature and practice which regards as counter-productive approaches based on problem-solving or 'deficit-based' thinking, and the whole notion of diagnosis, cure and recovery. Cooperrider *et al.* (2001) and Weisbord (1987) are two examples of this thinking. Cooperrider *et al.*, for example, write: 'A compulsive concern with what's not working, why things go wrong and who didn't do his or her job demoralizes members of the organisation, reduces the speed of learning, and undermines relationships and forward movement' (2001, p.20). Weisbord describes how the medical model (problem diagnoses, and cure through a recovery strategy) proves less and less satisfying for workplace improvement. 'If I could ask one thing of a crystal ball in every situation, it would not be "what's wrong and what will fix it?" but "what's possible here and who cares?"' (1987, p. 257).

Weisbord suggests that new approaches are needed which work away from solving the problem. These would include abandoning giving it to an expert, getting a task force, finding the technique to solve everything and doing it all immediately. Instead, new approaches would mean working towards creating the future, helping each other learn, involving everybody, finding a valued purpose and doing what is do-able (1987, p.279). A problem focus draws attention to inevitable breakdown rather than the strengths of the system, encourages a blame culture and creates an emphasis on 'looking good' rather than being good.

The impact of problem-solving is also highlighted by Barrett (1995) who notes that: 'while analytic problem solving has led to many of the advances we enjoy today, this approach to learning has limitations. We often approach problems from the very mind-set that created them in the first place' (2002, p.38). Cooperrider *et al.* (2001) believe that the habit of focusing on problems rather than possibility actually decreases organizational capacity by emphasizing how to fail rather than how to succeed. They go on to reflect on the fact that problem-solving approaches to change are:

- painfully slow – 'asking people to look backwards to yesterday's causes' (2001, pp.22–23)

- rarely result in new vision – 'by definition we can describe something as a problem because we already, perhaps implicitly, assume an ideal' (2001, p.23), and we search to close the gaps

- generate defensiveness in people – 'it is not my problem but yours' (2001, p.23)

- can reinforce hierarchy – 'where "less than ideal" individuals learn to accept their label and are encouraged to enter "treatment programs" under expert supervision' (2001, p.24)

- instil a sense of despair – poor morale and paralysis

- stimulates endless 'failure' conversations, which in turn construct and reinforce the message of failure – 'seeing the world as a problem is very much a way of organizational life'.

These limitations of a problem-focused approach to improving services underscore the need to take a new approach of organization development interventions. Organization development has been defined as 'a process for teaching people how to solve problems, take advantage of opportunities, and learn how to do that better and better over time' (French and Bell 1999, p.xiii).

Appreciative Inquiry

An alternative approach to one focusing on problems, which stresses a more positive way of thinking, is Appreciative Inquiry (Appreciative Inquiry Commons 2006). Appreciative Inquiry is a strengths-based approach to action research. Developed by Cooperrider it is based on the assumption that the organization 'is a miracle to be embraced rather that a problem to be solved' (French and Bell 1999, p.208). Although organization development and participative strategies in general are a challenge to undertake successfully in large, bureaucratic agencies, and managers are frequently not trained to carry them off, they can be used successfully (Cohen and Austin 1997; Pine *et al.* 1998).

Appreciative Inquiry has developed from social construction theory, action research and strengths-based approaches to organizational development. The number of people working in this way in the public and private sector is growing, facilitated by an open approach to sharing ideas and developments and willingness to practice the method in different settings. There is no single way to run an Appreciative Inquiry, only principles to be upheld.

Appreciative Inquiry begins with the assumption that something in the organization is, or has in the past, functioned well. With this method, stakeholders are invited to recall and explore the times when their organization was at its best. Working together, they turn their understanding of these highlights or exceptional moments into a picture or image of how they would like to see their organization in the future. This is a vision that everyone can share and help to put into practice. Advocates of this approach believe that building on acknowledged strengths creates enthusiasm and commitment and change becomes inevitable. It invites people to think differently about organizations and the people in them, and to recognize the impact of labelling performance and the way that interventions are handled. Crucially, it recognizes the complexity of working with organizations and takes this into account in moving forward.

What does an Appreciative Inquiry look like?

An Appreciative Inquiry follows five distinct stages and is carried out according to some basic principles (see Watkins and Mohr 2001). Within this framework, it can be applied in any context of whole organization, partnerships, divisions, teams or groups. Methods will differ according to the size and scope of the inquiry. In some models, everyone comes together in the room for one to five days to work through the process together; in very large-scale inquiries, parts of the process (e.g. appreciative interviews) are delegated throughout the organization over a number of weeks and then brought together to be developed further. However the inquiry is structured, participants will work through the following stages (adapted from Cooperrider *et al.* 2001):

DEFINITION

Decide what to learn about/inquire into in consultation with people in the organization. This sets the focus of the inquiry and determines the specific questions on which people will be interviewed.

DISCOVERY/EXPLORE AND UNDERSTAND

Conduct the inquiry, involving participants in interviews, sharing stories about the organization at its best, and working together to draw out themes about success.

DREAM/IMAGINE

Generalize from these themes to create a picture of how the organization would look if these elements existed now or in the future. This is rooted in the participant's knowledge and experience of what the organization has been, and could be, capable of.

DESIGN/CREATE

Develop ideas and practical steps about how to create this picture of the organization now. Work out what needs to happen (people, structures, resources) next to achieve this in practice.

DELIVERY

Put these ideas into practice, building on what has been learnt in the previous phases.

Using this method, a growing number of public and private sector organizations in the US and, more recently, in the UK, have successfully engaged their staff in designing and creating positive changes, working from their strengths and past successes (see French and Bell 1999; Department of Health 2003b).

The following US example illustrates Appreciative Inquiry in action:

> Picture a 'failing' social services organisation. Employees are demoralised and weary; morale is low. Staff are leaving; those remaining feel undervalued and isolated from the organisation, from colleagues, and from the service users. The outside pressures to improve services threaten and divide. Now imagine walking into this organisation a year later and discovering the changes.

> 'When I entered the building I sensed that something had changed. There was lightness in the air. Employees greeted me, each other and the children with a smile and sincerity. Joy and unity had been restored. Resignation and defeat had been transformed into communication, learning, commitment, responsibility, partnership, accomplishment and delight.' (Miller et al. 2004, p.369)

This is what happened in a Headstart (pre-school) programme in East Parish, Denver. The Community Development Institute (CDI) provided interim 'recovery' management after funding was withdrawn. After several months deploying regular training and strategic planning techniques 'with little or no results', the project leader turned to Appreciative Inquiry. Nine months later they were seeing startlingly positive results and new hope for the service as staff became re-engaged and enthusiastic about their work. They are convinced that Appreciative Inquiry helped the staff to turn this service around (Miller et al. 2004).

Applying Appreciative Inquiry in social services in the UK

Radford describes the use of *Appreciative Inquiry* as both a theory of change and a methodology for discovering, understanding and fostering innovations. It involves the 'art and practice of asking questions that strengthen a system's capacity to discover and develop its potential. It is not about ignoring problems; it is about approaching them from a different perspective' (Radford 2004). An example of these principles applied with teams of staff engaging in a wide-ranging family reunification program improvement effort is described in detail in by Barbara Pine and Lynne Healy in Chapter 2.

What might this mean for local authority social services in the UK? Appreciative Inquiry is based on the deceptively simple idea that organizations grow in the direction of the questions they ask and on which they focus. An inquiry (gathering information for the purpose of learning and changing) into past or existing strengths is itself a powerful intervention which begins to shifts the organization in a new direction. Imagine what it would be like if people in social services teams and authorities were talking, not about problems and deficits, but about their achievements, the things that had gone well and of which they were most proud. There follow two examples of what might happen.

A social services team might set aside some time to inquire into its performance, in a process that involves every member. Having identified the focus of the inquiry (e.g. communication, allocating and reviewing work, team performance in general), they agree specifically worded questions for the interviews with each other. They talk about the times when their team was (or is) working at its best, and list what they value and would like more of in their team. Briefing is given about conducting and recording the interviews. They are carried out during a specific meeting or as and when the opportunity arises over an agreed period.

The responses are then brought to a meeting of the whole team. They work together to understand the features of the team at its best, and use what they learn to envision how it would look if these things were always present. So, for example, what will be happening, how are people behaving, what are they doing, how they will work together and so on. Having worked together to create this picture of the team succeeding, they move into the design stage by looking at what needs to change to make this happen, including personal commitments to specific actions. The process is cyclical and they can return to any of the stages to work on specific aspects.

Another hypothetical example shows the impact of Appreciative Inquiry on a bigger scale:

An 'improving' local authority might arrange a process for its staff to undertake interviews/share their experiences about times when the organization (or a specific part of it) was at its best. This might be done by everyone or a representative slice of the organization, including councillors (elected representatives of local councils) and service-users, and again could be achieved by dispersed interviews followed by specific events to work on the emerging themes and lessons from the stories. In both examples, the process is participative, creative and focuses on identifying and increasing best performance. This approach immediately affects the way that performance is described and addressed. For example, the changes include the following:

- The language of 'failure' is rejected. Strengths of the people and the organization are highlighted and celebrated.

- Interventions are mutual; facilitators work collaboratively with the whole system, including service-users, councillors and the staff who will achieve the organization's recovery.

- Participants develop a shared view of the changes needed to improve their organization. Specific actions are developed for real situations. Everyone is involved in, and committed to, the organization's recovery.

- Energy and enthusiasm for change is created, together with commitment to take the changes forward in very practical ways. Changes planned and achieved under these circumstances are more likely to be sustained.

Mohr (2001) has applied this approach in many settings with many different inquiry topics, in large and small groups in the US. He identifies the following conditions as those that 'seem to be present when Appreciative Inquiry has been most effectively incorporated into a process of organizational learning and change' (p.4). The following points summarize these conditions:

- The organization honestly acknowledges any difficulties that currently exist. This approach does not advocate denying negative emotions or problems, but encourages participants not to dwell on them.

- The organizational culture is open to, and supports, participation by all, and is therefore, prepared to listen to and work with what the participants say.

- Change is seen as an ongoing process, not a one-off event.

- Leaders believe in the organization's capability and believe that a positive approach can be effective.

- The organization provides structures and resources to support the inquiry and to follow it through.

Conclusion

This chapter has highlighted a range of issues about improving services and performance and describes a positive and creative approach to managing change. There are some key messages from the chapter. These include the fact that how failure is perceived, discussed and acknowledged is crucial. There are many versions of success, from specific improvements to wide-ranging features of organizational life, and there is no universal recipe for achieving improvement – context is all. Linear models of change are inappropriate for complex systems and piecemeal attempts are more likely to fail. Key elements of effective turnaround strategies are:

- early warning
- swift action to stabilize crisis situations
- visionary leadership
- whole systems approaches
- participation, engagement and learning.

There are tensions between mechanistic solutions and those that advocate learning and more participative approaches. Approaches which emphasize diagnosis and cure can isolate problems and, in failing to recognize the complexity of the whole system, are often ineffective. Finally, methods that focus on solving problems work against organizational improvement; new approaches focusing on strengths and positive change are proving to be effective.

The public sector in England is currently preoccupied with managing risk and meeting performance targets, which inevitability focuses attention onto gaps, problems and deficits. Current thinking discussed in this chapter suggests that it is counter-productive to put these at the centre of our improvement planning; and the real challenge is to seek out, acknowledge and build on strengths. There is too much at stake for everyone to ignore the signs that traditional approaches are, at best, slow and, at worst, ineffective in creating sustainable change. The UK needs to adopt developmental approaches to organizational change and the chapter has given the example of Appreciative Inquiry as one such approach. Such approaches offer staff, stakeholders, service-users and whole organizations the opportunity to engage with services in a positive way. They may be just what our beleaguered organizations need to give them a chance to improve.

The author wishes to express her thanks to the *Journal of Research Policy and Planning*, for allowing her to include material first published in the journal in 2004, and to the Department of Health.

Chapter 4

Ethical Issues for Social Work and Social Care Managers

Lynne M. Healy and Barbara A. Pine

Introduction

The ethics-related demands on social work/social care managers are considerable. These managers must understand professional and organizational ethical obligations, make moral choices, set the tone and climate to facilitate ethical practice by others, ensure congruence between professional codes of ethics and the organization's mission, programs, and work environment, and protect the organization from legal risk related to ethical lapses. This has been described by Dawson and Butler as being "morally active" as front-line managers: "Faced with competing demands that require sorting into some order of priority and confronted daily with vital human needs that somehow have to be met from restricted resources, health and social care managers need an ethical framework" (2003, p.237).

According to Levy (1982, p.144), "Executives are the duly appointed monitors of the manifest values and ethics of social organizations, and the symbolic representations of them in and outside the organization." They should be guided by administrative ethics, defined as 'the formal and informal restraints that give legitimacy to the actions of an administrator'" (Reamer 2000, p.70).

While the importance of managerial ethics is clear, just as clearly some managers fail to practice ethically. The many scandals in corporate management have rocked faith in managerial honesty. These have been compounded by similar episodes in governmental and even non-governmental sectors including the human services. Well-publicized cases including the Enron company, the savings and loan scandal, the United Way of America and others reveal that managers have misused funds, misconstrued the financial health of private and non-profit orga-nizations, buried research on useless or even harmful products, intimidated and fired whistle-blowers, and practiced corruption. Thus, organizational leaders must earn the confidence of the public and their clientele through ethical practice.

Although the number of public scandals may suggest otherwise, there is increased interest in managerial ethics today, both in business and in social work. This is related to many factors, including but not lim-ited to the publicity surrounding scandal in the social services. Among other factors are the following:

- The emergence of new ethical challenges created by changing technology such as life-support systems, in-vitro fertilization and other medical advances. The agonizing examples of the Karen Quinlan case that began in 1975 (Ascension Health 2004) and the more recent Terri Schiavo case in 2003 (Liptak 2003) in Florida, both involving issues of right to die vs. maintenance of artificial life support of comatose patients, captured the public's attention.

- New social and health problems such as HIV/AIDS have raised complexities to confidentiality and public health safety.

- The increasing scarcity of resources for public and non-profit organizations has heightened attention to issues of distributive justice and rationing of services.

- In many countries, there is increased regulation of the profession of social work, with accompanying accountability mechanisms through licensure, registration or accreditation; all of these include provisions on ethics.

- Court decisions on professional liability, such as the
  well-known Tarasoff case in which a psychologist was held
  liable for failure to warn a potential victim of violence, have
  increased the financial and organizational risks of poor
  ethical decision-making. (Weil and Sanchez 1983)

In the UK, similarly, advances in medical science and new health and
social care issues and societal expectations have raised new dilemmas.
Lack of resources, increased regulation and a more litigious culture have
all contributed to raise managers' awareness of the ethical dimensions of
their role. For example, individual patients have been taking action
against National Health Service Trusts who fail to provide particular
drugs (e.g. for breast cancer) or treatments (e.g. for infertility) when similar trusts elsewhere in the country would provide treatment. The
consumers of services have viewed what has been described as a "post-
code lottery" as unethical and found support for their view in the courts.
Managers have been held accountable for their decisions.

Perhaps as a response to these factors, attention to ethics within the
social work profession at national and international levels has grown,
reflected in new codes of ethics and in a growing professional literature
on the topic. For all these reasons, concern for ethical principles, long a
hallmark of the social work profession, is increasingly important for
social work/social care managers. But advancements in ethical rules for
practice have emphasized direct work with individuals and families.
Practitioners who function in managerial roles often express frustration
or confusion when looking to social work codes of ethics for guidance
with their ethical dilemmas.

In this chapter, we examine the dimensions of managerial responsibility for ethics. We then identify some of the key ethical challenges
facing managers in the human services. Drawing on literature on managerial ethics, on social work ethics, and on codes of ethics we expand
principles for ethical decision-making in social work/social care management and identify mechanisms to assist ethical management practice.

Managers' responsibility for ethics

While the social work profession has focused its attention on ethics in
direct care, social services and social care managers face particularly

difficult ethical challenges. Managers are decision-makers, and decisions often involve moral choices. Managers have multiple and often competing obligations to a wide range of stakeholders. As organizational leaders, they also have multiple sets of ethical obligations, especially those linked to public service (such as accountability for the public good) and those that are part of their professional identity. Managers have power and thus have responsibility to exercise that power in ethical ways, by recognizing rights, being fair and just, and avoiding harm. As Ife stated, the greater power of the manager's position suggests "an unequal power relationship with at least the potential for oppressive practice and the denial of human rights" (2001, p.179). Thus, an important concept in managerial ethics is the concept of greater responsibility (Congress 1997). Yet, management roles and the nature of authority within the social sector are complex and fragmented. The practice environment is uncertain, with frequent severe threats to funding levels. As if that were not enough, legal risks to organizations and staff have increased, as is discussed further in Robert Madden's Chapter 7 on legal issues.

At the most basic level, managers are responsible for practicing ethically. As leaders, their actions have a spread effect and when managers practice ethically, they also model integrity and ethical behavior. Managers have a central role in setting the tone for ethics in their agencies (Brody 1993; Seden 2003). They have the opportunity to provide leadership to regular review and improvement of the organization's ethics-related policies and procedures. In addition to policies, managers must create the climate that makes ethical practice possible. This entails removing barriers to ethical practice (such as unreasonable efficiency pressures) and creating conditions that promote ethical reflection and reasoning within the organization.

An additional and often overlooked ethical responsibility is to ensure that the organization is in moral alignment: that there is congruence between the policies and practices of the organization and its mission and goals. Thus an agency devoted to expansion of flexible working conditions for women must have flexible workplace policies for its own staff; an organization devoted to advocacy for disabled people must strive for full accessibility in its own setting, and so forth.

Moreover, there are numerous arenas for tension and challenges in fulfilling the ethical responsibilities outlined above. They include:

- those associated with goals and functioning of the organization, including the congruence between the "espoused" and "enacted" values of an organization (Martin and Henderson 2001a, p.66)

- those associated with employer—employee relations

- those associated with the allocation and management of the organization's resources (program decisions and stewardship of finances)

- those associated with service-provider—client relationships

- those associated with relationships with other agencies, both collaborators and competitors, and

- those associated with agency-community relations.

Organizations and ethical responsibilities

Social work and social care managers function within organizations. Scholars differ over the obligations of managers and organizations in the arena of ethics. Joseph discusses literature that calls decisions of organizations "social decisions" that are non-individual and based on rationality. Social decisions are governed by rules of rational efficiency (utility) while the actions of individuals are governed by ethical responsibility (1983, p.52). She discusses and critically appraises Ladd's view that organizations "have no moral rights and responsibilities" beyond those defined by legal obligations (p.53). According to this view, organizational decisions should be made on the basis of rationality and utilitarianism. A contrasting perspective, is "that the organization, similar to an individual or collectivity, is a moral agent, ethically responsible for its actions" and that "human service organizations are responsible for their actions, a responsibility that stems from their purpose and public commitment" (Joseph 1983, p.53). Perhaps both aspects are relevant in that the rational view still leaves room for interpretation which the manager must deal with because managers both shape and are shaped by organizational structure and culture (Handy 1995).

More current organizational developments also compound ethical challenges. These is a growing emphasis on cost containment by organizations and the larger societal environment; an increase in the number of profit-making social service providers; and "ethical issues related to team and interdisciplinary action in organizational settings" (Joseph 1983, p.56). Joseph finds that the first two trends conflict with the value orientation of the social work code of ethics. The third raises issues of potential value conflicts with other professions, as not all ethics codes agree. Indeed, Martin and Henderson (2001a) point out the importance of exploring and recognizing that the values of various organizational participants may differ, both within and between professions. "Assuming that values are held in common may bring difficulties because it implies that there is agreement about ways of doing things that are consistent with these values" (p.57). They point out (as do other authors) that, within an organization, values are influenced by interactions among societal values, organizational values, group or team values, and individual values.

The often-maligned organizational form of bureaucracy comes under criticism as antithetical to ethical management. Manning (2003) identifies some of the facets of bureaucracy that may interfere with ethical leadership: routinization, fixed rules, secrecy, "moral anesthesia," structures for decision-making and specialization. It should be noted that bureaucratic rules were established in part to eliminate favoritism and aspects of unfairness that predominated in less rule-based structures; thus, it is unfair to conclude that bureaucracy in and of itself is contrary to ethical practice (Lipsky 1980; Hasenfeld 1983).

Managerial behaviors and ethical climate in organizations

It is not possible to overstate the importance of ethical management practice since managerial behaviors can positively and negatively affect ethical functioning in a social service or social care organization. As Dawson and Butler (2003) assert, managing is essentially a moral enterprise. As identified in Table 4.1, managers have many opportunities to act positively on the ethical front, beginning with their own practice and extending to their responsibilities for policies and procedures. In contrast, the negative behaviors of managers, ranging from specific unethical acts to disinterest, may create a climate of widespread tolerance of unethical practices among staff, or frustrate staff members in their own attempts to resolve ethical dilemmas. Rigid ethical rules, broadly applied, can also have a chilling effect on practitioners.

Table 4.1: Managerial behaviors and organizational climate

Behaviors that contribute to a positive ethical climate	
Behavior	*Example*
Manager models ethical behavior	Supports another agency's proposal to open a group home for the mentally ill in her neighborhood, even though it might lower property values
Manager puts in place/supports structures that encourage discussion of ethical issues	Establishes an ethics committee; conducts an ethics audit
Manager investigates suspected unethical behaviors	Conducts prompt and fair investigation of ethical violations
Agency policies and procedures are consistent with its mission and with general principles of ethical practice	Turns down a grant from a corporation whose business conflicts with the agency mission (such as a tobacco or arms company)
Behaviors that contribute to a negative ethical climate	
Behavior	*Example*
Ordering staff to do something unethical	Orders staff to lie in case record about degree of neglect, or number of client sessions delivered
Knowingly tolerates unethical behavior	Ignores evidence that one of the volunteer leaders is embezzling funds meant for children's program
Shows disinterest in ethical issues	Dismisses staff questions about ethical dilemmas
Overly rigid ethical rules—especially those that do not respect cultural difference	Writes policy forbidding staff from accepting anything from clients, even a cup of coffee, conflicting with the values of the ethnic groups served by the agency

Ethical complaints against managers

While the list of possible areas for ethical lapses and challenges is daunting, the experience of ethical complaints against social work managers appears less so. Strom-Gottfried (2003) examined 894 ethical complaints brought to the National Association of Social Workers in the US from 1986 to 1997. Out of these, 294 (32.9%) were brought against social workers in private practice; 47 percent were brought against staff within agency settings, including 179 (20%) against private non-for-profit agencies; 76 (8.5%) against public agencies; and an additional 165 against agency staff in which the auspices were not specified in the case record. More than 40 percent of complaints were brought by clients and another 11.4 percent by relatives of clients.

The second most frequent source of complaints was employees and supervisees against their supervisors or managers: 19.5 percent; in addition 10.4 percent were brought by colleagues of the accused. Strom-Gottfried notes, however, that "cases filed by employees against their supervisors or managers were the least likely to yield violations" (2003, p.88). Only 16 percent of these cases, as compared to 35 percent of cases brought by clients, were upheld as ethical violations. It is probable, however, that many of the unsuccessful ethical complaints were indeed cases of poor administrative practice or unfair personnel actions that fell outside the strict guidelines of ethical violations. The low rate of findings, therefore, should not necessarily be cause for concluding that managers are less likely than direct care workers to commit violations of ethics.

Principles of ethical management

In this section, we define ethical dilemmas and briefly discuss the theories underlying ethical decision-making. Then, we discuss in detail the ethical obligations of social work/social care managers and the sources from which these responsibilities derive.

What are ethical dilemmas?

It is important to state first and foremost that managers make many difficult decisions that are not ethical dilemmas. And, indeed, not all ethical decisions are dilemmas. An ethical dilemma is a decision that involves competing ethical principles and one in which the "correct" choice is not easily evident. Often, a dilemma means choosing between two or more negative alternatives and prioritizing one ethical value over another. Quoting Cooper, Reamer stated: "At base, these situations involve ordering our values and principles, consciously or otherwise. They are, therefore, problems of ethics" (2000, p.73). Managers often face dilemmas that are simply practice dilemmas—choices between several ways of accomplishing a task—but without significant ethical dimensions. Other choices that involve ethics are not dilemmas when there is a clear choice that is right, over one that is wrong. Faced with a choice of whether or not to embezzle funds, it is quite clear that embezzlement is wrong; thus, this situation in managerial ethics is not a dilemma. It is important not to overstate the reach of ethical dilemmas. As expressed by Reamer, "some ethical issues are fairly straightforward and others, however, are dauntingly complex" (2000, p.83).

Theories of ethics

Although extensive discussion of ethical theory is beyond the scope of this chapter, it is important to note that considerable scholarly work exists on philosophies and framework of ethics (Banks 2001; Bauman 1993; Beauchamp and Childress 2001). Ethical theories provide ways of organizing thinking and analyzing alternatives; they do not usually, however, usually provide clear directions for decision (Reamer 2000). The major theoretical division is between deontological and teleological approaches to ethics. Deontological theories are absolutist; certain actions are deemed always right or always wrong, regardless of the context or circumstance. Teleological theories are relativist and reject the idea of fixed ethical rules. Context and consequence are considered and weighed in judging actions (Loewenberg, Dolgoff and Harrington 2000). Decisions can be justified by a variety of rationales, including greatest good for the greatest number and greatest good for those who are oppressed. In his work, *A Theory of Justice*, Rawls (cited in Reamer 2000) explicates an approach that justifies inequality when it addresses unfairness suffered by persons through no fault of their own. Thus, those disadvantaged by accident of birth are entitled to special consideration from those advantaged through no "fault" of their own. Of particular interest to managers is the distinction between act and rule utilitarianism (Reamer 2000). In *act utilitarianism*, the rightness of an act is determined by goodness of its consequences in that individual case or set of circumstances (p.79), while in *rule utilitarianism*, the consequences that may result if one generalizes and acts similarly in all situations must be considered. In organizational contexts, we might expect the direct care social worker to be more apt to apply act utilitarianism while the manager must consider rule utilitarianism. An example of the distinction is given later in the chapter, showing that while an individual case decision to change a client's caregiver because of her discomfort with having a person of another race might be justifiable to meet the client's need for service (act utilitarianism), extending this policy to all clients would introduce racial bias into agency services—an unacceptable condition when adopted as a *rule*. Such an individual *act* would be deemed illegal in the UK, as it would be seen to be racially motivated. As Barris Malcolm discusses in Chapter 7 of this book, there are stringent laws in the UK to prevent discrimination on grounds of race, gender, religion, or sexuality.

Means and ends, not means vs. ends

The teleological approach is commonly referred to as situational ethics. In the situational approach to ethics, managers may justify ethically questionable means to reach worthy goals. Studies done in other professions indicate, for example, that many physicians in the US find it acceptable to write a false diagnosis on an insurance claim if it will improve patient access to treatment. And, in a study of the ethics of professional planners, findings showed that 33 percent of professional planners found tactics such as leaking private documents acceptable if done on behalf of a disadvantaged group, while only 16 percent judged the same behavior ethical if it favored a business-oriented organization, demonstrating a clear ends justify means mode of thinking (Howe and Kaufman 1979).

While social work and social care managers may indeed find comfort in the Rawlsian principles of justice, whereby special treatment is acceptable when it benefits those otherwise denied equal opportunities through no fault of their own, this is not the same as justifying unethical tactics toward good ends, as the following example illustrates. A child welfare social worker reported that she was ordered by her supervisor to exaggerate the extent of child neglect in a case and to state that she had observed things that she had not actually observed. When the worker objected, her supervisor took the case to a higher-level manager; this manager, too, ordered the social worker to put false information in the case record. We can assume in this case that the managers were striving for a good case outcome—child protection. To ensure that the court would support a protective order, they felt that stronger statements about parental neglect were necessary. Clearly, ordering a staff member to lie is unethical and an unacceptable tactic, no matter how noble the end. The ethical manager strives for ethics in both ends and means.

Sources of ethical principles for social work and social care management

Managers can draw on various sources for ethical principles, including managerial science, public service ethics, and the professions. In a discussion of the importance of ethics to leadership, Northouse posits that the ethical leader "respects others, serves others, shows justice, manifests honesty, and builds community" (2000, p.258).

Management and public service

In Britain, the Parliamentary Committee on Standards in Public Life, chaired by Lord Nolan (Nolan 1996), set up to address the values needed in public office, identified a set of principles for leaders in the public sector. It should be noted that the Committee was convened due to concerns over cases in which the personal interests of senior officials in the public sector had superceded the public interest. The Committee identified the following principles of ethical public service: selflessness; integrity; objectivity; accountability; openness; honesty and leadership (see Martin and Henderson 2001a, pp.60–61).

The value of accountability is often linked to the ethic of efficiency, interpreted as valuing the safeguarding of public or non-profit resources and achieving outcomes at the lowest possible cost. Indeed, the pressures of efficiency can be intense for public managers. Serving in a time of service and budget cutbacks, one public social agency manager noted that he was alarmed when he realized that he had been proud of the efficiency with which his unit had removed dozens of families from the welfare roles in response to new regulations. Although a committed social worker, he reflected that the ethic of efficiency can at times overtake one's focus on professional goals (personal communication). As expressed by Coulshed and Mullender:

> In social work and social care, it takes managers with vision to bring the customer care and staff care agendas to the center of attention. It also takes vision to shift managerial concerns beyond narrow conceptions of balanced budgets and procedural conformity onto quality standards that reflect the aspirations of all the interested parties, including service users and their families, for whom the best outcomes of care may not always be those that look the tidiest on paper. (2001, p.88)

The profession and ethics

The applicability of professional codes of ethics can be approached from two perspectives. First, do social work codes of ethics apply to social workers who are in managerial positions? Alternatively, we can ask whether social work codes of ethics are helpful to managers in resolving ethical dilemmas. One study of the ways in which public managers addressed ethical dilemmas revealed minimal impact of professional codes of ethics. To the surprise of the researchers, managers who were members of professions, including law, medicine, engineering, and psychology, "seldom mentioned the professions and the codes of ethics related to those professions as having any influence on their actions" in resolving ethical dilemmas (Gortner 1991, p.43). These professionals identified themselves as managers and reported that they did not find their professional codes helpful in addressing managerial situations. Interestingly, in instances that called upon the managers to act in their professional capacities (for example, as a lawyer rather than a manager), they reverted to reference to their professional codes. These findings raise questions about the adequacy of the social work codes of ethics as guides for managerial ethics. This will be examined below, although we begin from a premise that one's professional base forms the foundation for her or his managerial roles and that, despite their limitations for management practices, codes of ethics are essential tools for guiding ethical practice.

Tools to aid ethical management in social work and social care

There are several types of tools aimed at helping ethical management in social work and social care. Among them are codes of ethics, value hierarchies, ethics committees, and ethics audits.

Social work codes of ethics

The codes of ethics of the National Association of Social Workers (NASW) and of the British Association of Social Workers (BASW) are in agreement about the basic values of social work. Both codes indicate that these values are: human dignity and worth; social justice; service; integrity; and competence. The NASW Code of Ethics adds as a sixth value "importance of human relationships." The values provide a framework for social work/social care management, but only at the most general level.

The social work codes of ethics have grown in their detail and complexity. Hallmark social work ethical principles such as self-determination, informed consent, confidentiality, and non-discrimination are carefully spelled out. It is not possible to discuss each of these social work principles in detail here. However, the manager's multiple roles and ethical obligations for upholding traditional values can be demonstrated using the example of the principle of confidentiality. The manager has a duty to respect confidentiality in his or her practice by respecting the confidences of staff as well as clients and by informing others when conversations and documents are not protected. The manager has the important additional responsibility to develop, implement, and oversee policies that protect confidentiality rights of those served by the agency. And the manager must ensure that the practices and policies of the agency support social work staff in their efforts to maintain confidentiality and informed consent, such as through developing and providing helpful consent forms, training on exceptions to confidentiality, and creating a climate in which client information is respected and protected. The management applicability of other values such as prohibition against participating in fraud and dishonesty and commitment to nondiscrimination, is perhaps even more evident.

At the same time, we caution against transposing all provisions regarding clients to relationships with staff and volunteers. The NASW Code of Ethics, in particular, contains extensive cautions and prohibitions about dual and multiple relationships. Rigid interpretation and application of these principles to manager-staff relationships could result in an overly hierarchical and mechanistic organization and one that discourages promotions from within. While it is important for managers to remain sensitive to potential conflicts of interest and *harmful* dual relationships (such as sexual harassment or private business dealings), they must also ensure a flexible and participative environment that allows for growth, development, and contribution by staff and volunteers.

Careful management of potential conflicts of interest is essential for managers. It is important to avoid favoritism and to uphold fairness in all professional actions, from personnel to contracts and purchasing. A case in the state of Kentucky suggests that the standard for public social service managers can be very strict. The Court of Appeals rules that the Executive Director of the public Department of Social Services violated a state ethics code when she solicited money for Christmas presents for foster children from business having contracts with her department. While a lower court had ruled that there was no ethical violation because her action was not motivated by personal interest, the Appeals Court rules that "the ethics code serves to prevent apparent as well as actual conflicts of interest regardless of the motive involved" (Wolfe 2001). The implied authority of the executive to grant or withhold contracts could be assumed to pressure businesses into contributing.

In addition to ethical considerations, managers need to be cautious about dual relationships that lead to blurring of their roles and responsibilities. A familiar scenario in management of non-profit agencies is the confusion of roles and responsibilities of board members and the executive. The following case illustrates the point:

A small and relatively new non-profit agency was struggling to survive in a difficult funding climate. The agency developed out of the commitment of the founder to address the needs of an underserved community; he recruited friends and supporters to help, and, as the agency became a registered non-profit, asked some of them to serve on the Board of Directors. Members were recruited to the board with no specific terms of office; as is true of many new small agencies, policies were not yet written for board functioning, elections, etc. Board members sometimes took on hands-on projects for the agency, such as assisting with grant writing. The Board President took on more and more such projects and began to come to the agency almost daily. He began to criticize and overrule decisions made by the director about details of building management and then staff supervision. He then announced to the director that since there was empty space in the new building and he was reorganizing his own small business, he was planning to move his office into the agency building.

While the case may not have serious ethical violations, the relationships between the board members and executive director had clearly become intertwined to the extent that both executive and board functioning were impaired. Thus, in terms of its impact on the organization, it is an example of harmful dual relationships.

Distributive justice is a particularly important administrative ethical responsibility. Whereas direct service practitioners often approach cases with the goal of optimizing outcomes for an individual client or family, managers must recognize the multiple claimants on the organization's resources. The NASW Code of Ethics specifies that managers should seek adequate resources and that fair allocation procedures should be used:

a) Social work administrators should advocate within and outside their agencies for adequate resources to meet client needs.

b) Social workers should advocate for resource allocation procedures that are open and fair. When not all client needs can be met, an allocation procedure should be developed that is

nondiscriminatory and based on appropriate and consistently
applied principles. (NASW 1996, para 3.07).

Although less specific, the BASW Code of Ethics calls for managers to
"promote equality policies and practices and advocate for resources to
meet service users' needs" (BASW 2002, para 4.4.1c). The principle of
honest stewardship of agency resources is nicely stated in the NASW
Code, stating that "Social workers should be diligent stewards of the
resources of their employing organizations, wisely conserving funds
where appropriate and never misappropriating funds or using them for
unintended purposes" (NASW 1996, para 3.09g).

Climate creation—a core managerial ethical responsibility we identified early in the chapter—is emphasized in the BASW Code. First
among the special principles for managers are responsibilities:

a) To work for the acceptance by employers of the values and
principles and requirements of the Code; and

b) To eliminate all factors within their control which prohibit or
discourage employees' adherence to the Code. (BASW 2002,
para 4.4.1).

Similarly, NASW states: "Social work administrators should take reasonable steps to ensure that the working environment for which they are
responsible is consistent with and encourages compliance with the
NASW Code of Ethics" (NASW 1996, para 3:07d).

Both codes identify fair personnel practices and policies as an ethical
responsibility, with particular attention to eliminating all forms of discrimination. The NASW Code, in fact, states that "Social workers should
accept employment...only in organizations that exercise fair personnel
practices" (NASW 1996, para 3.09f). This section carries extra implications for administrators/managers, who have power and authority to
influence the policies of their organizations and carry out these policies.
Thus, 3.09(f) can be reinterpreted for social work managers to specify
that they must ensure that the personnel policies of their organizations
are fair and that these policies and the way they are implemented remove
all discriminatory elements. Both codes contain specific provisions that
managers should ensure adequate professional supervision for social
workers.

A further consideration for social work managers in the UK context is the number of codes that can apply to operational decisions. There are now four Care Councils each with codes of conduct for social workers which are as relevant to social work managers as professional codes such as those of BASW. Additionally, when managers in both the UK and the US are working across agency boundaries in joint work, the codes of practice of other professional practitioners, for example nurses or teachers, must also be considered. This existence of a proliferation of guidance makes the manager's job even more complex. Therefore an ethically principled or "morally active" approach based on values is particularly important, to avoid a defensive, procedural approach and to enable the manager to reflect carefully on the equity and fairness of decisions. Dawson and Butler (2003, p.256) argue that a manager needs to be "ethically literate" to take "responsibility for their actions in the social contexts that surround them."

In summary, social work and social care managers should find that the social work codes do contain applicable principles for management, both in the specific sections on managerial responsibilities and in the general principles that underlie ethical social work, such as confidentiality, self-determination, and informed consent. It is also likely that knowledge of the codes of ethics will shape managers' expectations of their social work staff members' behavior (Perlmutter, Bailey and Netting 2001). However, not all provisions that specifically apply to client service can or should be transposed to the managerial functions. It is in fact dangerous to view the manager—staff, manager—policy maker, or other relationships between the manager and stakeholders as a replication of social worker–client relationships.

Value hierarchies in social work and ladders of ethical principles

As implied in the definition of an ethical dilemma, the most difficult ethical situations are those in which there are conflicting ethical principles. This suggests a need to rank order ethical principles to assist in determining which principles take precedence when not all can be optimized. One such rank ordering, called the Ethical Principles Screen has been developed by Loewenberg et al. (2000). The Screen gives priority to Protection of Life, followed by Equality, Autonomy, Least Harm, Quality of

Life, Confidentiality, and Truthfulness/Full Disclosure, in that order (p.69). An earlier version included the element of following the rules and regulations of the employer. Its omission from the current version certainly suggests a lower priority than the seven principles included. Managers may find this priority ladder helpful. However, it should be recognized for what it is—the opinion of one set of ethics scholars on the relative importance of the ethical principles. It is interesting, as noted above, that their own rank ordering has changed somewhat in the various editions of their ethics text, as it underscores that hierarchies of ethics are contested. A useful exercise within an agency would be to engage staff or members of an ethics committee (discussed below) in discussion of the Ethical Principles Screen and their own weighting of the principles.

Ethics committees

Formation of standing committees on ethics within social agencies can assist staff with resolution of ethical dilemmas (Reamer 1987). Particularly helpful are committees comprised of staff members from different levels of the organization who come together to discuss ethical problems facing the agency and its practitioners. The committee is available to social workers and managers as they encounter dilemmas that cannot be easily resolved, such as those involving conflicting principles.

Ethics committees in the US grew in popularity in health care settings partly as an outcome of the Karen Quinlan case, mentioned earlier. The New Jersey Supreme Court, while ruling that Ms. Quinlan's father had the right to determine that she be removed from a respirator, recommended that hospital ethics committees be formed to make such decisions (Ascension Health 2004). Although such committees are now common, their jurisdiction is by no means absolute. In fact, "most experts now agree that any authority an ethics committee has is limited and must appropriately respect the decision-making authority that properly belongs to patients, surrogates and care providers" (Ascension Health 2004).

Social workers and administrators will find ethics committees helpful in their deliberations, however. In one case, an agency that provides home care services for the elderly maintains an ongoing ethics committee. Staff members feel comfortable in bringing specific cases for discussion, knowing that the decision will be mutually arrived at and not subject to rigid rules. Some of the cases are relatively easy, such as assisting a social worker in deciding whether it is appropriate to accept a modest gift from a client; others involve the more challenging situations of self-neglecting elderly who wish to remain at home in spite of declining abilities—the conflicting principles of autonomy, protection of life, and least harm (Brown and Seden 2003; M. Gavin, personal communication, October 2004). Ethics committees are particularly common in hospital settings, where end of life and life support issues occur frequently.

Ethics audits

A more recent tool is the ethics audit, a comprehensive review of an organization's ethical practices and policies. A complete audit begins with examination of "an organization's faithfulness to its mission and the way it treats its staff, volunteers, donors and clients" (Allen 1995, p.51). It continues with review and critique of practices in board relations, marketing, financial management, personnel practices, and "the organization's ability to cultivate a climate in which trust, respect, professionalism, a sense of community and other important values are prominent" (Allen 1995, p.51). Examples of audit instruments are one developed by the Colorado Association of Non-Profit Organizations (CANPO) for use in any non-governmental organization (Colorado Association of Non-Profit Organizations 1994); and one tailored to social work developed by Reamer (2001) for the National Association of Social Workers. Both include checklists that can be followed in conducting an audit and suggestions to ensure that the audit results are used to make needed organizational changes.

A simple case illustration—or is it?

The following case is used to demonstrate a number of the principles discussed in the preceding pages. Although it appears to be a relatively simple case, it demonstrates the complexities of ethical decision-making from the vantage point of the manager.

CASE: Self-determination, the client comes first or nondiscrimination
A community based agency serves elderly persons. A social worker is organizing a friendly visitor service to reach out to the people in their own homes. The program is entirely voluntary; elderly persons who would like a friendly visitor register with the agency, and community members are solicited to volunteer as visitors. A procedure has been developed to match elderly with a volunteer. Both parties fill out papers, detailing interests and other personal facts. The agency then matches a volunteer with a client based on the paperwork and arranges for a first meeting. A 92-year-old woman has recently had her first meeting with the matched volunteer. The next day, she calls the social worker to say that she wishes to withdraw from the program. When the social worker asks why she wishes to withdraw, the elderly woman states that she is uncomfortable with a black companion as she has never before had a black person in her home. Therefore, she does not wish to continue. (Adapted from a case contributed by Leslie McDonough.)

What should the social worker do? Options are to attempt to mediate the situation and work to overcome the woman's prejudices; assign a white volunteer as her friendly visitor instead of the black woman originally assigned; or to respect the woman's right to choose who comes to her home, but refuse to adopt agency practices based on race and withdraw the client from the program.

While difficult for a direct care worker to resolve, this situation becomes more complex for administrative decision-making and, in fact, illustrates a number of the issues discussed in this paper. The social worker may focus on the needs of the 92-year-old client and the elements of the social worker codes of ethics that specify that the client comes first. For a manager, however, issues of precedent, fairness and nondiscrimination, and social justice compete for attention. The manager must consider the impact the decision will have on staff, on the community, on current and future volunteers, as well as the impact on the client. A manager might argue that while the client has a right to self-determination, the client does not have a right to determine that the agency compromise its commitment to nondiscrimination. The issue of setting precedents for decisions illustrates the possible contrast between the *act utilitarianism* that may be applied by the direct care worker and the *rule utilitarian* concerns of the manager. Additional factors that may add complexity to this situation (or others) are the age of the client (does the fact that she is 92 merit consideration?), whether the service is voluntary or mandated (would the client's expression of her self-determination be more compelling if this were a mandated service—perhaps justifying respecting her small effort to exert control over her life?); whether the service provider is a paid staff member or a volunteer (does taking race into account have a negative impact on the provider in terms of career, self-esteem, regard within the professional community, etc.?). As Northouse observed, "justice requires that leaders place fairness at the center of their decision making, including the challenging task of being fair to the individual while simultaneously being fair to the common interests of the community" (2001, p.274).

If the Ethical Principles Screen (Loewenberg *et al.* 2000) is used in this case, we can see that a number of the principles are potentially involved—equality/inequality; autonomy and freedom; least harm; and quality of life. Potentially, the value of truthfulness could be involved if the manager decided to meet the client's need, but document an alternative reason for the change of visitor. This relates to the issues of openness and transparency in decision-making. When making ethical decisions, administrators are urged to be open. Which decision would the manager be willing to announce to the public in this case? Would the case decision differ if the manager were sure it could be kept quiet? Can secrecy in such decisions ever be justified? The case also raises the issue of moral alignment mentioned earlier. The manager must take responsibility for ensuring congruence between the agency's mission and goals and its operating principles and practice—congruence that will be challenging to achieve in this case.

This is surely an example of a case that would benefit from open and frank discussion by managers and social workers in an ethics committee forum. On the face of it, the case is fairly simple. It demonstrates, however, the complexities of ethical decision-making and the challenges of optimizing social work ethical principles.

Conclusion

In concluding, there are several important cautions and areas for future consideration concerning codes of ethics and the scope of ethical decision-making for agency managers in the social context. Social work managers must remember that interpretation of ethical principles is not fixed but evolves and shifts in response to changes in society and new perspectives on what is acceptable or possible. The impact of globalization is likely to make this more complex. Over the past several decades, social work professional organizations in the US, the UK, and elsewhere have rewritten their codes of ethics, adding increased specificity and expanding the areas addressed. Ethics and values, however, are not only or even primarily about rules. A scholar recently noted "Teaching values, then, is central to our nation's well being and can't be reduced to—or confused with—the mere proclamation of rules or codes" (Scapp 2004, p.13).

As social work codes of ethics have grown in complexity, so have concerns that rule-based ethics may turn professionals into technicians. Banks warns about the dangers of the "rulebook" approach, criticizing detailed codes of ethics as "over-prescriptive and appearing to limit the role of professional judgement" (Banks 2004, p.123). She cautions that such codes may give professionals a false sense of security that all is well if the "rules" are followed. Furthermore, they may discourage development of "the capacity for ethical reflection and judgement" (p.123) that is so crucial in a care-oriented profession. The drive for increased accountability in the human services has led to emphasis on specific case outcomes and documentation of practice; it may also have contributed to the growth of the more detailed ethical codes. The impact of the accountability emphasis is complex. On one level, accountability and outcomes-focused practice protects clients from poorly focused services. On the other hand, practice targeted at measurable outcomes may be driven by efficiency and utilitarian emphases. Thus, professional values and ethical reasoning have important roles to play in ensuring a focus on care.

It is critical that social work/social care managers understand that ethical management is more than the absence of scandal or lawsuits. Ultimately, it is about just and good client-oriented, mission-focused social agency management that contributes to enhanced human wellbeing. In writing about ethics and leadership in public service, Luke (1991) emphasizes that the policy outcomes of managerial decisions are an important component of ethical behavior. Describing a shift from "behavioral ethics to policy ethics," Luke says:

> Policy leaders—elected and appointed—must consider ethical implications of policy choices. In their regard for the quality of life and well being of society, policy leaders must pay attention to the long-term consequences and externalities of their policy decisions. As a result, ethics in public administration involves not merely the avoidance of dishonorable behavior or the virtuous behavior of an individual manager. It also involves new ethical principles of action that can guide leaders in making policy choices in an interconnected global society. (1991, p.166)

Luke's ideas present an important frontier for social work and social care managerial ethics. The profession cannot be satisfied with a manager who goes no further than to do nothing wrong, although he or she accounts wisely for funds, treats staff fairly, and avoids conflicts of interest. With an expanded understanding of ethics, we must look at the impact of their managerial service: was life improved for those served, and was society made better in some way? Manning agrees, indicating "there is a moral necessity to contribute to the common good through the social responsibility that is attached to leadership" (2003, p.257). Ultimately, this may have more importance than the more narrow rule-based view of ethics; however, good policy consequences should not be used to justify individual behavioral indiscretions.

Finally, social service organizations and their leaders do not exist in isolation. The struggle for many social work/social care managers will be how to manage ethically and justly in an unjust society. Managers who persevere and remain proactive on ethics may discover that ethical management builds and strengthens community, both within the organization and in the larger environment (Allen 1995; Northouse 2000). By maintaining a focus on ethical principles rather than rules, and encouraging discourse on difficult ethical questions among staff and constituents, the manager may indeed create a more mission-compatible climate for the practice of social work management.

Chapter 5

Managing across Interagency Boundaries: A Learning Agenda for Change

Vivien Martin

Introduction

This chapter is about the challenges that face human services in developing interagency services. It explores the context of developing services across organization divides within the UK, mainly in relation to England. The chapter outlines the government's modernizing agenda for human services and poses the challenges which moving forward brings for managers and service providers. These include the agenda to involve citizens in planning and evaluating their services, developing partnerships, sharing philosophies and strategies and, above all, pooling budgets. There are barriers to change, including issues relating to an appropriate workforce, as well as factors that can facilitate change, including improvements in organizational arrangements and communications. These obstacles and facilitators for change also have relevance for social work managers in the US, where both government and private funders are promoting a range of collaborative initiatives to address complex social problems (Mizrahi and Rosenthal 2001).

A major vehicle for change is 'transformative learning'. This approach to learning draws on theory developed by Mezirow (1991) who suggests that individuals can be transformed through a process of critical reflection in his theory of transformative learning. Leading the learning agenda is a pivotal role for managers at all levels. Only through a learning agenda can both those who use and deliver services work together for change.

The expectations of those who need human services

People who need human services require and expect services that meet their needs. Essentially, this should be a sequence of care from the initial contact until the service is complete. Historically, in the UK, services have often been grouped into organizations to rationalize service provision and delivery rather than to create smooth pathways for service-users who need more than one service. Consequently, people often find themselves having to knock at the door of a series of different organizations and talk to a series of individuals, explaining their needs to each one and giving a range of personal information time after time. Service-users have constantly told researchers and government that they want timely and effective services that improve their quality of life, organized in ways that make them easy to use (see, for example, Department of Health 2001a).

The context of human services in the UK

Human services across health and social care in all four countries of the UK have traditionally been delivered through a range of organizations, each of which has operated with a degree of interdependence within a local health and social care economy.

Both health and social care services have been provided in all parts of the UK by a variety of different public, private and voluntary agencies. The same is true in the US. The providing organizations differ considerably in size, capability, funding arrangements and the extent to which they are subject to public accountability. Whilst in the UK, a number of these agencies operate under the overall umbrella of local government (in what is known as a local authority), many lie outside their jurisdiction, including National Health Service provision and the wide range of voluntary organizations. As a result, the allocation and disposition of resources to each of the contributory areas of service provision is subject to the accountability frameworks, funding regimes and operating practices of each of the 'providing' organizations. These features may vary considerably in different agencies.

There are several factors that have influenced the development of services. Many larger organizations have been formed from services that group naturally together, for example, social services departments or hospitals, Many of the individual organizations which group together usually structure themselves to focus on their specialist area of work with the aim of providing better services for people who need them.

Sometimes, the different ways in which organizations construct an interface with service-users and with each other have inadvertently created a range of barriers to the provision of high quality 'joined up' services. Some professionals, for example, associate themselves more with their professional groups than with their employing organizations, and may create boundaries around areas of work. This can increase difficulties in delivering services that cross these boundaries. Even when organizations are created to reduce barriers, managers find there is work to do to enable practitioners to understand each other's roles and abilities (Charlesworth 2003b; Ward 2003).

Modernizing public services

Contemporary policies have attempted to address the problem of barriers to seamless services across organizational divides by encouraging the integration of previously separated services. Consequently, the 'joining up' of public services is part of the political drive to modernize service provision within all the different countries of the UK. As the government paper underpinning proposed changes to human services in England stated in 1998, the aim of modernizing human services should be to create 'services that are suited to the needs of the people, not the convenience of providers' (Cm 4169, 1998, *Modernising Social Services* p.38).

The changes in social work and health services are only part of a wider political debate around the role of public services. Politicians of all parties claim that the overriding aim of the modernization of public services is to reduce social inequality and thus to improve the health and wellbeing of individuals and of society as a whole (see for example,

Department for Environment, Transport and the Regions 1998). This has been underpinned by a move away from reactive services towards a preventative approach that seeks to improve the conditions in which people live as well as respond to their immediate issues (see, for example, Department of Health, Department of the Environment 1997).

Demand for more coherence has been fuelled by highly publicized service failures, particularly incidents involving abuse of children or vulnerable adults, such as the case of Victoria Climbié, which was discussed in Chapter 3 of this book (see also Cmnd 5730 2003). In many of these cases, investigation revealed a need to manage issues that exceeded the capacity of any one organization or profession. Following the Climbié Inquiry, new guidance on interagency working has been issued in England, but success is still going to depend on the extent to which organizations and individuals make the operation in practice effective (*Working Together to Safeguard Children*, HM Government 2006a).

In the field of mental health, policy changes which attempt to create a better quality of life have increased the need for care in the community through closure of the old-fashioned, mental health institutions. Though the ideal of increasing care in the community is laudable, implementing these changes has not been without its problems, notably a reduction in funding of the continuing care for patients who have been discharged from hospitals and the ill-preparedness of communities to receive them.

Another factor that has influenced change has been the general increase in consumer expectations of what constitutes quality in public services. Policy makers have responded to these expectations by setting agencies the task of publishing charters for service delivery. Human services are now required to consult more widely with citizens and to be more inclusive in involving local people in development of local services. This increasing involvement in decision-making has raised expectations of wider choice for consumers and threatened an upsurge in demand on resources.

Attempts to control costs inevitably include consideration of different approaches to managing service provision. These, and other issues were laid out in the government's paper, Cm 4169, 1998, *Modernising Social Services*. This Government White Paper detailed service failings in social care and set out an agenda that was intended to bring services up to the standards required. *Modernising Social Services* emphasized the need to improve protection and services for children alongside improvement of workforce standards, partnership working and improvement of delivery and efficiency of service. Setting of standards was considered a priority and there was a new requirement for managers to gain a qualification. A similar paper was produced in Scotland (Scottish Office 1999).

In relation to health services, *The National Health Service Plan* (Department of Health 2000a) detailed the government's plan for investment and reform that was intended to lead to more staff in the National Health Service in England and Wales. Staff would also be working differently, with more decision-making located in local health and care communities. It acknowledged that structural and cultural change would be required to align responsibilities at the local level and to enable resources to be devolved. Strategic Health Authorities were to replace the former regional structures and to work closely with the Workforce Development Confederations, responsible for workforce planning. The new Primary Care Trusts, which replaced the structure for general practitioner services, for the first time included social services in their governance. Closer working between health and social care was supported by the appointment of Regional Directors of Health and Social Care.

To facilitate changes, the Health Act 1999 (England and Wales) and the Health and Social Care Act 2001 removed legal obstacles for joint working across health and care public services in England and Wales. Changes included supporting commissioning arrangements for partnership agencies, merging some services to provide a 'one-stop package of care' enabling the establishments of Care Trusts to provide integrated care and, above all the pooling of budgets between health and social care agencies. The development of Primary Care Trusts provided for closer working at the most usual first point of contact for those needing services. Funding was targeted at improvement of quality and efficiency of care through development of services including rapid response teams, intensive rehabilitation services, recuperation services, one-stop services for older people and integrated home care teams. Joint commissioning for mental health and services for older people was introduced to bring those services closer together. Health Improvement Programmes were established to tackle major health issues including substance misuse, teenage pregnancy and cancer care (see *Modernising Social Services, National Priorities Guidance*, Department of Health 1998b).

Pooling budgets to improve inter-agency working – some key issues

Prior to the policy changes brought about by New Labour in the late 1990s, it had often proved difficult to pool resources to provide seamless services because of the differing statutory requirements and legal frameworks of these mainly public bodies. Funding often hindered collaboration when organizations were working under different statutory and legal restrictions. These constraints were overcome in principle with the Health Act 1999 legislation that allowed the pooling of budgets between the National Health Service and social services. This allowed for both one-off and recurrent funding to be passed from the National Health Service to social services and voluntary organizations, or from social services to the National Health Service. These new arrangements raised several issues.

The transfer of funds

From a control perspective, the transfer of funds between organizations is, in theory, a relatively straightforward matter. However, as Mark Ezell explores in Chapter 11, in practice many complexities can arise, especially where diverse sources of funding are involved. Within the statutory sector in England, certain procedures have been laid down in government guidance from the Department of Health issued in 2000. Once the objectives of the transfer have been agreed, the funds can be transferred. Providing the funds transfer according to the guidance laid down by the Department of Health, an audit trail can be established. Within the recipient organization the transferred funds can be controlled within the normal budgeting processes established for that organization (see Department of Health 2000c).

Objectives and measurable outcomes

There are, however, other difficulties inherent in pooled budgets. Some of these arise from failures to agree initial objectives. A budget is a monitoring and control mechanism for measuring a plan of forecast activity. Such plans require objectives that are set out in terms of measurable outcomes that are usually, but not always, financial.

A number of difficulties typically arise in establishing common objectives for a pooled budget. For example, even in a budget for a service to be delivered jointly by two publicly funded organizations, the National Health Service and a local government social services department, a number of problems might arise. National Health Service care is traditionally free at the point of delivery whereas, although social services for children may often be free for children who are deemed to be 'in need', especially those at risk of significant harm, social services for adults are means tested. Even some children's services, such as day care and respite care, may require some payment. Difficulties arise when care provision crosses these traditional boundaries, for example, in deciding who should pay for personal service support when people are unable to care for themselves.

Potential for unequal partnerships

There may also be unease about the potential financial and strategic domination of one partner over the other. One agency for example, may play a lead role and tend to favour its own concerns and interests. If the lead partner sets the pattern for all of the systems, this often can be read as a takeover rather than formation of a new organization. There is also a danger that old patterns of work will be retained in the style of the lead organization so that the potential benefits of bringing together the different services offered within the partnership will be lost.

Problems in establishing service charges

There are often difficulties in establishing service charges. These can result from a wide range of factors, including differences in pay scales, overhead charges, methods of calculating workloads and formal agreements over work practice. Different performance indicators may be in use, leading partners to value (or have valued for them) different measures of what might be considered successful outcomes.

Overcoming issues of professional identity

Apart from the issue of budgets, there are other hurdles which need to be overcome. Sometimes professional status can create barriers to working across professional boundaries. Professions in health and social care environments have traditionally had different approaches to provision of care and have sometimes been slow to recognize the contribution made by professionals outside their own service. There are also often differences in values or in focus of service provision that mean it is difficult to make progress together, in partnership, until some common understanding and agreement has been established. Such agreements may be inhibited by clashes between different cultures within organizations. One annual report of the Chief Inspector of Social Services in England, for example, noted slow progress in changes because of the continuing failure to recruit and retain appropriately qualified staff and the failure to change existing service models (Department of Health 2000–2001).

Improving the workforce

Since 1996, the Social Service Inspectorate and the Audit Commission have carried out joint reviews focused on how well people are served by their local social services, including how well resources are used to provide 'Best Value'. One of the key barriers to working together has been the shortage of skilled staff, an issue noted in an annual report of the Joint Reviews of the Social Services Inspectorate and Audit Commission (Social Services Inspectorate and Audit Commission 2001–2002).

The report commented on the need for change in the everyday working practices between agencies and noted that sufficient attention was not always paid to ensuring improvement of core service provision. Instead, much of senior management time was spent in negotiating with staff in this highly political environment. Managers were urged to work closely with other agencies in commissioning, planning and developing new service structures. These activities needed attention to detail in sharing information, joint decision-making and effective performance management (Social Services Inspectorate and Audit Commission 2001–2002).

Similar concerns have been expressed in relation to the children's workforce, emphasizing the importance to improving children's outcomes of building better integrated services. This requires strengthening interagency and multi-agency working, and developing new workforce roles (*Children's Workforce Strategy*, HM Government 2005).

What helps organizations work together?

Sometimes it seems that there are more barriers to change than positive pathways but there are indications about what makes for positive working together.

In a competitive world, organizations may choose to work together for mutual gain. This is likely to occur when an alliance offers potential strategies that identify with products or outcomes rather than with the processes that have been developed to create those outcomes. It is these processes, however, that are an organization's 'core competences' and which provide valuable capability. For example, one organization might have a core competence that enables them to apply a high quality new technology; another might have a core competence in providing services to very large numbers of people or across a wide geographic area. It is often these core competences that provide the opportunity for organizations to consider a strategic alliance for mutual benefit. Such an alliance is not easy to maintain unless each partner recognizes that the other partner(s) add significantly to the achievement of shared purposes, maybe by adding an essential element or by increasing capability in some way. In health and social care, it would seem that organizations would have much to gain through partnerships that could 'join up' services that are frequently sequential in a service-user's pathway. Alternatively, joining together might enable a service to become more widely available.

Organizations with common purposes can also often find reasons to work together. When the ultimate common purpose is to reduce social inequality and to improve the health and welfare of citizens, such as occurs in public services, this would seem to provide a reason for partnership formation, especially wherever this would create opportunities to improve services. In reality, however, key organizational objectives are usually more focused on the nature and outcomes of a particular service. Identifying themselves with a particular locality may also be more important to some organizations. A number of mechanisms have been developed to help to overcome these obstacles to collaboration. In their study of 70 coalition leaders, Mizrahi and Rosenthal (2001) found that commitment to goals was ranked highest in a list of elements that contributed to successful partnerships.

Mechanisms for overcoming barriers – shared principles and charters

One strand of the government's aim to drive forward the agenda of interagency working has been to produce charters for providers and service-users. In 1999, to develop joint standards for the provision of services, the government produced a national charter for people who need long-term care in England (*Better Care, Higher Standards,* Department of Health and Department for the Environment, Transport and the Regions 1999). The charter was grounded in nine principles of public service. These stated that service providers should:

- set standards of service
- be open and provide full information
- consult and involve
- encourage access and promotion of choice
- treat all fairly
- put things right when they go wrong
- use resources effectively
- innovate and improve
- work with other providers. (pp.2–3)

These principles explicitly required providers to work together and to use resources effectively. The national charter also set out values that should underpin local charters. These included:

- treating people with courtesy, honesty and respecting their dignity

- helping people to achieve and sustain the maximum possible independence

- working in partnership with users and carers to provide the services they need

- involving users and carers in decisions and giving them sufficient information to make informed choices

- helping users and carers to have a voice through advocacy and other representative organizations

- treating people fairly on the basis of need and not discriminating against them on the basis of age, sex, race, religion, disability or sexual orientation, and

- ensuring that people feel able to complain about the standard of services provided and that they should not be victimized because they complain. (p.3)

Local performance standards have been set for each of these values. If organizations can adopt common values and use these in designing and developing care provision, this can provide a framework that will help to overcome apparently conflicting priorities. The rapid growth of inter-organizational partnerships in the US has been paralleled by a growing literature on interagency collaboration as well as a number of tools for assessing their success. Such tools can provide a learning agenda as partners seek to work together more effectively. A Collaboration Checklist identifying 12 factors that influence the collaborative process has been developed by Borden and Perkins (1999).

Pooled budgets in practice

The Health Act 1999 enacted legislation that provided greater scope for the resourcing of partnership schemes in England. Subsequent guidance suggested how jointly financed developments might be implemented through pooled budgets, lead commissioning and integrated provision. Mechanisms have been developed to improve co-ordination and to deliver 'seamless' service. These include joint funding of professional posts and the setting up of joint National Health Service and Social Services Trusts. Not only do these include joint funding but they demand the development of partnership agreements between local authorities and community care providers and provision of both health and social care at one location to provide cost-effective and efficient services and communication (Department of Health 2000c).

The complexity of bringing together funding from different sources is explored in depth by Mark Ezell in Chapter 11. Although there are a number of examples of these processes in operation in England, it is clear that the problems inherent in financial planning and control require a great deal of effort by all parties concerned. In some cases, the management practices and systems operated by the lead partner in a particular situation are adopted willingly by the others, and other stakeholders work to those systems. Sometimes, several systems are run in parallel and lateral co-ordination mechanisms are added to smooth the boundaries between them. Alternatively, a new system can be designed to meet the needs of the situation. Whichever of these approaches is adopted, there will always be major challenges to be met, such as co-ordination, data collection, information generation and the management of the core tasks, before high quality levels of service delivery can be achieved. The positive part that technology can play in such arrangements is discussed by Myron Weiner and Peter Petrella in Chapter 10.

If several systems operate in parallel, the potential for confusion is high. Clarity will depend on the success of mechanisms put in place to structure lateral and vertical communications. If a new system is designed, lessons from implementation suggest that there is a need for piloting it to iron out any faults, for winning hearts and minds, building in training and recognizing the potential for a period of confusion as people learn to work differently. A good example of lessons in implementing a new system of working can be found in the evaluation of the implementation of the *Framework for the Assessment of Children in Need and Their Families* in England and Wales (see Cleaver *et al.* 2004).

There are a number of areas where good design and work on ensuring compatibility are needed. When organizations come together in partnerships, there is often incompatibility of different software and operating systems that make it difficult to communicate and to share information (Ousley, Rowlands and Seden 2003). These have to be made compatible. Such issues and the importance of getting the right technological assistance are explored further by Myron Weiner and Peter Petrella in Chapter 10.

Operating difficulties are not necessarily only related to computer-based systems. It is likely that partner organizations will have different communication protocols governing who communicates with whom and how the communications are carried out. Some of these differences may emerge from different cultures within the partner organizations that may influence the expectations, for example, of whether communications are predominantly formal or informal. It might also be difficult to establish audit trails for accountability if the partner organizations have very different traditions. Managers will need to use their skills to identify and overcome these barriers and establish common systems.

Ultimately, it is people, not organizations, who work together. People make partnerships work. Organizational leaders and senior managers set the direction within which organizational partnerships can be formed. Leaders and managers at all levels develop the interpersonal relationships that enable collaborative working (Murphy 1993; Harrison et al. 2003).

Leading a learning agenda to support collaborative working

As lessons from implementing new ways of working have shown (e.g. Cleaver et al. 2004), one of the major facilitators of change in organizations is to establish a learning culture. The essence of such a culture is that the need for learning is acknowledged and shared by all staff at all levels. If people are to think and work in different ways they need to learn to do things differently. Government policies have acknowledged the need for learning throughout working lives (Department of Health 2001b). This approach to life long learning has also been supported by a Human Resource programme (Department of Health 2002) which focuses upon improving workforce planning, modernization of training and education, modernization of services and enhancement of staff skills to enable them to work differently. In order to achieve so much change, as Martin suggests, leadership is crucial:

> Leaders work with others to visualise how change could make an improvement, they create a climate in which the plans for change

are developed and widely accepted and they stimulate action to achieve the change. Leaders who can work with others to achieve improvements are needed at all levels of health and care services. Leaders are needed to make the small day-to-day changes that ensure services continue to meet the changing needs of the communities they serve. Leaders are also needed to achieve the more dramatic step changes that have to be accomplished to change the direction or focus of services when new approaches are introduced. (2003, p.5)

In the study by Mizrahi and Rosenthal (2001), mentioned above, leadership was second after shared goals as a priority for successful partnerships. The critical importance of leadership was discussed in detail by Barbara Pine and Lynne Healy in Chapter 2. As that chapter suggested, leaders are required to set a complex proactive agenda (Austin 2002). In effecting a learning agenda, leaders have several roles and tasks. First, leaders have a key role in developing a shared and compelling vision of the organization to clarify purpose and to enable strategies to be developed so that the desired change can be achieved (Rogers and Reynolds 2003a). The sharing of this vision must include those who use services, who need to be involved in the design and development of services (Connelly and Seden 2003).

Second, excellent leadership skills are needed in managing change. Improvement requires change, and change cannot happen without people who are able to lead and provide direction for the workforce and take them with them, and create feelings of satisfaction (Healy *et al.* 1995). Leaders can develop the capacity of organizations to change and to work in partnership with those who use their services and other agencies by negotiating to find ways of working across barriers (Rogers and Reynolds 2003b; Pine *et al.* 1998).

Lastly, leaders at a senior level need to work with their middle managers to ensure they are proactive and take effective and efficient action to achieve the organization's objectives. As Julie Barnes explored in Chapter 3, all aspects of performance management are crucial to ensure that all of the resources of an organization, including the human resources, are used to carry out the core work of the organization and to provide 'Best Value' for those who finance services and those who are in receipt of them.

Using transformative learning to effect change

The permanent whitewater of change (Vaill 1997), cited by Barbara Pine and Lynne Healy in Chapter 2, is a dominant feature of social work and social care organizations. As Vaill implies, concerns are emerging about the extent to which staff and service-users are able to engage in the fast pace and complex nature of changes in service development. Change involves people and their energy, their enthusiasm, their values and their abilities to think and to do things differently. Transformational leadership is required to bring about change (see Chapter 2) and learning is at the heart of the process of change. When people learn, they make changes in themselves and have the potential to apply that new understanding to how they live and work. Learning is therefore central to both personal and organizational change.

Any learning can transform people but the deeply personal nature of some learning has implications for those leading and engaged in transformational change. Learning is often a significant experience for individuals who may feel vulnerable or lose confidence if long-held beliefs are challenged. This kind of profound learning that leads to a fundamental change of view is called *transformative learning* (see Mezirow 1991).

Most people accept that they have to learn and develop throughout their lives and that incidents and events they experience will often provoke such learning and development. In spite of this, often these incidents puzzle people or cause emotional reactions like anger, fear or frustration. Sometimes individuals feel that they will lose something that they value or that they will face difficult challenges in the proposed new conditions. When ideas and values are challenged, individuals have to re-think their priorities and reconsider their value frameworks. This process is integral to any changes involved in moving from single to interagency working. There are sometimes very difficult challenges for organizations which embark on such transformational change with the expectation that members of staff will engage in the personal learning journey that is needed to work in changed conditions.

One major barrier to be overcome is the reconstruction of the reference points and mindsets of staff. When workers are confronted with a different perspective, brought by working for organizational leaders who hold a different view of the world, they find their own previously held viewpoint challenged. This can lead to a profound learning experience in which they review the assumptions and beliefs that they had relied on as a personal 'frame of reference'. If the learning is effective, people realize that some of their fundamental values are out-dated or inappropriate for the life they now live and the work they now need to undertake in the interagency arena.

Such learning has to be placed in the context of what is known about how adults learn. Mezirow, for example, has suggested that adult learners bring to situations of change an ability to view life from a wide perspective:

> to the degree our culture permits, we tend to move through adulthood along a maturity gradient which involves a sequential restructuring of one's frame of reference for making and understanding meanings. We move through successive transformations towards analysing things from a perspective increasingly removed from one's personal or local perspective. (cited in Jarvis 1987, p.18)

Transformative learning can change more than the way in which a person works; it can change the ways in which people live their lives. When there is significant change in the workplace, employees who are experiencing transformative learning during the change can become vulnerable in other aspects of their lives, if they become exposed to unanticipated and unsupported personal development. Leaders and managers can address this risk by being sensitive to the potential vulnerability of staff who are prepared to engage wholeheartedly in learning in order to work in different ways. Workers can be helped to be less vulnerable if managers provide a clear focus and opportunities to discuss what needs to be learnt. It also helps if leaders and managers acknowledge that they too have a lot to learn alongside all other staff when new processes and practices have to be designed and developed.

Learning to change

In the current policy agenda of 'joined up' working, there is an opportunity to review the contribution that a number of fields of study might make to inform the emerging development of multi-professional and multi-disciplinary fields of practice.

Change has become such a constant part of work in health services and social work services that most organizations have a range of change projects in progress to manage aspects of change. These projects usually have arrangements for formal evaluations to capture the learning that has been gained. In the context of project management, learning is usually recognized as a normal part of working life (see Martin 2002) and mechanisms to support staff can be developed. In the wider context of everyday work, learning can be supported and encouraged by ensuring that there is some planned time for groups to reflect and review their practice and some protected learning time for individuals.

Service improvement will not be achieved unless the people who *work together* in human services are willing to *learn together*. There are many ways in which individuals might be encouraged and supported to learn, but potential barriers to learning include self-perception and personal aspiration, both very much influenced by the context in which an individual works and receives feedback about his or her work. Learning is central to service improvement and in order to gain staff participation in learning these staff must feel valued and supported. Managers have a pivotal role in ensuring that the learning experience is positive and does bring about change to improve services.

Learning can lead to many different types of change in individuals, influencing abilities, ways of thinking, awareness of the nature of knowledge and awareness of differences in perception. Learning might be evident in changes in the ways people think and act, both as individuals and in the complex multi-professional and interdisciplinary settings of health and social care services.

Modernizing human services puts a particular emphasis on the ways in which people from different traditions work together. It recognizes that there are different starting points in how professionals approach their work. Social workers, for example, expect to engage in inter-organizational working as a normal activity when they collaborate with others to achieve positive objectives for, for example, older people, or those with a disability. Increasingly, it is recognized that children in need, for example children in out-of-home placements, often require different services in order to meet their optimal levels of development (Aldgate 2006). There is, however, always a tension between each profession maintaining its own discrete, specialised expertise and a more holistic approach whereby different professions pool their knowledge to promote the general wellbeing of children or adults. In Scotland, inter-agency working is a fundamental plank in the Scottish Government's *Getting it Right for Every Child* initiative which will set a shared system of universal and tiered assessment, planning and recording for all children (Scottish Executive 2005).

Increasingly, in this changing context, there is recognition of the role that education can play. In particular, the development of inter-professional education has attempted to address changing expectations:

> Inter-professional education has developed over the years... It has worked to restore equilibrium as working relationships have been destabilised, the unquestioned authority once enjoyed by the established professions challenged, hierarchies flattened and demarcations blurred, as new professions have grown in influence, consumers have gained power and a better informed public has expected more. (Barr 2002, pp.13–14)

Unfortunately, there is often a gap between the aspirations of an holistic, inter-professional approach to human services developed in educational institutions and the reality experienced by students in work placements. The workplace experience is often of a service under extreme pressure to deliver and without time or energy to be able to work in anything other than familiar and well-understood ways. If inter-professional education is to contribute to inter-professional working in the workplace, it may be necessary to develop opportunities for those entering professions to gain work experience in a managed environment that is able to demonstrate the benefits of inter-professional working for service-users. An example of an approach to address some of these issues is to be found in the development of standards for interagency working developed at Salford University with funding from the Department of Health (Shardlow *et al.* 2004).

Much of the work in health and care services is practical and is carried out through interpersonal contact. This raises a number of issues in terms of learning. All of our actions are informed by mental models, concepts and theories, whether these are consciously selected or unconsciously accepted. These conceptual ideas are sometimes referred to as the 'fields of practice and study'. Any changes in how individuals think about and do things at work can involve challenges to the beliefs and values that have guided their practice. Beliefs and values that professionals hold are formed during foundation education which is shaped by professional bodies and service demands but usually delivered through tertiary education with professional supervision of experience in practice. These actions take place in a 'field of practice'. Students learn to link ideas from the 'field of study' to activities in the 'field of practice'. As human services work involves both theory and application in practice, both types of learning are important.

One of the difficulties that we all face is that nothing stands still for very long, and both theory and practice are constantly changing. It is not sufficient only to continue learning about the field of study as the field of practice continually changes and evolves. Theory becomes out of date as new ideas and discoveries replace older theories. Practice also changes as new procedures and processes replace older ones in response to development in knowledge about the impact of people's actions. Individuals also have to change and develop practice to accommodate new technology and processes.

Bohm challenged the idea that knowledge is ever permanent and absolute and proposed that there is nothing that we can consider permanently 'known'. He used his background as a physicist to give the example of the atom, which was originally thought to be something that could not be split. Later, physicists found that atoms were made up of electrons, protons, neutrons and empty space – and then there were further discoveries (1994, p.102).

The temporary nature of knowledge is acknowledged in phrases like, 'the current state of knowledge about…' or, 'we used to think…', often used when an individual realizes that things have changed so much that it would no longer be appropriate to think like that. Two very good examples in human services are changes in attitudes to diversity in the workforce (see Chapter 6 in this book) and the growth of technology (see Chapter 10 in this book). For many people, these shifting ideas about thinking and knowledge seem rather alarming. It can seem that the solid ground on which we believe our knowledge to rest is being lost. It may seem dangerous to regard knowledge as transitory when so much of our technology, our disciplines and professions, our cultural traditions, our experience of life, appear to be firmly grounded in our collective knowledge. It is also true, however, that knowledge must be regarded as transitory but also cumulative, when the impact of new discoveries, new ideas and developments are considered.

Once knowledge is accepted to be changing all the time, it follows that the personal knowledge of individuals may be out of date. The knowledge that informed actions five years ago might no longer be a sound basis for decisions today. In health and social care, professionals, clinicians and others, whose work is informed by traditional bodies of knowledge, are increasingly aware of the need for continuing professional development. This need is now build into post-qualifying requirements in relation to the continuing registration of the social work workforce in the UK. Continuous learning is essential if health and social care services are to reflect changing understanding of the knowledge that informs practice at all levels. High quality services cannot be sustained unless human services staff from different disciplines are consistently engaged in learning, individually and together.

Those who use services and the learning agenda

One of the main concerns in the modernization of public services is to provide a context for service provision and delivery in which all linked services are joined up so that, from the perspective of those who require services, services are experienced as seamless. This cannot be achieved unless those providing each domain of service understand why and how services need to link so that the experience and expectations of the service-user can be met.

Services are delivered through interpersonal relationships and therefore the learning experiences of both providers and those who use services must be part of service development. Through our experience as patients or social work clients, we learn more about ourselves and about the ways in which we provide health and social welfare services in our society. Some patients and clients come to see professionals having conducted their own research on their problems. Sometimes, they are better informed about their particular condition than the professionals and clinicians who offer services to them. Undoubtedly, such self-tutoring has been facilitated by the internet. Accepting a role of learning from 'expert' patients and clients is a new aspect of working life for many staff and it can be uncomfortable for those who are not accustomed to having their knowledge or expertise challenged, as Janet Seden and Trish Ross outline in Chapter 9.

Providers of health and care services are increasingly required to consult with service-users and involve them in shaping services both for individuals and in their locality. There are many ways in which this requirement can be met. Some of these are explored by Janet Seden and Trish Ross in Chapter 9.

Implementing the modernizing agenda

Modernization is based on a philosophy that attempts to marry emancipatory and social justice practices with quality improvement in health and care services. This brings an implicit dilemma. Theories relating to quality improvement are almost always based on capitalist assumptions of consumerism in a market-led society in which powerful forces work to create and sustain demand. By contrast, modernization of human services seeks to promote social equality and to involve service-users in design and development of local services. Unless citizens are educated sufficiently to understand and resist the powerful pressures brought by marketing practices, wider involvement in shaping public services will increase the extent to which notions of quality reflect consumerist ideals.

There will always be a tension between choices based on the greatest good for the greatest number and the individual choices that are usually accompanied by differentials in purchasing power. Services that are essentially limited by resources inevitably reflect the philosophies and values that underpin decisions about what represents good value for money. Concepts such as 'Best Value' are an attempt to straddle these two extremes and are an important part of the attempt across the UK to increase the power and participation of citizens in matters that affect their quality of lives. In relation to social work and social care in England, there is a requirement on local authorities: 'to find out what local citizens' service needs are, and what they think of how the council is doing' (Cm.4169, 1998, p.34). Implicit in the development of consultation is the belief that professionals have much to learn from those they serve. Reconfiguration involves linking service areas and different organizations to create easier access and smoother pathways for service-users. None of this is possible without the involvement of staff who are able to change the ways in which they think about their work and the ways they work with each other. It is also not possible to effect change without involving both staff and service-users in a joint learning agenda with the ultimate aim of improving the management and effective delivery of human services in a manner which maximizes positive outcomes for those who receive them.

Chapter 6

Managing Diversity in Social Services Settings

Barris Malcolm

Introduction

The UK and the US are among the most multi-racial, multi-ethnic, and poly-ethnic countries in the world, with people of all races, colors, ethnicity, religious beliefs, and political ideology represented in their populations. Indeed, diversity in people and cultures has greatly enriched British and American societies over many decades, by bringing global ideas, perspectives, and productive contributions to all areas of contemporary life. Like most modern, liberal democratic, and pluralistic societies, the UK and the US accommodate this diversity by establishing rights and freedoms guaranteed to citizens. However, achieving social justice, cohesion, and equality remains a challenge even though both countries have continued to wrestle with accommodating and managing diversity, passing laws aimed at ending discrimination and providing new parameters for social relationships particularly in the work environment.

In the US, the population is rapidly approaching 300 million people and the society is becoming increasingly diverse (Bureau of the Census 2000). Unprecedented numbers of immigrants and refugees have arrived in the past two decades, increasing the number of foreign born to 12 percent of the population, a figure that has more than doubled since

1970 (Healy 2004; US Census Bureau 2006). There are six main receiving states: California, Texas, New York, Florida, Illinois, and New Jersey. Another ten states now have the fastest growing immigrant populations. Most newcomers are from Latin America and Asia (Capps *et al.* 2003). These newcomers join long-established minority populations in the US, resulting in a demographic profile of a national population that is 12.2 percent black, 14.2 percent Latino, 4.2 percent Asian and others, of mixed race, American Indian and other minority groups (US Census Bureau 2006). Latinos/Hispanics have recently surpassed blacks as the largest minority group. Currently, 67.3 percent of the population is white/non-Hispanic and by 2050 Americans of color are expected to outnumber those who are white (Center for Mental Health Services 1998; US Census Bureau 2006).

In the UK, with its population of nearly 60 million, ethnic minorities represent about 7.9 percent of the population, or about 4.6 million. Most are concentrated in urban areas; nearly half of all ethnic minorities live in greater London. The largest minority group is Indian, followed by Pakistanis and then by black immigrants from Caribbean countries (British Studies 2003). The arrival of unaccompanied asylum-seeking children, adult refugees and asylum seekers in the early part of the twenty-first century and the mechanisms for supporting them have become a matter of political debate. At the same time social workers are actively involved in the processes of both assessment and support. The role of social work in immigration policy has presented new practice dilemmas and concerns and ethical issues for individuals who query the appropriateness of their role (Humphries 2004). Additionally, people are arriving from increasingly diverse parts of the world which means that cultural sensitivity and competence are particularly important (O'Hagan 2001; Leigh 2002).

This ethnic diversity in both countries demands that human service agencies formulate appropriate responses in the design and delivery of programs as well as in the structuring of agency policies and practices to ensure that the needs of both those being served and those providing the services are met (Committee on Racial Equality (CRE) 2001; Healy 2000). This chapter focuses on managing diversity effectively among employees and service recipients in human service organizations in the

UK and the US. As the social environment changes, human services managers need to be more knowledgeable about ways to lead and manage, as well as to serve, people with diverse backgrounds and culture (Schein 1992; Ginsberg and Keys 1994; Healy 2001).

Managing diversity in the workplace is complex, posing many challenges and opportunities for human services/social care managers committed to the social justice ideals of the social work profession. Taylor (1993) has pointed out that effective management of diversity facilitates achievement of three types of organizational goals:

- those having to do with moral, ethical and social responsibility

- goals to meet legal obligations

- goals related to performance.

Thus, the "culture-shaping" role of these managers is a very important job function (Keys and Ginsberg 1988; Cahn and Richardson 1993; Weinbach 2003).

This chapter first defines diversity and then reviews previous approaches to managing it. Second, it applies a number of existing theoretical frameworks and typologies to illustrate managing diversity in work environments and suggest ways forward, the goal for managers being diversity competence, or the capacity, skills, and resources within the agency to provide effective services to people of diverse backgrounds (Lum 2003). Finally, it aims to impress upon social work/social care managers in human service organizations the need for their leadership in identifying, redressing, and eliminating existing gaps and deficiencies in cross-cultural knowledge and standards for professional competence in the organization.

Defining diversity

Diversity traditionally refers to "distinctive categorical variety or multiformity between and among individuals or groups making them unique" (Webster's Dictionary 1996). According to the 2001 Educational Policy and Accreditation Standards (EPAS) promulgated by the Council on Social Work Education (CSWE), and the Standards for qualifying social workers in the UK's four countries (TOPPS 1999), diversity refers to differences, as in race, ethnicity, gender, age, martial status, national origin, culture, family structure, religion, sexual orientation, disability, and HIV/AIDS status (Council on Social Work Education 2001). The National Association of Social Workers Standards for Cultural Competence in Social Work Practice also defines diversity in broader terms (beyond race and ethnicity) to include "the sociocultural experiences of people of different genders, social classes, religious and spiritual beliefs, sexual orientations, ages, and physical and mental abilities" (National Association of Social Workers 2001). As implied by these delineations of difference, diversity is not neutral. It has been, is, and will continue to be the focal point of many social and political debates. It bears strong implications for access to, and allocation of, resources, and accommodation, in particular opportunities in employment and receiving services (Dominelli 1998).

Thus managing diversity in the interest of minorities and traditionally oppressed groups must remain a major thrust for social work/social care managers as they work toward ensuring equal access and opportunity, according to law and professional obligation, influencing organizational policy and culture in support of diversity. Accommodating and maintaining support for diversity and multiculturalism require skilled leadership and a commitment of resources, especially as once sanguine and cooperative attitudes are increasingly replaced by apathy and outright hostility (United Nations 1998). In the US, there has been a strong backlash against affirmative action in several universities (Gibbs 1999; Gibelman 2000). Even in existing pluralistic, democratic, and multicultural societies, where formerly there were acceptance and tolerance of social and cultural diversity, there is growing hypersensitivity and objection to certain cultural and religious freedoms. Public discourse in many countries has also grown negative and intolerant, with support for extremist ideologies, xenophobia, anti-immigrant sentiments, anti-Semitism, and homophobia becoming stronger each year (Human Rights Watch 1997, 1999; Tang 2003).

Managing diversity can be difficult, requiring a shift from old paradigms to new ones, which may create uncertainty, discomfort, or opposition. Diversity critics have argued that beyond the principles of freedom and equality there is no compelling reason to justify granting any special rights or opportunities to minorities, or that diversity of any kind carries no real significance for political arrangements. Legal scholars also point to the moral hazard of attempting to protect any specific historical, legal, social, or economic rights of cultural or minority communities as this often impinges on the rights of the majority community (Shachar 2001). As pointed out by Kymlicka (1998) and others, there is a dilemma because while in societies such as the UK and US, where the commitment to individual autonomy is both "deep and wide", crossing ethnic, linguistic, and religious lines, it can also result in the eroding of individual autonomy in ethnocultural communities. Some legal scholars have therefore argued that minority rights supplement, rather than diminish, individual freedom and equality. Other legal scholars have countered with the argument that the reserving of special rights for minorities may so perilously rent the social integration and solidarity necessary for political life that contest, resentment, and recrimination may ensue (DeCoste 2001).

Moreover, not all Americans subscribe to the egalitarian political morality implicit in the American Constitution, or to subsequent civil rights laws (Seligman 1973) and the same may be true of British citizens. Witness the recent success of the BNP in local elections in England and the growing concern that others express about this party's views. As a recent US survey showed, there is growing unpopularity of previously supported preferences for minorities. Calls for repealing of laws that give preferential treatment to African-Americans and women in hiring have grown louder and these laws are more often challenged in the courts.

It is ironic that even as the world has become progressively more global in perspective it has also grown more segmented and nationalistic. In the aftermath of the terrorist attacks of 11 September 2001, the debate about whether Islam belongs in Europe has become increasingly controversial (Power and Dickey 2003). A significant outcome of these events and the two ensuing wars, in Iraq and Afghanistan, has been the increased attention and effort given to increasing self-awareness, respect, and cultural sensitivity, and the growing support for multiculturalism and, for example, satisfactory rapprochement between Muslims and the rest of the world (Baines 2002). These developments create new demands on the social work profession and its ability to heal fractured lives, rebuild communities, and transform people so that culture wars may give rise to culture conversations based on substance rather than power politics (Adams 1996; Fisher and Karger 1997; Thompson 2002). Clearly, managing diversity in the current geopolitical environment requires stronger and deeper grounding in theories that so strongly influence human behavior in the social environment.

Past approaches to managing diversity

The literature on diversity has become a burgeoning industry (Arredondo 1996; Barry 2001). Many authors have addressed managing diversity in human service organizations, with much of the work focusing on legal mandates for diversity, gender, and race disparity. During the 1990s, in the US, diversity and cultural sensitivity trainings were "buzz" words in many human service organizations. Government and publicly funded organizations, including non-governmental agencies receiving public funds, were required to offer these trainings once a year as part of funding requirements. Cultural audits were carried out to examine agency statistics on employee demographics, complaints of bias and the agency's response to them, and cultural sensitivity training sessions (Beckett and Dungee-Anderson 1996). These funding requirements spawned many diversity and cultural sensitivity consultancies in the US.

Group training attempted to increase cultural awareness among participants and usually consisted of intensive half or full-day sessions about the beliefs of individual cultures, respecting differences, and avoiding taboos and offensive words or gestures. A typical cultural sensitivity training would use a variety of approaches including practice exercises, group discussion, documentaries, and reports from representatives of cultural, racial, or ethnic groups of focus. Some consultants use manuals or tools that ask participants to talk and/or write about personal encounters, experiences, relationships, or observations that show evidence of bias. In such settings, some participants (male, white, heterosexual, young, etc.) may be viewed (or view themselves) as the group being targeted by the training exercises. Minority participants on the other hand, are often viewed (or view themselves) as victims lending temporal authenticity to both the teaching and the learning experiences (Bryant 2001; Shachar 2001; Prevatt-Goldstein 2002; Thomas 2005).

In some organizations, cultural sensitivity and diversity training is presented in other forms such as a special diversity day event featuring a lecture, panel presentation, or group discussion. Members of racial or ethnic groups may be invited to wear native costumes, share cultural arti-facts, and prepare and share special ethnic foods. However, care must be taken for these events not to become divisive when those from other groups in the organization are not invited to participate by celebrating their own cultures. Moreover, the challenges of managing diversity require a much deeper and broader understanding and set of approaches as will be discussed below.

Dimensions in managing diversity

Perlmutter *et al.* (2001) discuss three theoretical orientations to diversity in the workplace: legal, which emphasizes knowledge about and adher-ence to the law; anthropological, which focuses on awareness of cultures; and finally, the socio-psychological orientation which focuses on diver-sity as in differences and similarities between individuals, groups, and in organizational values, knowledge, and skills. Social work and social care managers must have knowledge and skills spanning all three orienta-tions; organizational change efforts aimed at valuing diversity must include the structural as well as the social if true multiculturalism is to be achieved. Cox (1994, p.229) delineates the characteristics of a multi-cultural organization as one:

- that fosters and values cultural differences
- that integrates informal networks
- without bias in practices and policies
- where there is little intergroup conflict because of diversity efforts.

Perlmutter *et al.* (2001), citing the Equity Institute (1990), discuss a four-level typology of diversity involvement in organizations that managers and workers may find helpful in assessing the extent of multiculturalism and structural diversity in their agencies. In this typology:

Level 1 is the *equal employment organization,* and is exemplified by an organization in which managers exert minimal efforts, and commit few resources to recruit, hire, and promote minorities and women. An equal employment organization accommodates diversity as a token, and does so mainly to satisfy federal, state, municipal, or stakeholder demands.

Level 2 is termed an *affirmative action organization,* and refers to an organization that actively recruits, hires, and promotes minorities and women. Managers of affirmative action organizations discourage all explicit racism, sexism, and other forms of discrimination, in written policy, in communication, and actions. In affirmative organizations assimilation is the avenue for making progress, and a few minorities and women may be granted rapid promotions to improve the image of the organization by being seen as exemplars of progress and diversity, but are held back or denied access to the most powerful and top positions. In affirmative organizations, minorities and women who are unable to assimilate are kept back, or summarily replaced.

Level 3 is termed the *self-renewing organization,* and is exemplified by an organization that systematically assesses its culture, and uses this information for formulating new strategies for enhancing diversity-competent staff. Managers of a self-renewing organization commit the necessary time and resources for creating and sustaining a working environment that is sensitive, tolerant, and supportive to employees from various backgrounds.

Level 4, the highest level, is the *pluralist or multicultural organization* exemplified by an organization that is open, affirming, supportive, and diversity-competent. Managers in these organizations practice diversity in hiring and promoting staff, prohibit discrimination in any form in the workplace, and affiliate with like-minded organizations.

This section will now discuss the three dimensions or orientations to diversity–legal, anthropological, and socio-psychological and their relevance for social care and social work managers.

Legal dimensions of diversity

In the US, public and private institutions with 15 employees or more must abide by anti-discrimination laws and provisions. Chief among these are laws that govern equal access to employment opportunities and protection from unfair treatment in the work environment, mainly the Equal Pay Act of 1963, Civil Rights Act of 1964 (Title VI) with its various additions and amendments including Title VII, and the Equal Employment Opportunity Act (EEO) of 1972. Other relevant laws include Affirmative Action (Executive Orders 11246 and 11375); Title IX of Education Amendments of 1972; the Pregnancy Discrimination Act and the Age Discrimination in Employment Act of 1973, Vocational Rehabilitation Act of 1973, the Americans with Disabilities Act (ADA) of 1990, Civil Rights Act of 1991, and the Family and Medical Leave Act (FML) of 1993. (See also Chapter 7 by Robert Madden.)

In the UK, there are also nationally produced equal opportunity and anti-discrimination guidelines in the Race Relations Act (1976), and the 2000 Amendment Act, which are monitored by the Commission for Racial Equality. Managers need to take account of the Human Rights Act (1998). There is a whole raft of employment-related law which managers need to know about. This includes the Sex Discrimination Act (1976); Employment Equality (Sexual Orientation Regulations (2003); Race Relations Act (1976) (Amendment Act 2000); Employment (Equality (Religion or Belief) Regulations (2003), Disability Rights Commission Act (1999), and Disability Discrimination Acts (DDA) (1995; 2005). Basically, in the UK, any discrimination in the workplace on the grounds of race, disability, sexual orientation, or belief is unlawful and the Equal Opportunities Commission can look at both the general operation of the law as well as individual complaints just as the Commission for Racial Equality can. Such stringent controls influence everyday situations in social care settings, as the example in Chapter 5 illustrated.

The legal dimension of diversity focuses on knowledge of, and compliance with, these and other relevant laws that pertain to employment. It is in the interest of their organizations for managers to be cognizant of the requirements of, and operate in compliance with, these laws. Discriminatory practices in employment refer to adverse decisions made against an employee or a prospective employee based on any of the three following elements. First, decisions based on membership of an individual to a certain group rather than on the ability of that individual to perform the job. Second, decisions based on assumptions about the inferiority of one group compared with other groups that may contribute to the denial of equal treatment. Third, making decisions that are harmful or negative to the interests of an employee costing her or him a job, a higher position, or better pay.

The civil rights approach in the US emerged after much advocacy and civil unrest by African-Americans and women's rights groups. Of particular relevance is Title VII of the Civil Rights Act, which addresses equal access and opportunity, and states that an employer, employment agency, or labor union may not discriminate against an employee because of an individual's race, color, religion, sex, national origin, in any term, condition, or privilege of employment (Buchholz 1992). Title VII also legislates against discriminatory practices in hiring, firing, wages, fringe benefits, classifying, referring, assigning, or promoting employees (Buchholz 1992). The concept of equal opportunity is consistent with free enterprise, competition, and the merit system. Human service managers must also be aware of the role of the Equal Employment Opportunity Commission (EEOC) in enforcing the laws, and investigating complaints filed by individuals.

Although the Civil Rights Act forbids preferential treatment, it recognizes that groups who were discriminated against in the past, such as African-Americans and women, needed special provisions, collectively called affirmative action, to relieve deficiencies. There are a number of different approaches in the implementation of affirmative action programs ranging from concrete efforts to expand the pool of applicants to include minorities and women, preferential hiring of minorities and women, and use of quotas with specific goals for hiring minorities and women (Seligman 1973). Affirmative action has come to be viewed by some constituents in the US as reverse discrimination (adverse decisions against white individuals and males) (Issacharoff 2002). There is similar debate around affirmative action in the UK. Human service managers must therefore know how to prepare for responding to these challenges if so charged and brought to court. Until the law permitting affirmative action programs is abolished, the best a manager can do to defend the organization against such a charge is to consult legal advice to establish appropriate guidelines and to apply these guidelines consistently in recruiting, interviewing, hiring, promoting, and firing.

The Americans with Disabilities Act (ADA), passed in 1990, is viewed as a revolutionary public policy in the US that eliminates discrimination on grounds of disability in federal programs and programs that receive federal funding. The Act parallels the provisions against race and gender discrimination but, in addition, requires employers to make individualized and reasonable accommodations for working based on the specific needs of qualified disabled persons. The Act also requires that public facilities, including service and social services institutions, be accessible to individuals with disabilities. Human service managers also need to be aware that the ADA specifically identified institutions relevant to social work as day-care centers, senior centers, food banks, adoption agencies, shelters for homeless individuals, hospitals, and professional offices (Orlin 1995).

Sexual orientation has gained increased attention, leading to recognition of homosexual and bisexual individuals as minorities in a diverse workforce. Many homosexuals choose not to disclose their sexual identity and may live in constant fear of being "outed". Others openly disclose their homosexuality (coming-out) and may run the risk of being discriminated against in recruitment opportunities, promotions, work assignments, and restrictions on social opportunities in the workplace. Homosexual employees experience discrimination, unfair treatment, hostility, and even violence such that managers must create and maintain hospitable and fair work environments, with respect to equal employment opportunity and employee benefits (Colbert and Wofford 1993). Beyond the basic civil rights protections, legal rights and protection for homosexuals in the US are piecemeal, varied, and at risk because they are based mostly in executive orders, state and municipal ordinances, private employment contracts, and in case law (Colbert and Wofford 1993).

Anthropological dimensions of diversity

All of us are multidimensional, complex, and unique with identities formed through intersect of race, ethnicity, class, gender, language, religion, national origin, sexual orientation, ability, and other cultural influences. The anthropological perspective takes the macro approach and focuses on cultural and sub-cultural group awareness, or on cultural relativism (Hing 2002; Hogan-Garcia 2003). The operative paradigm of the anthropological perspective is that human beings are genetic and cultural hybrids and therefore no person, group, race, or ethnicity is homogeneous or pure.

Hogan-Garcia identified 12 common aspects of culture or ethnicity as including history, social status, value orientation, language, family life process, healing beliefs, religion, arts and expressive forms, food, recreation, and clothing (2003, p.14). Butera (2001) has identified the three dimensions that have guided thinking about race, ethnicity, and cultural diversity as: 1. assimilation, 2. cultural pluralism, and 3. multiculturalism. Assimilation (melting pot theory) has become unpopular. Assimilation places high value on individual, racial, and ethnic differences, regarding them as unique social characteristics, to be added to rather than altering mainstream culture. As its name implies, the melting pot theory assumes that as each of the racial and ethnic groups voluntarily conforms to mainstream values and culture, their distinctive cultural differences will be absorbed and disappear.

Cultural pluralism theory (social mosaic) posits that rather than being encouraged to melt together, cultural differences between racial and ethnic groups should be recognized as unique endowments that ought to be highlighted. According to cultural pluralism theory, rather than becoming assimilated into an "American culture," new immigrants should be encouraged to consciously maintain separate identity within explicitly defined territorial boundaries and ethnic communities creating a mosaic of coexisting but distinct cultures.

Multiculturalism theory is a product of postmodernist and social constructivism and consequently is grounded in the assumption that no single culture is superior or inferior to another (Williams 1996). It therefore challenges all notions of cultural hegemony and ethnocentrism. Accordingly, multiculturalism theory is based on assumptions that individuals are multidimensional and complex, but yet with unique qualities and identities formed through intersection of time, empire, race, ethnicity, class, gender, language, religion, national origin, sexual orientation, ability, and other cultural influences. Multiculturalism therefore acknowledges that different individuals make unique contributions to a larger and evolving national culture that is greater than the sum of any single component. The focus of multiculturalism is therefore harmonious coexistence and the shared experiences of living in a social community. According to Parekh (2000), multiculturalism is the proper terms of relationship between different cultural communities. As a theory, multiculturalism reconceptualizes the understanding of cultural identity by redefining the role and place of cultural membership in the individual and collective life. Achieving multiculturalism is, therefore, a main objective for achieving self-awareness and being trained in cultural sensitivity.

Socio-psychological dimensions of diversity

Practice wisdom in social work suggests that self-awareness is a logical place to begin the process of assessing the congruency between beliefs and ideals espoused as part of the development of knowledge and practice skills within a social justice framework (Hawkins, Fook, and Ryan 2001). Self-awareness involves the critical examination of personal beliefs about race, ethnicity, cultural identity, family history, values, perceptions and experiences, biases, and ignorance. The process involves deconstructing of reified social constructs such as "race", "color", "theory of whiteness", "privilege", "ethnicity", "class", "nationality", "sexual identity", "oppression", and "language". To deconstruct is to ask questions such as, "How, why, by who, and for whom?" of particular social constructs. Often this challenging exercise involves the retracing of origins, family history, and background and the history of our nation.

Becoming self-aware about how one views cultural diversity is naturally an individual, internal, and introspective process, but it is described in a number of sociological and psychological theories. For example, post-structural theorists such as Hartman (1991) and Postman (1992) have pointed out the significant role language plays as an "ideological instrument" in creating worldviews. Hawkins *et al.* argue that language determines what is named, how it is named as well as denoting "structures and power relations through assignation of subject/object status, activity and passivity" (2001, p.3). The process may be disturbing, but the act of examining one's history can also be transformational and liberating if old paradigms become deconstructed and replaced with new ones. For example diversity seen in the old paradigm merely as "being different" can, in a new paradigm, be understood as "variety or synthesis."

Becoming self-aware is also educative because it exposes people to new facts. For example, racist ideas founded on myths can be countered with science that shows that human beings share most of their genetic material and display personality traits and behaviors that are common or universal. By deconstructing social constructs that have had negative connotations, such as "race", "blackness", "minority", "aliens", and "immigrant", and derogatory terms used in references to homosexuals, one learns that these are merely linguistics. This is also the main point among feminist post-structural theorists who have examined how use of language creates and supports gender imbalances (Berlin 1990; Sands and Nuccio 1992; Graham 2002). The process of deconstructing is empowering and emancipating because concepts, terminologies, classifications, categorizations, and stereotypes are seen for what they are as linguistics, artificially contrived, and atypical (Berquist 2001; Pease 2002). Most of these constructs have no scientific basis and therefore have no inherent power to control an individual.

Building or changing self-awareness may be greatly helped by the application of relevant theories including interpretive theory (Guba and Lincoln 1994; Harper and Leicht 2002), labeling theory, role theory, and symbolic interaction (Robbins, Chatterjee, and Canda 1998). Tenets from these theories are helpful toward understanding that, religious beliefs and theology notwithstanding, human society is fundamentally a social construction derived by interaction, process, and negotiated order (Harper and Leicht 2002). It is therefore also important to note that negotiated order includes reaffirmation, change, or destruction of existing social arrangements and cultural meanings. Language, communication, and the careful choice of words are also important elements in the deconstruction and reconstruction of new paradigms and meaning.

The result of such self-awareness is the ability to suspend judgment, to be more open, accepting, sensitive, and tolerant to cultural variety, yet without abandoning social work values of social justice, social change, problem solving, empowerment, and the defense of human rights. Increased self-awareness can, therefore, produce individuals who are committed to supporting diversity, which is a social work ideal and obligation. However, in planning diversity training, caution should be taken. An exercise examining self-awareness may be too personal and self-revealing in a group setting such as in a single-session diversity training exercise. Such activities need careful planning and facilitation, especially with groups that are racially or ethnically diverse, otherwise participants may remain silent or the session may deteriorate into a shouting match or blaming session. Such a process may best be undertaken through didactic sessions, guided readings, journal recording, and discussion in closed group sessions over an appropriate period. Shaping self-awareness is the most difficult step; however, once achieved it becomes easier to focus on cultural differences and multiculturalism.

Diversity competence

The aim is for agencies to achieve diversity competence, which has been defined as the capacity, skills, and resources within an organization to appropriately assess, plan, define, design, implement, and manage relevant and effective social services or personal interventions to persons with diverse backgrounds (Lum 2003). Achieving diversity competency is both an individual and an organizational goal; human service/social care managers play key roles in both (Iglehart 2000; Kettner 2002).

Managers' roles

It is the responsibility of managers to know organizational needs in terms of appropriate staffing and resources. It is also their responsibility to acquire, train, and support the right complement of staffing and resources to satisfy the needs of the organization and its stakeholders. They also must ensure that staff are kept up to date by continually expanding and improving diversity knowledge and competencies. Finally, they must ensure that statutory, licensure, and funding requirements for diversity and cultural competencies are satisfied.

Human services managers bear the ethical responsibility to ensure that staff members are committed to understanding issues of diversity as these may affect various aspects of their work. This involves, but is not limited to, the hiring and training of diversity-competent workers, conducting research, and understanding how diversity affects the dynamics in organizations, groups, families, and at the individual level in terms of access to services, opportunities, and resources (Haley-Banez, Brown, and Molina 2003). Managers might refer to the previously mentioned standards for cultural competence (National Association of Social Workers 2001) which identify ten diversity competence standards for social workers in the US, but which may also be relevant to British social workers and social care managers. Further reference is made to diversity in the National Association of Social Workers Code of Ethics (NASW 1998) and in the Standards for qualifying social workers in the UK (TOPPS 1999).

Individual diversity competence

The National Association of Social Workers (NASW) defines cultural competence as "the integration and transformation of knowledge about individuals and groups of people into specific standards, policies, practices, and attitudes used in appropriate cultural settings to increase the quality of services, thereby producing better outcomes" (NASW 2001, p.11). In social work, individual cultural competence refers to those attitudes, behaviors, knowledge, and skills that demonstrate sensitivity, respect, and ability to communicate and to work successfully in cross-cultural settings (NASW 2001). Cultural competence may therefore also include linguistic ability for communicating in different languages or dialects, as well as the ability to distinguish between customs, belief systems, norms, and behaviors of different cultural and ethnic groups.

From the direct practice perspective, diversity competence has been the subject in a large number of texts, articles, and manuals (Fong and Furuto 2001; Hogan-Garcia 2003; Lum 2003); it has also been addressed from a management perspective (Chernesky and Bombyk 1988; Loden and Rosenor 1991; Asamoah 1995; Healy 1996; Haley-Banez et al. 2003; Weinbach 2003). Cultural competence, or diversity competence, is now a common expectation for social work practitioners. Training for diversity-competent practice differs from training in diversity and cultural sensitivity because it refers to particular knowledge and skills needed within an organization to make it culturally relevant for working with particular racial, ethnic, cultural, or language groups (Council on Social Work Education 2001).

In clinical practice, diversity competence refers to clinical knowledge and skills acquired by social work practitioners for delivering appropriate care and services, and regulated by licensure of the organization and individual practitioners. In the US, social work practitioners are not only required to possess the appropriate clinical knowledge and skills, but to be diversity competent. Practitioners

> are expected to exhibit awareness of any possible negative emotional reactions toward American Indians, Alaska Native Peoples, African Americans, Asian Americans, Hispanics, Latinos/Latinas, gays, lesbians, bisexuals or transgendered persons, persons with physical, mental/emotional, or learning disabilities, particularly with regard to race and ethnicity. (Haley-Banez *et al.* 2003, p.45)

Having to serve such a wide range of cultural subgroups and individual variations, being diversity competent is becoming important because people bring their cultural heritage to the clinical setting. In part, diversity in cultural heritage and beliefs may account for variations in how consumers communicate symptoms and the ones they report (Lago and Thompson 1996; Kurz, Malcolm and Cournoyer 2005). Research shows that some aspects of culture underlie culture-bound syndromes (some symptoms are more common in some societies than in others). More often culture bears upon whether people even seek help in the first place, the types of help they seek, their coping styles and social supports, and how much stigma is attached to certain conditions. It is also important for practitioners to be cognizant that all cultures feature strengths, such as resilience and adaptive ways of coping, which may buffer some people from developing certain disorders (US Department of Health and Human Services 2004).

Systems approach to diversity competence
According to the National Association of Social Workers (2001), there are five essential elements contributing to a system's ability to become more culturally competent. These are: 1. value diversity, 2. developing the capacity for cultural self-assessment, 3. becoming conscious that conflict is intrinsic when different cultures interact, 4. making cultural awareness an integral part of the system, and 5. designing delivery

services to reflect competence and better understanding of the diversity between and within cultures in those systems.

Perlmutter *et al.* (2001) point out that managers often attempt to address diversity competence in the organization in one of two ways. First, the *access-and-legitimacy paradigm* (Gummer 1998), an approach by which managers attempt to achieve diversity by matching the demographics of staff in their organizations with those of consumers or constituent groups. The second and more desirable approach is called the *discrimination-and-fairness paradigm* by Gummer (1998), and refers to efforts by managers to focus on career development and mentoring of workers, notwithstanding the risk of losing trained individuals. Perlmutter and her colleagues (2001) suggest a third approach, termed the *learning and effectiveness paradigm*, which recognizes that inevitably workers draw upon their cultural background, affiliations, identity, and experiences when making job-related choices and decisions. Diversity with regard to gender is especially complex in the UK. For example, Rogers and Reynolds (2003b) point out that, in Britain, women are at a disadvantage in promotion to senior management positions in social care. Citing a workforce study by Ginn and Fisher (1999), they note that, while women comprise between 86 and 95 percent of the workforce, they represent only 60 to 70 percent of management. A number of factors are thought to account for this under-representation, but the key factor is their responsibility for child care and its impact on their full-time career history as compared to that of their male counterparts.

Fernandez (1991), as well as Cox (1994), argues that organizations need a plan for diversity competence that integrates the perspectives of employees into the organization's goals and thereby diversify, enrich and probably redefine its mission, strategies, and constituents. What is being advocated is a systems approach to managing diversity. Strategies include leadership of steering and advisory groups, research to set benchmarks and achievement of measurable objectives, training and education, and organization development approaches aimed at culture change (Cox 1994).

A recent diversity survey of 200 organizations including trade unions, equality agencies, and government agencies found 69 percent of respondents stating that diversity policies had enhanced their corporate reputation; 62 percent said these policies helped in attracting and retaining highly talented personnel; 58 percent reported that diversity policies had improved motivation and efficiency; 57 percent reported increased innovation; 57 percent also reported enhanced service levels and customer satisfaction; and 57 percent stated that they had helped them overcome labor shortages. The report also recognized that difficulty persists in measuring the effects of diversity policies, and identified other obstacles to the success of diversity policies such as the challenges in trying to change company culture, and a lack of awareness among employees (Europe Information Service 2003).

Diversity Best Practices, a US-based service organization established in 1999 to foster shared insights on increasing diversity in the workplace, was given an outstanding organization award for its corporate vision statement, which asserted its belief that "diversity is a business imperative and an ethical and social responsibility, grounded in core values of team spirit, service spirit, and spirit of progress." To show company commitment to diversity, its Diversity Leadership Council was chaired by the corporate executive officer, all of its over 15,000 managers completed training in equal-employment and affirmative-action programs, and the annual compensation of its senior executives and managers is based on their diversity achievements, regardless of the company's financial performance (Reed Business Information 2003).

Conclusion

Social workers are trained to respect the inherent dignity and worth of the individual and to behave respectfully and caringly toward every individual, without regard for personal difference in color, race, gender, age, or culture. Social work/social care managers know that managing diversity involves more than hiring according to affirmative action and gender equity requirements, and the seasonal recognition and celebration of differences. Every organization has a culture, analogous to a societal culture, guided by theories and intangible yet powerful assumptions about power relationships and social energy that motivate and control behavior (Kettner 2002). Often, minority individuals or groups are deliberately excluded from, marginalized by, or treated as tokens by the cultural mainstream within organizations. It therefore requires personal commitment and skilled leadership on the part of administrators to fully utilize the skills and potential of all employees as individuals and as members of a team.

System theory provides an effective diversity paradigm by showing that open systems are the more desired state as people bring to the workplace not only new energy, education, and skills, but lifetime experiences as men, women, black, white, young, aged, disabled, heterosexual, gay, lesbian, transgendered, married, divorced, or living with HIV/AIDS.

In the context of a healthy work environment, men want to be regarded as allies and not foes of women, to enjoy the same freedom as women to express emotions, to grow and be supported at the workplace and at home. Women want to be treated as equal partners, to enjoy the active support of male colleagues, and for family and home responsibilities to be valued in the work environment. Minorities want to be respected and treated as equal partners, to be valued for who they are, to enjoy open and honest relationships with colleagues, and to be actively supported by white colleagues in combating racism. At the same time, white staff members want their ethnicity acknowledged, want to build relationships based on shared goals, concerns, and mutual respect and want not to be seen as racists and accountable for the misfortunes of all minorities. They also want greater comfort in their relationships with members of minority groups. Gay men and lesbians want to be recognized as whole human beings, and not for their sexual orientation, to be supported by colleagues who do not want to change or fix them, to enjoy equal opportunity in employment, and to see increased awareness among heterosexuals of the negative impacts of homophobia and moralizing behavior. Heterosexuals want to increase their awareness of gay and lesbian and transgendered individuals, to understand the legal, social, and personal consequences of being gay, and to engage in discourse about homophobia with gay and lesbian individuals. Younger as well as older workers want to participate in work that is challenging, meaningful, be treated with respect and sincerity, and be valued for their experiences. People who are disabled want to be acknowledged for their abilities and not pitied or labeled by their limitations, to be included, and be challenged and supported by colleagues and their organization. Able-bodied workers want to feel comfortable with disabled colleagues, to accept them for who they are, and show appreciation, give honest feedback and appropriate support without being patronizing. Persons living with HIV/AIDS want to be encouraged in advancing their careers, continue to participate actively in the work, and be supported in gaining access to research, medicines, and treatment. They also want the reassurance that they can count on the backing of their colleagues in the end stages of their lives (Aufiero *et al.* 2002). They do not want to be judged, blamed, nor pitied because of their disease.

As discussed in this chapter, managing diversity also focuses on fundamental changes in self-awareness, processes in deconstruction, cultural audits and the building of organizational culture. These changes are essential for diversity competence and multiculturalism. Human service managers are entreated to explore how diversity can be supported and constructively harnessed to create harmony, improve the quality of work, and increase service effectiveness. The late US president John F. Kennedy once stated:

> Too often we hold fast to the clichés of our forbearers. We subject all facts to a prefabricated set of interpretations. We enjoy the comfort of opinion without the discomfort of thought... For the great enemy of the truth is very often not the lie: deliberate, contrived and dishonest, but the myth: persistent, persuasive, and unrealistic. (Miller and Nowak 1977, p.123)

Spoken over four decades ago as a critique of race relations and poverty in the US at the time, these words are as relevant and profound now, as contemporary societies become increasingly diverse, multicultural, multi-ethnic, and international.

Social work and social care managers are uniquely prepared as diversity leaders since in both the US and the UK professional training includes knowledge and skills in work with oppressed populations, understanding human behavior in different social environments, analyzing and advocating social welfare policies, community organizing, and practicing ethical behavior.

Chapter 7

Liability and Safety Issues in Human Services Management

Robert G. Madden

Introduction

There is an oft-quoted political maxim that "to govern is to choose." In human services management, managers must make choices informed by knowledge of what is required by law. They must recognize the legal risks, both personal and organizational, of each option being considered. In government-funded and public agencies, managers are charged with understanding the purpose and scope of the services as defined in statutes and regulations. In addition, all human service managers must operate within standards established by the law. Understanding the law is an essential component of the knowledge base necessary for managers to make informed choices and to manage organizations effectively.

Human services managers are also responsible for creating a safe environment for staff and clients. Clearly, it is not possible to prevent all incidents. However, there are basic policies and standards that enable the management of an agency, whether this be governmental or non-governmental, to demonstrate reasonable professional behavior and thus reduce liability risk. When a worker or a client suffers some harm, liability is evaluated based on whether there was a negligent act or an omission that constitutes a breach of professional responsibility.

This chapter will explore legal subjects in human services common to the UK and the US. It is helpful to think about legal responsibilities for each area competing for a manager's attention. What procedures should be in place to ensure the fairness of the hiring process? What constitutes due diligence in checking references of potential employees? What are the best practices in disciplinary matters? Are there legal standards defining the services offered by the agency or the eligibility for benefits? What policies are in place to ensure the safety of workers and clients? How much discretion does a worker have in determining what services to provide for clients? Do supervisors understand the legal risks of failing to monitor the practice of workers? Do staff document practice in a thorough and consistent manner? Are services offered consistent with the prevailing standard of care? These and many other questions require an understanding of the law and the variety of ways human services are shaped by legal principles.

The context of legal issues in human services management

The variability of laws, legal structures, legal proceedings, and legal traditions in the UK, the US, and other countries makes the task of writing a chapter on legal issues in human service management daunting. While it would require volumes to detail all relevant laws, it is possible to explore common issues facing managers of human service programs. In fact, the challenge of this chapter is analogous to the challenge facing managers: Without being able to know the details of all the laws affecting practice, which legal concepts are crucial to the performance of management activities?

The law may seem inaccessible for those without legal education. The language, location, and sheer volume of material can be intimidating. University education can provide coursework in the law but the truth is that the details of many laws are largely specific to the setting. How does the statute define the conditions under which a child can be removed from a parent? What are the specific factors that a judge considers in approving a guardian or conservator for an elder member of the community? How does a child qualify for special education services or a family qualify for welfare assistance? What are the limits of confidentiality when a client is in a high risk situation? Statutes and regulations governing such issues are usually only retained by a manager when they are used on a frequent basis. Rather than studying specific statutory language, managers need to develop what Vernon (1993) calls a "professional ease" with the law. An understanding of basic legal principles facilitates the manager's task of becoming competent in the law.

Legal competence, like competence in any area of practice, involves mastery of certain knowledge and skills. One must develop a basic familiarity with the role of law in society. The law is an institution that organizes society by enforcing expectations, maintaining order, and structuring relationships. Managers must have knowledge of the laws that sanction or require practice interventions and the regulations that specify the procedures to be followed in working with particular populations or settings (McDonald and Henderson 2003). The competent human service manager must possess a strong knowledge of practice standards in order to ensure that program staff are operating within the accepted professional standard of care. It is also important for managers to build their understanding of the role of lawyers and legal reasoning. In working with legal professionals, there may be difficulty communicating due to different terminology, values, and orientation (Preston-Shoot, Roberts and Vernon 1998b). Managers must make a commitment to learning legal terminology and understanding the priorities and obligations of legal professionals.

In addition to legal knowledge, human service managers must develop the skills to interact effectively with the legal system. First among these skills is the ability to research the law including the locating and analysis of legal materials (Madden 2000). Many human service professionals accept legal rules, administrative regulations, and court decisions passively. There is an opportunity missed when this stance is taken. Developing the skills to play an active role in the legal system can empower managers to influence social policies that affect clients and practice and to influence the outcomes for service-users in particular situations. This might involve educating lawmakers, judges, or administrative authorities about the needs of clients and the implications of decisions or policies on the people served by the program. Human service workers may be able to share the stories of their clients, using client narratives to influence positive decisions by legal authorities. Human service managers may supervise staff preparing for support roles with clients experiencing court proceedings. Finally, human service managers may be called to testify in court cases and to support staff to do so. Developing the skills to be an effective witness and to build proficiency in this role can be a precious opportunity for advocacy.

Authority and discretion

The authority to take action in human services arises from a combination of government sanction and professional judgment. Governments sanction the provision of services or mandate practice based on laws and administrative regulations, often developed as policy and procedures in agencies in the UK. The government regulates eligibility to practice in some cases by the licensing, registration, accreditation, or credentialing of workers. Also, in providing funding for programs, a government sanctions specific services. However, these sanctions are mostly general in nature and leave room for professionals to use their education and experience to make various practice decisions within the general scope of their authority. This is referred to as professional discretion. The most important regulating system for professional activity, including discretion, is the presence of professional standards of care, ethical codes, and current research on best practices.

Professional discretion

Human service workers are endowed with powers and limitations or, as expressed by McDonald and Henderson, "duties, powers, responsibilities, remedies" (2003, p.79). The legal system may intervene when there is an abuse of power, a failure to perform a legal duty, a negligent act or omission, a breach of a legal expectation, such as confidentiality, or vicarious liability where an agency assumes responsibility for the actions of its employees (Raisbeck 1977). A professional acting within these standards must have discretion to apply legal rules and determine when specific legal procedures should be followed. The essential task for human service workers is to determine when and to what extent a court or other legal authority would grant them the authority to use their discretion to apply a legal rule (Madden 2003, p.75).

There are two aspects to the analysis of discretion. First, managers must evaluate whether all procedures were followed. Were clients informed of their rights and afforded the opportunity for a fair process? Were the specific mandates of the law followed in making the practice decision? Often front-line workers act out of passion, their good intentions clouding objective analysis. The task of the manager is to know the relevant legal standards in order to structure the determination of whether a practice decision is consistent with legal procedures or rules and thus a legitimate exercise of professional discretion.

For example, in a child welfare case, the statute may require a human service professional to report any case in which there is a reasonable cause to believe that abuse or neglect or significant harm has occurred or is imminent. The government sanction to breach confidentiality to make a report is explicit in the law. Professional discretion issues emerge in the assessment of when the behavior in the family reaches the threshold of being a "reasonable cause to believe" that abuse has occurred. Human service managers should support practice policies within the agency that ensure staff members are employing professional standards and are acting in accordance with professional ethics (see also Chapter 4).

Legal oversight of social services

If one searches for the causes of manager stress, it would be wholly justifiable to place considerable blame on the increasing legalization of society and the fight for civil rights. This might sound offensive at first, but consider the argument. In the US, public agencies were dominated by human service professionals whose practice expertise rarely was challenged by courts (Mosher 1987). Courts were cautious about establishing a precedence of second-guessing professionals that could cause a flood of new cases. This changed in the US with the civil rights movement. Lawyers and other advocates working for individual rights for vulnerable populations began to challenge professional judgments. They criticized many professional decisions as patriarchal, based on arbitrary criteria. In response to the call for increased accountability, programs to help vulnerable populations became increasingly rule-based and thus became easier to challenge in court by seeking judicial review (Tyler 1992). Did a decision by a human service worker result in the violation of the client's civil rights? In those areas where professional discretion results in a deprivation of someone's liberty, courts in the US are especially likely to review the decision to evaluate whether the professional acted in compliance with legal criteria.

In the UK, the issue of oversight by the legal system is more related to the concepts of professional duty. Without the same legal principle of constitutionally protected civil rights, English law specifically defines the power of the human service agencies and the conditions that trigger the use of the powers. As a result, the legal system reviews the question: "Have the powers provided by law been exceeded or utilized lawfully?" (Preston-Shoot, Roberts and Vernon 1998a). Here again, the issue of professional discretion is significant. When the legal system evaluates accountability in human service agencies, it generally applies legal rules, statutory language and procedures rather than looking at the complex issues involved in a case (Preston-Shoot *et al.* 1998b). Human service managers must be prepared to justify practice decisions based on familiarity with legal mandates and the reality of working with populations and settings that require professionals to exercise discretionary authority.

The introduction of the Human Rights Act (HRA) 1998 in the UK has served to unify some of the issues around competing legal frameworks that regulate human services managers and practitioners. The Human Rights Act (1998) affects judgements made in relation to all other law, as they need to be HRA compatible. It has major implications in relation to the actions of public authorities and can be used as a sanction against poor practice. For example, in *R. v North and East Devon Health Authority* (ex parte, Coughlan [1999] 2CCLR 285) a health authority was prevented from closing down a residential unit after legal action taken by residents (McDonald and Henderson 2003).

Understanding legal rules and mandates

It is important but insufficient for human service managers to be familiar with the legal statutes and regulations that sanction the functions of the organization. For those in public settings and where statutes specifically control the parameters of practice, the laws may provide detailed information concerning the rules, eligibility guidelines, policies, and procedures. At times, the law prescribes certain conduct (e.g. children in foster placement in the US must be seen at least one time per month by a caseworker and in the UK the placement reviewed within the first 48 hours). At other times, the law may proscribe certain conduct (e.g. it is a criminal act in the US for a mental health worker to engage in a sexual relationship with someone under care). For agencies that are not directed by statute, there are many ways in which legal oversight occurs. First, many agencies receive grants, third party payments, or public money contracts. In each case, there are specific guidelines that have the force of law behind them. In all settings, the law reinforces the standard of care. When an agency or its employees acts in a manner that is outside accepted practice standards resulting in harm to a client, redress may be sought through a lawsuit.

Sources of legal obligations
Statutory law

Statutes are passed by legislative bodies and are often the most general statement of the law. Frequently, when the law is to be administered or overseen by a public agency (or a combination of public agencies, e.g. Children Act 2004 (England and Wales)), the legislation empowers the minister/administrator to develop more specific regulations, sometimes referred to as secondary legislation. For example, in order to receive funding for mental health services to indigent populations, a local agency must agree to periodic audits of their records performed by the administrative agency. The administrative agency might also write guidelines for record keeping and standards for practice that must be followed by the local agency in order to receive funding. These details would not be found in the original legislation but they are promulgated by the responsible public agency within the parameters of the original language of the enabling legislation.

Case Law

An additional source of law that human service managers need to be familiar with is referred to as case law or common law. The common law develops from a series of cases that examine the same law or regulation.

There are two important prerequisite understandings that managers must acknowledge to be legally competent. First, much of the law is written in vague language that does not answer the questions arising out of a particular situation in practice. Second, every legal case involves a unique story. The presentation of the competing narratives of the case by the lawyers using the adversarial system pushes the law to develop gradually. Judges must abide by legal precedent, the concept that compels a court to follow its own decisions and the decisions of higher courts within the same jurisdiction. But a judge may be persuaded by arguments that a different law applies, or that the facts of the case distinguish it from the established rule. What is most important is that human service managers become familiar with important legal cases in their area. By reading the reasoning of the decisions, the general legal rules become clearer. Although common law requires us not to use one case as evidence of a general rule, cases that consistently reinforce the same interpretation of the law increase confidence in how a court might rule in the future. Managers can use this knowledge to make decisions that will be consistent with the most widely accepted rule of law.

Human service professionals are assigned duties and responsibilities arising from the statutes but often these are defined further by case law. For example, in the Gloucestershire case in the UK (*R. v Gloucestershire County Council*, ex parte Barry [1997] 2WLR 459) the local authority's decision to withdraw services because of its financial situation was challenged. The House of Lords ruling on the matter decided that local authorities can take resources into account when assessing need and deciding what services to provide, but clarified how any eligibility criteria had to be reasonable and detailed how they must not be used to fetter discretion in individual cases (McDonald and Henderson 2003).

In many jurisdictions in the US, a client who threatens harm to self or others creates an obligation to take action to prevent the harm from occurring. Most jurisdictions have passed statutes protecting clinical information shared with those providing psychotherapy services, giving clients the privilege to keep the information private. These privileged communication statutes include a number of exceptions, one of which may allow for disclosure to prevent harm. However, the statute alone does not provide guidance as to what conditions trigger this duty. In case law, courts have examined the duty and clarified it. In the case of a threatening client, the threat must be assessed by the mental health professional as credible, and the threat must have been directed against a specific identified (or identifiable) person(s). These *conditions* create a conflicting set of legal duties: the duty to maintain confidentiality and the duty to prevent harm when the professional is aware of the threat. Human service managers with knowledge of both the statute and the case law can make informed decisions about how to proceed.

Professional practice standards as legal requirements

Human service managers are responsible for maintaining quality standards of practice within their program. The most important way that practice standards act as legal requirements is through the oversight of civil courts applying principles of negligence law. If a client of a human service agency is harmed as a direct result of the actions of an agency employee, there may be a lawsuit or civil complaint filed. The goal of these complaints is either to seek damages as compensation for the injuries suffered, or to demand that the agency take some action. These legal claims are called torts. A tort is an action, or the failure to take action, that violates a standard of reasonable behavior and causes harm to another party (Madden 2003). The two most relevant types of tort claims are negligent and intentional torts.

When a human service manager understands the elements of a negligence claim, it can structure the planning, monitoring, and evaluation of services and staff. As stated, negligence actions require a duty of care owed to an individual and a subsequent breach of that duty. Clients would always be considered a party to whom the agency staff owe a duty of care. What is the scope of the duty owed? Consider, for example, the case of a neighbor slipping on the unrepaired carpet covering the front steps of your home and suffering injuries. An ordinary negligence action would examine whether your behavior (not fixing the rug) was reasonable given the circumstances. This analysis might include evidence of how long the dangerous condition existed and whether you had knowledge of the defect.

In the case of professional negligence, the standard is what was reasonable for a similarly trained professional in the same circumstances.

The evidence of reasonableness might include testimony from an expert establishing the standard for the profession. For example, in a case of a child who suffered bladder control problems at night, it would be a professional standard for a counselor to refer the child to a physician to rule out physical causes. If a counselor failed to make a referral, treating the enuresis as a psychological condition, and the child turned out to have a life threatening tumor, the family would have a good chance of proving a violation of a professional standard. A violation of the standard of care can also involve the failure to follow accepted procedures such as the failure to return the telephone calls of an actively suicidal client, or the failure to follow policies or procedures. In addition to the finding that a professional has violated the standard of care, there must be proof that the actions of the professional caused the injury. Finally, there must be actual damages suffered by a client in order to sustain a professional negligence lawsuit.

Intentional torts are a less frequent concern of human service managers than negligence actions. These torts involve deliberate behaviours that intentionally cause harm to another such as assault, libel, slander, or intentionally inflicting emotional distress. Human service managers must be alert to actions that could give rise to lawsuits. Sometimes intentional torts arise out of conflictual supervisory relationships such as publishing knowingly false information about another person in a reference letter or at a public meeting; or creating an emotionally toxic environment to try to force an employee to resign. In addition, agency employees may act intentionally to harm a client. While infrequent, these situations can be devastating to reputations and expose an agency and an individual manager to large damage awards.

Day-to-day management concerns

Human service managers can reduce the possibility of a court finding against staff by being attentive to several fundamental management activities. First, the day-to-day operations of the program must be well planned and organized in a way that is consistent with legal rules and mandates, such as health and safety regulations. Workers must be adequately supervised, practice must be carefully documented, and policies must be clear, widely disseminated, and meticulously followed.

As a general statement, good management practices result in reduced liability for an organization. However, the motivation for establishing and insisting on compliance with policies and procedures should not be liability prevention. Instead, the primary goal of managers should be to prevent harm to clients and to workers by insisting on good practice. Policies serve the function of standardizing responses and reducing the chances of negligent acts or omissions. They formalize expectations and detail responsibilities. However, there is a fine line between positively ensuring compliance and creating an anxious fear of litigation or public inquiries. When liability prevention is the goal, there is a defensiveness to practice. An agency that has this posture does not prioritize the needs of the clients and the management oversight generally is perceived by the staff as disempowering (Obholzer 2003). The goal of effective management should be to build the policy structure within which staff can understand the parameters of their authority, rely on protocols for handling difficult practice situations, and be trusted to use their professional discretion within this framework.

Documentation of practice

It is a frequently repeated maxim in human services that in legal matters, that which is not documented is not done. Documentation of practice through recording is important for a variety of reasons. In many areas, there are statutory requirements to document events, such as plans for children in out of home placements in the UK. What agencies are to record and the quality of compliance will be monitored and reinforced through inspection by government bodies such as the Commission for Social Care Inspection in England and the Social Work Inspection Agency in Scotland. The time at which managers are most concerned with the quality of documentation is when a legal authority is seeking the file or when someone is questioning the services provided to the client. However, managers should be attentive to the quality and timeliness of documentation at all times. The possibility of being accused of fraud is a strong disincentive to alter records after they are subpoenaed or otherwise requested. Therefore, waiting for a crisis before checking the content and currency of case records generally results in inadequate documentation.

For example, in the US, when a client presents a risk of harm to self, the worker must have documented observations about client affect, mood, and behavior. The suicide assessment information should be documented if the client presented with suicidal ideation. The safety plan, report of contact with family members, input of supervisors, and consultations with psychiatric professionals would also be noted in the client file. Specific information such as the time of each contact would be important evidence to support appropriate professional response. If the client left the program at midday but the call to the family was not made until early evening, it could be argued that the worker failed in the duty to prevent the harm of the client's suicide from occurring.

Kagle (1991, p.141) identifies three primary goals of record keeping in human services: accountability, efficiency, and client privacy. All of these goals are important for managers. Record keeping enables supervisors, administrators, and funding sources to hold programs accountable for the services being provided by each worker to clients. The ability to document the number of clients served and the outcomes for those clients can demonstrate the effectiveness and of the agency. Documentation provides the data concerning client progress toward goals and thus can influence decisions regarding the efficiency of particular treatment approaches and program initiatives. It can also be useful for the manager who supervises the actions of the practitioner and the progress of the work. Finally, careful documentation formalizes the process of record keeping, ensuring that client information is managed so as to protect privacy.

Therefore, the most important record keeping issue for managers is to establish policies for monitoring accountability. How often was each client seen? What is the client's progress in working on goals? What is the plan for further actions? This information is used to ensure quality services and to safeguard clients. However, it also is critical to account to funding sources (government agencies, foundations, insurance companies) that the services were provided to the clients in a manner that meets the requirements of the contract or grant. Managers need to include record reviews as a standard part of the procedure when planning strategies to monitor worker performance. In one agency, human service workers providing support services to an immigrant population did most of their work off site in the community. Due to budget cuts, the agency reduced administrative staff and several of the community workers were not monitored for several months. Two of these workers subsequently left the agency. When a funding agency audited the program, the records of these community workers were missing and the former workers could not be located. The agency had been paid for services but there was no documentation that the services were provided and the funding agency threatened to require reimbursement for all services that could not be documented.

The legal system uses human service records in a variety of ways. Human service organizations need to consider the way professional documentation is collected and retained in order to be ready to supply records when appropriate. Data collection, recording, and the use of information therefore must meet the requirements of legislation relating to record keeping, such as the UK Data Protection Act (1998), which identifies what kind of information should be recorded and provides guidance in relation to information sharing and disclosures.

Managers need to create systems for documentation that ensure the records contain facts and observable details rather than opinion or speculation. One of the key ingredients in record keeping is the concept of attribution. All statements made by clients and other pieces of information in a record should include a statement identifying the source of the information. For example, a young boy, Joseph, was being seen in a youth agency. Joseph complained that his mother never let him go outside to play. A well-known drug dealer, Mr. Jones, lived in the building and there were people in the hallways "getting high" and exchanging drugs. In the agency record, it would be important to identify the source of the information, attributing the statements to Joseph. In addition, it is important not to name Mr. Jones in this record. Instead, it would be advisable to identify him merely as a neighbor or resident of the building. All case records should be treated as if, one day, they could be part of a court case or otherwise made public. The names of non-clients are not relevant to documenting practice and staff should be trained to keep their files free of these extraneous details.

Supervision

When agencies fail to review the performance of front-line workers, the program confronts a heightened risk of liability for negligence. For example, an experienced social worker took a part-time supervisory position with an agency that provided services to men infected by HIV. The agency had been formed by a dedicated but not professionally trained man. No written case records were kept concerning the counseling and support services provided by the workers. Soon after assuming the position, the supervisor met with each counselor but was unable to gain much perspective due to the lack of documentation regarding each counselor's professional work. About one month later, a complaint was lodged against a worker at the agency. One of the workers had begun a sexual relationship with one of his clients. The supervisor had met with the worker only two times and did not realize the worker's confusion concerning professional boundary issues. When the worker quit the agency and was not able to be contacted, the client filed a complaint against the agency and the supervisor for failure to properly monitor the actions of their employee.

The concept of supervisor liability is relevant to discuss at this point. The theory is that the supervisor assumes a duty of care to the clients of the supervisee. This duty involves the monitoring and evaluation of practice to ensure that no one is practicing in a way that would be harmful to clients. The client generally might argue that, as a result of the inadequate supervision, the worker's harmful behaviors were not corrected and the client suffered damages as a result. In the case of the supervisor named in the case above, there was no record to demonstrate that the worker's performance was monitored and evaluated.

The second legal theory relied on by clients who are suing human service organizations is *respondeat superior* (let the master respond) (*Black's Law Dictionary* 1983). This legal theory holds organizations responsible for the actions of their agents. It would be unfair for an organization to avoid liability by claiming that the harmful act of one of its employees was not its responsibility: it was the individual employee who was at fault. The law views the organization as responsible for the actions of its employees and volunteers as long as they were acting in the scope of their responsibilities.

The realization that human service agencies are subject to lawsuits or other legal complaints based on the actions of individual workers is sobering and should motivate managers to attend to the supervision system. However, recognizing that sometimes clients are harmed by workers who are not closely supervised should be the stronger motivation. Fear of liability often creates defensive supervision whereas quality control approaches can enable a system focused on a developmental model, promoting professional growth while protecting client rights.

Compliance with legal mandates

Human service managers have the responsibility to ensure that workers are complying with legal mandates and with practice standards. This responsibility includes building a knowledge base in statutory language and administrative regulations. Frequently, managers only know the broad strokes of the law, failing to familiarize themselves with specific legal language. Managers should collect legal statutes relevant to the agency and keep them within reach. As situations arise, returning to the actual language of the statute or regulation can be instrumental in arriving at an informed decision. In the recent past, most statutes and regulations have become available on the internet. Managers can collect and organize legal materials from primary sources such as government administrative agencies and statutes. Competence in legal research skills is now essential for the effective human service manager.

A case example helps to reinforce the importance of knowing specific legal language.

A family counseling agency faced a difficult decision. One of their counselors worked with a man who was in the process of getting a divorce. His wife, Irene, was invited into sessions on two occasions. Irene presented as angry and somewhat out of control, culminating in a scene where she threw a chair at her husband, damaging a wall, and breaking a number of objects in the room. About one month later, the counselor was contacted by a child protection worker who informed her that she was investigating a claim of child abuse involving Irene. The worker was seeking information as to whether to remove the child from the Irene's care. Should the counselor share information about Irene's violent temper with the child protection worker?

In this case, looking at the language of the privileged communication statute enabled the counselor to see that there was an exception to confidentiality in cases of danger to a person and in cases where the law mandates the report of child abuse. But the language of the statute alone is insufficient. The wording of the exception allows the counselor to share information but does not require it. Does the counselor have the right to disclose the information under the mandated reporting exception even though she did not make the child abuse report? As should be evident, the statutory language is helpful but not determinative. In consultation with the agency director and a legal consultant, the counselor decided to share with the investigation worker that Irene had a potential for violence. This disclosure was judged to be enough information to fulfill the purpose of the disclosure: protection of the child. However, in order to provide additional details, the counselor needed to wait for a signed authorization from Irene or an order from a judge. Access to the language of the statutes allowed the counselor and those she consulted with to make a decision that was within legal mandates but did not exceed the permitted disclosure.

Compliance with agency policies

Practice policies are designed to ensure that workers follow procedures and act in a manner consistent with professional standards. Some policies, such as the content of medical records, may be defined by statutes and others are drawn from the standard of care for the profession. Managers have the responsibility to provide leadership in policy development, training, and compliance. Agency policies can involve a myriad of issues depending on the services of the program. In some cases, the services are available only to those meeting eligibility criteria such as residence, age, diagnosis, or income level. Agency intake policies require documentation of these eligibility standards. The agency may have policies regarding fees, scheduling of appointments, performance reviews of staff, travel, or transporting of clients. There may be protocols for handling emergencies such as suicidal clients or violence on agency property.

Managers do not often think of these agency policies as legal requirements. However, the legal system views agency policies as evidence of standard practice. The policies should therefore, reflect national standards and professionally sanctioned protocols. The legal system is interested in agency policies when something has gone wrong. The agency is being sued for negligence or malpractice. A worker who has been fired is claiming discrimination and has asked a court to reinstate him. A child has suffered a serious injury while participating in a recreational activity sponsored by the agency. An elderly client who receives case management services from your agency is hospitalized with malnutrition. A child in a family you are working with is severely injured by her father who has been drinking. In each case, a court may be asked to review the actions of the workers involved with the clients. The general standard is whether the actions of the worker were consistent with accepted practice standards. If it is demonstrated that agency policies were not followed, it is likely the agency will face liability.

The initial challenge for human service managers is to develop relevant, comprehensive and state-of-the-art policies. Researching best practices, making use of outcome based treatment protocols, and ensuring that agency policies are consistent with legal mandates is a demanding and ongoing management function. For example in both the US and the UK, legislation on the privacy of medical records requires agencies to follow policies regarding the confidentiality of records and sets up specific procedures that must be implemented in health and mental health agencies. The privacy acts (the Health Insurance Portability and Accountability Act (1996) (HIPAA) in the US and the UK Data Protection Act of 1998 (DPA)) also govern communications with insurance and managed care companies paying for services. HIPAA, DPA and other similar regulations must be incorporated within the policies of programs covered by the acts.

The need for dissemination of policies

An agency with well-written, nuanced, researched, and current policies has only done one-third of the job. The second task of the human service manager is to disseminate these policies to the staff and provide reinforcement through ongoing opportunities to retrain staff on agency policies. A case study below illustrates this issue.

In addition to making certain all staff are aware of all policies, new employees and temporary staff such as student interns must be informed of policies as part of their orientation to the agency. If management does not actively disseminate policies and regularly reinforce them with staff, compliance can suffer dramatically. Also, all policies must be examined for consistency with professional ethical codes and standards of practice. The policy prohibiting home visits was inconsistent with the staff's view of their professional responsibilities and agency mission.

A social work intern was working in a section of a large city characterized by a high crime rate and drug-related violence. He and another student were assigned to work with a family, but the family had difficulty keeping appointments at the agency. The interns decided to meet with the client family at their flat. Several months later, they were pleased with the gains made by the family and decided to present the case to the staff. At the presentation, the agency director stopped by to listen. He was upset to learn the interns had been doing these home visits and informed them that, due to the violence in the neighborhood, there was an agency policy prohibiting home visits. The students were shocked to learn this, but more shocking was the reaction of the staff present in the meeting. Half of the ten agency employees reported that they did not know about this policy.

Monitoring compliance

The third responsibility of the human service manager regarding agency policies is monitoring compliance. In this task, the manager faces the challenge of designing systems to monitor policy compliance of the staff without creating either excessive paperwork or producing a staff that feels a lack of autonomy and trust. The key strategy is to set a clear expectation concerning policy compliance and to provide the support and structures necessary to carry out this mission. Staff need to be convinced of the relevance of the policy to good practice. If it is presented merely as a legal requirement, staff resistance will be high. Recognizing the way agency policies support good practice and presenting them in that manner can improve staff compliance with these requirements. Also, actively involving staff in designing agency policies and regularly reviewing their efficacy gives staff ownership of the policies and improves overall compliance.

Maintaining safety for clients and workers

The responsibility of human service managers to provide a safe environment for clients and workers has received increasing attention in recent professional literature (Leather 1998; Spencer and Munch 2003; Newhill 2004). For most management students, the image of managing a human service agency probably does not include pricing security cameras or planning lock down drills for a program. However, the reality of current practice requires managers to be attuned to a variety of risks to clients and workers and a duty to act to reduce these risks. The legal issue arises from basic tort law. Should an injury occur to a client or an employee, the legal review process will investigate whether the agency owed a duty to provide a safe environment and, retrospectively, whether it was reasonable to expect that certain precautions should have been taken or certain policies should have been followed.

Safety for clients

Consider the issues related to clients who are injured while involved in a program activity. When an agency creates a program inviting clients to participate in services or activities, a duty of reasonable care is created. The legal system reinforces this expectation through damages awarded to those who have been harmed. The litigiousness of the past two decades has led some agencies to discontinue programs. This response overstates the real risk and leads to a defensiveness in programming. A better response is to examine carefully all programs and activities to determine whether sufficient safeguards are in place. For example, in a youth agency that organizes trips to area amusement parks and museums, it would be advisable for a manager to review the staff to student ratio, to provide common colored tee-shirts to improve monitoring of youth, to use a qualified bus company, and other similar strategies to demonstrate adherence to safety protocols.

The law cannot expect that accidents will never happen and, even if all precautions are taken, someone could still file a lawsuit after suffering an injury in a program activity. It is precisely because there is no guarantee that a risk-aversive response to the threat or possibility of liability is not productive. Accepting that risk is inescapable, the best strategy is to increase safety and attend to the details of planning each activity with attention to safety concerns.

Safety for employees

There is something uncomfortable about the concept of creating a safe environment for workers, especially when the issue is client violence directed at staff. If a program hires a security guard, installs security cameras and new locks on doors, there may be a message implicit in these acts. The message may be that "we" professionals are outsiders in "their" community and we do not feel safe. Therefore, we are going to barricade ourselves in this fortress and allow entry to those who are judged to be of no risk. This can create a dynamic that is not conducive to developing and maintaining trusting relationships. However, if an agency does not attend to security, there may be legal consequences. In a recent case in the US, an agency was found liable for failure to monitor a parking area where an intern was assaulted on her way home in the evening (*Gross v. Family Services Agency and Nova Southeastern University* 1998). The court found that the lot had been the site of several crimes in the recent past and the agency had done nothing to improve the security of the area or to institute policies regarding escorts for workers leaving in the evening. The university had not ensured that the practicum was offered in a safe environment.

The courts are not likely to tell agencies what must be done or how much must be spent to safeguard staff and clients. The answer to the security concerns has less to do with money than attention. Regardless it is clear that courts will hold agencies liable for failure to maintain a safe work environment, especially where there was knowledge of a dangerous condition and no action taken to improve safety.

Violence in the workplace

It is important that managers not wait until an incident has occurred before addressing safety issues. There are some settings that are more high risk than others such as child protection, criminal justice, and mental health (Newhill 2004). But every setting and population carries some risk of violence. Managers should target their attention to three main areas: improving skills in assessment and de-escalation of crisis situations, developing policies to address safety issues, and providing adequate support to staff.

The staff of a program needs to be provided with professional development opportunities to improve their ability to assess violence risk in their clients. For example, workers need to recognize the types of practice situations, diagnoses, and exacerbating conditions such as intoxication when determining how to respond to clients (Duffy 2004). The failure to attend to adequate staff training could result in lawsuits by either clients or staff injured by violence. The analysis of the organization's culpability would focus on whether the staff was prepared to handle situations that could have been anticipated given the population or issues in service delivery.

A thorough planning process that involves staff can result in a reduction of the frequency and severity of client violence (Hunter and Love 1996; Flannery, Penk and Corrigan 1999). There has been increasing professional literature on the development of safety plans (see, for example, Newhill 2004). Human service managers should consider the establishment of a safety committee that can examine issues specific to the program and recommend policies. A safety plan should never be technically completed since there generally are ongoing issues related to the practical operation of the policies, compliance by staff, and the training of new workers. A side benefit of safety plans is that they demonstrate a commitment to staff wellbeing that can enhance job satisfaction and retention of workers (Vinokur-Kaplan *et al.* 1994). Safety is often on the minds of workers but the subject may be considered taboo to discuss publicly. Managers must assume leadership roles in the creation of safety plans to reduce the incidence of violence and to demonstrate reasonable professional practice in response to high risk situations (Scalera 1995; Spencer and Munch 2003).

Developing support policies

In addition to maintaining safety for clients and workers, a third zone of attention for managers is the provision of support to workers. The support can take two tracks. Workers who provide services to populations where there is an especially high risk of violence need backup plans. For example, clients who are involuntary, such as those mandated by court, may be angry about being coerced to attend. Those who are participating in drug or alcohol treatment may be more likely to arrive at the agency inebriated and may be more impulsive as a result. In child welfare and custody settings, the highly charged emotions that arise from the threat to parenting roles may trigger violent reactions (Griffin 1997). In these settings, managers must establish a plan for providing backup to staff. In some cases, this may mean assigning two workers to group or family work. It may involve an on-call supervisor in the building during agency hours to respond to crises. When appropriate, there may be security personnel hired to be present within the agency as both a deterrent and a response. Establishing policies concerning work done in the evenings or at other times when there are few other staff present can reduce some of the risks to individual workers.

A second type of support that needs to be provided to staff is a plan for providing services to those who have been victimized. As mentioned earlier, it may not be considered acceptable by some workers to acknowledge their feelings following an assault or even a threat. It is important for managers and supervisors to provide an environment where workers can receive support and have permission to process these feelings. Managers should provide an opportunity for debriefing immediately after an incident and should provide access to treatment. Here it is important to caution that the judgment concerning whether the incident was traumatic to the worker must be left to the worker. Supervisors who make assumptions or minimize the effect of incidents may be doing harm to the individual worker and may be subject to employment complaints.

There is also increasing concern about workplace stress and its impact on wellbeing for social work and care staff (Arnold, Cooper and Robertson 1998). Managers are in a position to influence the factors that contribute to practitioner stress and wellbeing (Elkin and Rosch 1990). While creating a positive work environment for staff is a component of best practice, the organization's responsibility is often brought into sharper focus when individuals take employers to court claiming compensation for work-related stress. In 2002, a former social worker in Worcestershire in the UK was awarded £140,000 in an out of court settlement and the Trades Union Council (TUC) won £321 million in compensation for workers in 2001. The front-line manager cannot avoid a direct responsibility for working to maintain systems, structures, and cultures that support their staff and protect their wellbeing (Seden and Katz 2003). This may include purchase of or referral to counseling or other support.

Responding to worker concerns

One additional source of legal risk is related to this discussion of safety and wellbeing issues. Human service managers should work to establish a system of receiving and responding to worker concerns. It is a benefit to the case of a plaintiff who is suing an agency when there is documentation that a dangerous condition existed but the administration failed to take any action to remediate the problem. The range of safety issues may include environmental problems such as air quality, toxic cleansing agents, building security, lighting, or other conditions that pose a risk to health or safety. In the day-to-day activities of busy managers, worker concerns may be marginalized and responses delayed.

Dangerous client situations

A protocol is an established manner to respond to a particular situation. When clients threaten harm to themselves or others, an agency should have a protocol that workers follow. It is common for clients to inform workers about intentions to engage in a dangerous act. As a manager, there are several concerns. No single staff member should be in a position to decide how to handle a homicidal or suicidal threat. Managers should be concerned over the breach of confidentiality that would occur if the agency chose to initiate action to prevent the harm from occurring. However, the greatest liability arises from inaction in response to information. A well-designed policy on dangerous client situations bases the decision on the shared assessment of more than one professional.

The features of an effective protocol for managing threats of dangerous behavior by clients includes a system for obtaining consultation with appropriate senior staff or consultants. The factors involved in the assessment of dangerousness should be detailed in the policy and considered by the team. If there is not sufficient expertise on staff, plans should include the use of mobile crisis teams, hospitals, or other mental health services. If a client threatens harm against an identified or identifiable person and the assessment indicates that the client is likely to act on the impulse, there may be an obligation to warn the intended victim. Similarly if a suicide threat is assessed as serious and imminent, actions may be taken to protect the client from self-harm including involuntary commitment or informing family members. Organizations should discuss their philosophical stance concerning clients who make a lucid, competent decision to end their lives. Inaction could expose the agency to legal complaints by surviving family members.

When an agency develops written protocols and other policies, it may increase some legal risk. An investigation by a lawyer or other legal professional would compare the protocol to the facts of what actually was done in the case being investigated. Any deviations from the written protocol may result in liability. Some would argue that agencies are safer, from a liability perspective, if they do not have many written policies to be held to. That point of view, however, assumes that written policies are not followed. If there are sound written protocols, with periodic retraining and reinforcement, they are likely to be used in crisis situations. These protocols serve as guidelines for how to respond within the professional standard of care. They can safeguard clients and staff and thus reduce overall agency liability.

Managers and employment law

Most managers are not prepared to deal with the challenges of practicing within the parameters of employment law. At each point in the employment relationship, recruitment, hiring, supervision, discipline, and termination of workers, supervisors must apply legal rules. This section reviews some of the major employment law policies and identifies basic guidelines for managing employment issues. It is important to recognize that each jurisdiction differs as to specific requirements so managers should pursue consultation with human resource professionals and local attorneys.

Well-defined job descriptions are the foundation for employment decisions for human service managers. The task of articulating responsibilities and expectations for each staff position should be a priority. The job descriptions are crucial when hiring, evaluating, disciplining, and terminating employees. At each stage of an employment relationship where there is a possibility of legal system review, the decisions of managers are most protected and affirmed when they are based on the written criteria for the position.

Hiring

The laws related to employment are similar in the UK and the US. In the US, the Civil Rights Act of 1964 prohibits discrimination on the grounds of race, sex, religion, color, or national origin, and later legislation extended protection to elderly and disabled people (Americans with Disabilities Act 1996).

In the UK, several laws protect the right to equal employment opportunity. The three primary laws address discrimination on grounds of race (Race Relations Act 1976), sex (Sex Discrimination Act 1975) and disability (Disability Discrimination Act 1995). Three commissions (Equal Opportunity Commission, Commission for Racial Equality and Disability Rights Commission) have been established to review cases, and to provide technical assistance and information. The European Convention on Human Rights is becoming a more influential source of discrimination law and enforcement in the UK as European Union collaboration continues to evolve.

When an agency hires an employee, it takes on a range of legal responsibilities. Managers must be familiar with issues beyond basic salary, benefits, and tax requirements. First, in the hiring process, it is important to know about the various statutes that prohibit discrimination and procedures that should be followed. This is the first use of the job description previously discussed. Selection and questioning of candidates should be guided by the essential functions of the position. Personal questions such as inquiries about family matters, age, religion, or disability-related issues are inappropriate and in some jurisdictions may be the basis of legal complaints. Managers should utilize human resource professionals and develop a set of candidate questions in advance to ensure that questions do not violate legal guidelines and to document equal treatment of all candidates. The specific criteria in the job descriptions provide the framework for objective analysis of each candidate. This process reduces the possibility of discrimination in hiring and provides documentation in the event the hiring process is questioned.

When considering a person with a disability for a position, the manager or search committee may make an offer of employment based on the applicant's ability to meet the job requirements as specified in the detailed description. Once offered a job, the person may request reasonable accommodations under the law in some jurisdictions. Even where a specific statute does not exist, it is within the mission of human services to seek a diverse workforce that can respond to the needs of the whole community. For example, an experienced case manager was offered a position working with homebound elderly clients. He had severe arthritis and was unable to type information into a computer. Although the agency maintained all files electronically, this was not an essential function of his job as case manager. It would be a reasonable accommodation to have him dictate his notes to be transcribed or to purchase voice recognition software for his computer. In this way, a valuable, relevant worker was able to be hired and the agency stayed within the legal requirements prohibiting discrimination on the basis of disability.

Monitoring the performance of staff

Supervision is often the victim of increasing responsibility combined with decreasing resources. The tradition of close monitoring of human service workers has wilted over time, although supervision in the caring professions is supported by a substantial literature (Kadushin 1995; Horwath and Morrison 1999; Hawkins and Shohet 2000) and there are many resources for support and training. As human service managers, it is vital to support structured supervision and regular evaluation. There is a potential for liability for agencies and supervisors when a supervisee acts negligently or inappropriately and causes harm to a client (as the description of *supervisor liability* showed earlier in this chapter). The supervision relationship should be guided by the job description. In addition, the supervision should occur on a regular schedule, include written evaluation, developmentally based goals to address deficient areas, and dates for subsequent reviews. The manager should require documentation of the evaluation process including specific areas of concern, examples of any areas in which the employee is not meeting the essential functions of the job, and a plan for remediation/retraining.

Discipline and termination of employment

Human service managers need to act deliberately but decisively when disciplining or terminating an employee. Too often, managers act in the style of their training in human service practice (treating a worker like a client) and continue to tolerate a staff member who is not performing tasks in an adequate or safe manner. The liability concern should be sufficient to prompt action. If there is a building record of poor performance that is not followed with management response and the employee in question causes harm to a client through an action or omission, the agency may face significant liability. Decisive action in employment cases involves clear documentation of how the worker inadequately fulfilled the essential functions of the position as defined in the job description, as well as documentation of the evaluation process and the status of the remediation plan.

In some cases, employees are protected by labor contracts or civil service systems. Other times, laws or practice may require an employer to provide due process protections to workers prior to taking any job actions. Basically, most due process protections include the right of the worker to an informal hearing and an opportunity to contest the job action. Usually there is a grievance or appeals system available to the worker. Employees are protected by the terms of the employee handbook that provides the details of the process. Managers must be cautious not to act in haste or with the emotion of the moment in making decisions on employee discipline and sanctions up to and including termination. The grievance procedures, suspension process and conditions for termination of an employee must guide the actions of managers. Often legitimate reasons exist for the termination of employees but they are able to argue successfully that written procedures were not followed. Although the law does not usually require the rehiring of these employees, substantial financial settlements may be awarded to departing employees.

Working with lawyers and the legal system

Human service managers have an important role to play in building a stronger collaboration with the legal system. The process is analogous to the approach to developing cultural competence (see, for example, Green 1998; NASW 2001). As an initial step, there must be knowledge of self; an understanding of the roles, rules, and sanctions for the agency services, and a clear sense of professional practice standards. Second, human service managers must construct a knowledge base about the law, including the statutes and regulations governing agency services and the orientation, process, and thinking of legal professionals. A third part of the path toward collaboration is the education of legal professionals about the helping professions and their underlying knowledge base including theoretical models such as human development, oppression, empowerment, and family systems theory. Finally, human service managers can move toward collaboration based on shared knowledge and understanding of roles and a common professional language (Preston-Shoot et al. 1998b).

Collaboration with the legal system is a worthwhile but insufficient goal. The legal system embodies many important values but there are many circumstances in which laws, legal procedures, or the actions of legal professionals produce harmful or anti-therapeutic outcomes for those participating in the legal system (Wexler 1990). For example, children and families going through divorce actions are often harmed by the legal process, and the addiction problems of some individuals are sometimes made worse through the interventions of the criminal justice system. Human service professionals must be active in seeking legal system reform to make the experience of the law more therapeutic for all parties (Madden and Wayne 2003). When clients are involved in legal matters in which they are without voice, marginalized, and discriminated against, when the experience of the legal system creates trauma or a sense of injustice, the professional value regarding advocacy for system change requires action to transform the features of the legal system that are oppressive and anti-therapeutic (Hatton 2001).

Conclusion

This chapter has focused on the various ways the legal system is enmeshed with the provision of human services and the management of organizations. Human service managers must accept the law as an integral component of the practice environment and commit to the development of legal knowledge and skills. Knowledge of the law includes the legal rules found in statutes and governmental regulations. It also includes understanding basic legal principles such as negligence, duty, liability, and due process because the answer to many management dilemmas cannot be found in a specific legal rule. The legal skills necessary for good practice include conducting effective legal research, applying legal principles to management situations, and relating legal rules to policy development.

Many human service managers learn law the hard way. They may handle employment situations poorly, fail to respond to liability risks, ignore the rights of clients, or find out that an agency policy is not consistent with a legal requirement. Through these experiences, they come to understand the way things should have been handled to reduce agency liability or to comply with a legal rule. This chapter has presented information about some of these areas that can prepare managers to begin the process of becoming legally literate in the issues related to managing in human services. Readers should not stop with this information. It is vital to learn the law of the local jurisdiction and the legal rules relevant to the population served by the agency. Like other areas of management, professional development in the law is a process that needs to be assessed continuously. Legal information changes over time and situations arise in managing that have not been dealt with in the past. Often there are periods of fairly frequent changes to the major legal frameworks for practice, as has been the case in England since the 1990s (Vernon 2005), and managers can feel they are "running just to keep up."

Human service managers who maintain a base of legal information and the skills and commitment to locate necessary legal principles will protect the rights of clients and workers, and reduce liability risks for their agencies and themselves.

Chapter 8

Managing Care Environments: Reflections from Research and Practice

Jill Reynolds and Sheila Peace

Introduction

This chapter considers the role of senior staff in managing the use of space and the physical environment within care settings. These day and residential settings come under the broad umbrella of social work and social care but the care may also be organized from within health. This is a subject that does not appear on the curriculum of many management courses in the UK or the US. However, it is critical in relation to social work and social care involving managers in residential homes, day centres and other provision where the physical environment can enhance or be detrimental towards service-users' wellbeing. In such settings many activities go on under one roof, particularly in group care or when the care is provided in a person's own home. The care environment is complex and can be bounded within space, place, time and behaviour. Activities and time available compete or have different meanings for the participants. The impact of environment on staff can also be profound. As Gibelman has suggested, 'the physical surroundings in which employees work influences their attitudes towards the job, the organization and the clients' (2003, p.109). Managers have different kinds of relationships with workers and with service-users. The environment in which care takes place often frames these.

For many social care employees there are everyday changes from places that are domestic to those that are non-domestic; from private to more public spaces; from those where people may be part of a group to those where they are very individual and from situations of formality to informality. Settings, situations and types of space shift constantly. The impact of these changing contexts on the role of managers forms the basis of this chapter. The intellectual background to our discussion is in the fields of environmental and social psychology, sociology, anthropology and human geography. We introduce concepts such as *territory*, *privacy* and *boundaries*, as they can underpin the ability to develop environmental quality. The chapter draws on the authors' work elsewhere, notably Peace and Reynolds (2003).

We use exemplars from residential care settings, drawing on the work of one of the chapter's authors concerning residential care homes for older people (Willcocks, Peace and Kellaher 1987; Peace, Kellaher and Willcocks 1997; Peace 1998). While contrasting use of the environment is very marked in residential care, our discussion also has application to the role of managers in other social work, social care and health settings.

Different faces of the environment

People's experiences of any setting will vary according to the reasons for their presence. Their control or power over their situation differs, and this may affect their access to a range of spaces or areas. In most working environments, there is what might be called 'public' space (reception and waiting-room areas for instance) and 'private' space (individual offices, interviewing rooms). While boundaries exist between these spaces, they may be invisible. Time of day also affects the use of space.

To illustrate this variation of use of space, consider the example on the next page of a resident of a care home for older people.

This scenario shows how one area can at the same time be a living, a working and a visiting environment. Mrs Wallis uses the hall area as a *living environment*, a place where she feels 'at home' through being able to control how she interacts with others in both public and private areas.

> Mrs Wallis likes to sit in the reception hall area for periods of time, where she can see others come and go. She avoids the adjoining entrance porch, where some people, mainly male residents, like to go for a smoke. From her seat she can see the dining room, and be ready to go there for the next meal. She can also see the administrator's office and the adjoining entrance to the office of the registered manager. Mrs Wallis can see the care staff carrying out tasks with other residents, as well as visitors arriving.

Others may not feel comfortable sitting near staff areas. Gender and cultural differences can affect where men and women find it appropriate to sit: Mrs Wallis, for example, did not want to sit with the men who were smoking in the porch. Others may find this area difficult to access for mobility reasons, and be dependent on a staff member's help. The design of the building may be crucial to its use: the number of stairs; the ease with which a wheelchair user can change floors; the gradients of hallways and external paths. These are all aspects of creating an enabling environment.

The reception area is a threshold, a point of entry that provides a 'public' boundary between inside and outside. There are other less public boundaries, for instance a separate entrance that staff use when coming on duty. For the care staff of the home it is a *working environment*. Their access and use may change from day to night where on-call sleep-in arrangements occur. These boundaries give information about the status and power of different people.

The positioning of an administrator's office near to the entrance is likely to mean that the administrator acts as unofficial receptionist, offering a welcome and giving information and directions. Whoever takes on this role – it might be a member of care staff in the midst of other activities – provides a link between people. They may facilitate access by using their insider knowledge of what is going on and who is doing what at that point in time. The care home is also a *visiting environment* and visitors have different types of access. Some are the family of residents, who may have been close informal carers when that person was living in their own home. They may just walk in and out, knowing where they are likely to find their relative. Other visitors may be more distant relatives or visiting for the first time, and unsure of procedures. Some will be informal and others formal and more official. They might be practitioners – social work, chiropody, hairdressing – as well as part of the local community.

The combination of living, working and visiting environments is common to many places in which care occurs and has to be managed. Similar variations occur in care that is provided to people in their own homes and in day-care facilities. An entrance hall has clear importance as a boundary yet, in considering the three kinds of environment, the boundaries may be less clear. The degree varies as to how far care environments involve people in these three different aspects, but the example of the residential care home helps to identify the complexity.

Some parts of a residential home are very clearly private places, such as residents' bed-sitting rooms. Yet they are also places that can be used for visiting and working. An understanding of who has control over this space will be an important guide to behaviour, reflecting the values and the culture of the home. Working space, such as the more public offices, may also need a level of privacy, depending on the activities for which they are used or the information held there. Function is thus important in determining the nature of space. Functions can change momentarily as people and places interact. The power that some people have – because of their role, status and the values they impose – can influence the atmosphere. For example, the pleasure of eating may be destroyed by the staff member who fails to see that a resident needs assistance or clears the plates in a hurry.

Organizations are multifunctional, so different aspects need to be managed in different ways. For instance, in the care home the management of care staff as employees needs to be considered differently from the management of the residents' day, although these aspects are connected. If the balance of how this is handled tips towards social control by staff, then the experience of residents may be endangered. Visitors have transitional but varying needs with different levels of attachment to the person visited – from a lifetime's relationship to a recent meeting. The management of all these different elements is complex and a situational approach to management is crucial. There is not a simple formula for resolving matters. Managers need to keep central the purpose of the service they are managing while balancing the needs of the various people involved so that they complement each other. Their approach contributes to the organizational culture and its impact for each situation. Before we examine different situations where managers may influence the environment, some of the basic concepts of this discussion – *territory* and *privacy* and their impact on behaviour – need further explanation.

Managing territory and privacy

The working environment varies in care work according to the role of the person and their closeness to offering a direct service. For people in a managerial or supervisory role, the context of work moves between formal and informal, in terms of duties or functions that affect perceived levels of professionalism, and public and private, in terms of the degree of privacy. Figure 8.1 shows a way of charting these contextual changes within a 'territorial net'.

A variety of managerial roles and functions can be located on this diagram. Talking with service-users and their families might be formal but managed privately, while a chat with senior colleagues might also be private yet informal. At the more public end of activities, a public meeting and a fundraising activity involve a contrasting range of formality and informality. In any one day a manager may move between such different functions and roles. Multiple constructions of culture and role inform different reactions to space, identity and setting. This framework can be used to explore how different forms of *territory* are established for different tasks in managing care.

In the working environment, territory is often defined as an area that each person can call their own and demarcate in some way; indeed research suggests similarities with natural environments where individual territory is important and confined areas can lead to disputes (Sommer 1969; Veitch and Arkkelin 1995). People may share offices or have different schedules but how space is allocated and set out is an issue that calls for awareness and immediate sensitive responsiveness from managers. Office desks are often personalized through books, files and arrangements of furniture, even in open plan offices. In a residential home, for example, there may be no official office space for care staff.

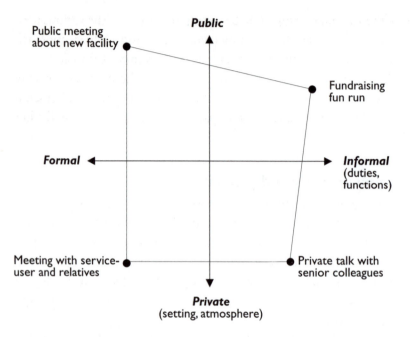

Figure 8.1 The territorial net (Source: Peace and Reynolds 2003, p.138)

Instead, the personal space may be a chair in a staff room, or access to a particular cupboard: either might be recognized as belonging with particular roles or individuals. In a small group home that aspires to be like any ordinary home, the notion of an 'office' as such may have been dispensed with and the space made available to the residents for telephone calls or to see their visitors. However, residents and staff may still see a strong invisible boundary, especially if staff who sleep-in on duty use a bed in this space.

Private space is an aspect of territory: a sense of ownership allows for changes of use and for times when individuals may engage in isolated, one-to-one or small group tasks. However, the degree of privacy that is possible depends on the level of control that an owner has over how space is used. Privacy often relates to forms of behaviour that people want to engage in either alone or with chosen others. The person does not want the public attention of others. Privacy can also relate to interruption or disruption. It may be that a task requires close attention and confidentiality because of the information being passed between people and how that information needs to be stored. There is a need for protected time, space and sound. Of course, while thinking of the values attached to privacy, it is also possible to see how privacy can entrap people in close contact with others and give opportunities for abuse – physical, sexual or psychological.

As will be discussed in more detail later in the chapter in relation to UK standards, legal requirements may also shape the use of space and the provision of privacy. Staff at one long-term care facility for older people in the US had prided itself on its open reception and administrative office area, allowing residents to freely enter in order to create a more homelike environment. The Health Insurance Portability and Accountability Act (HIPAA, also discussed in Chapter 7) passed in 1996 and effective as of 2003, requires health facilities 'to establish policies and procedures to protect the confidentiality of protected health information about their patients' (US Department of Health and Human Services 2003). The managers felt forced to reconstruct the office area to ensure that patient information that might be visible on a computer screen or on a desk was protected; offices were walled off from the patient areas, thus diminishing the homelike environment so prized by the residents.

Ideas on territory and privacy have been explored by Goffman, who uses the concept of dramaturgical role performance in his analysis of how people behave. Goffman (1961, 1969) argues that people stage-manage the impression that they want others to receive of them through their personal front, or manner, which can be influenced by the situation as well as affect how situations are defined. He looks at how people try to control situations and considers the impact of place on behaviour.

In relation to issues of privacy, Goffman's notion of regions of performance – *front region* and *back region* – is especially helpful. The *back region* is a place where people drop their performance for a period. Goffman talks of the ways in which different impressions are given in different spaces: the value often attached to the living-room in a domestic home, for instance, or activities 'behind the counter' at a reception desk. He makes the point that an individual may change the nature of a space simply by acting differently, giving the example of an executive's private office. This can be at the same time a front region area, where status is expressed by the quality of office furnishings, and a back region where the executive can relax, take her or his jacket off and act in a chummy way with fellow executives (Goffman 1969).

As well as physical demarcation, people use more subtle changes of behaviour to indicate how space is to be used. A manager of a learning disability service gives an example of an informal but private activity when a service-user asks to 'have a word alone' (Open University 2003a). The need for a private space might be anywhere that they will not be overheard. However, if the service-user starts to make a complaint, the meeting may change from an informal to a formal meeting. The manager might start to make notes and advise the person of the complaints procedure. The working context is not always well designed for requirements of privacy. In the television series about an emergency ward, 'ER', it is not unusual for staff in the operating theatre or in an emergency cubicle to say 'Can I speak to you in private?' which, as they draw apart from others, affords only notional privacy. These examples provide instances of turning a front region into a back region through redefining a particular space as private.

Whose territory?

Questions of territory and privacy are important in relation to the provision of social care because of power differentials. Perceptions over who 'owns' territory may come to dominate the value base within any care setting. Territory may be considered to be domestic or non-domestic and it is common to move between these two functions. This affects how people perceive issues of control, formality and autonomy. For instance, when a social worker arrives for a planned interview at a service-user's house she is entering someone else's territory. What are the opportunities or conventions regarding whether the television is on or off, whether hospitality is proffered or accepted; what smells or sights have an impact on what takes place? Whose boundaries are being crossed in such encounters?

The manager's space

Managers, like others, may have needs for territory and privacy. One manager we spoke to, in the course of our empirical investigations, worked in a team room with other project workers . She found this help-ful for knowing what was going on, being accessible to team members and creating a sense of team cohesion. However, she also found some disadvantages: she could easily be deflected from getting on with her own work, and was increasingly taking work home; she could get enmeshed in someone else's crisis with their caseload and she needed privacy for some telephone calls and discussion.

Two basic functions of privacy, according to Veitch and Arkkelin (1995, p.279), are the achievement of a self-identity and the manage-ment of interactions between the self and the social environment (for purposes of this discussion we can consider the working environment). The first function allows people to drop their social mask and frees them from concerns over how they look to others. A manager may not feel confident in making a taxing telephone call in front of team members, quite apart from confidentiality requirements. Privacy additionally gives busy managers the time to reflect on experiences and to formulate strategies.

On the other hand, the manager who maintains an office set apart from staff offices and client areas and seldom walks around creates an aura of distance from the work and working conditions. This may create resentment on the part of staff, expressed as, 'If only he or she knew what our conditions are like.' Peters popularized the term 'managing by walk-ing around' in his 1982 book written with Waterman (Peters and Waterman 1982). Managers are advised to get out of their offices and to go where employees are working in order to stay connected to the work environment.

The management of interactions also helps with self-identity. Pri-vacy is complex and too much privacy may be as unpleasant as too little. It is important that managers have some control and regulation over which people they are available to and when. This also requires negotia-tion with other people. As an alternative to physical boundaries through separate offices, people can use behaviour to regulate contact. In other words, the way you behave may lead other people to understand that you want to be on your own – what has been called an 'opening' or 'closing' of the self (Altman 1975; Veitch and Arkkelin 1995). In this way, managers can be selective about who has access to them, which can have a range of effects.

For instance, when a manager sits alone in the garden for ten minutes, or joins a group of residents for coffee, or writes a report at the dining-room table, she conveys different messages about her need for privacy. By considering the extent to which some managerial roles require inter-actions with individuals or groups, it is possible to see how privacy can be more or less important, and how both the design of the building and the philosophical underpinning of the staff group can affect its use.

An enabling environment for all

In each nation of the UK, the development of national minimum stan-dards for all residential services contributes to the quality of the environment. In England standards for adult care are regulated by the Department of Health (see Department of Health 2003a, 2003c)). The importance of a single bed-sitting-room for the living environment of older people in care homes has been commented on by residents since the days of overcrowded workhouses (Willcocks *et al.* 1987).

More recently, ideas about the value of private space have moved on to a recognition of the importance of spatial control that offers the opportunity for people to be themselves at different times of the day, in different moods, alone or with others, surrounded by objects that reflect something about them. In the US, too, more facilities are encouraging residents to bring personal items and furnishings, such as a favourite chair, within the limits of often small and shared rooms. However, in England, the expense of ensuring minimum room size and the availabil-ity of a choice of single rooms has proved controversial. Requirements for homes that existed before 2002 have been weakened in response to lobbying from care home owners (Department of Health 2003a).

Design is an important factor in improving people's wellbeing. Sur-prisingly, for much of the twentieth century, care service workers and those who used services were rarely asked for their views on the design of their environments (Sommer 1969; Willcocks *et al.* 1987). Design and advances in technology can be enabling, and the rights of people with disabilities to accessibility to and within buildings are being recognized through legislation (see, for example, Disability Rights Commission 2002).

The Americans with Disabilities Act of 1990 requires all new buildings providing care to be accessible by persons with disabilities. Existing structures must make reasonable modifications. The standards for child care centres, for example, state that 'existing privately-run child care centres must remove those architectural barriers that limit the participation of children with disabilities (or parents, guardians or prospective customers with disabilities) if removing the barriers is *readily achievable*' (US Department of Justice 1997). Examples given include changing door hinges to widen doors, rearranging furniture, and installing grab bars. Standards for government run centres are more stringent: 'centers run by government agencies must insure that their programs are accessible unless making changes imposes an undue burden' (US Department of Justice 1997).

Some of the best ideas regarding design and use of space can work for everybody. Detailed advice on the physical settings that work best for people with dementia is a useful example. For instance, arranging chairs around coffee tables to create a more natural feel encourages interaction; using signs and pictures on doors means they can be easily identified; different decoration schemes for corridors facilitate orientation; dead ends or areas that present confusing choices can be avoided; varying the levels and types of lighting can reflect changes in the season and time of day and furnishing spaces such as landings, alcoves and entrance halls may give people additional choice of sitting places which aid stimulation (see Clarke, Hollands and Smith 1996, pp.17–18).

Care taken to enhance the physical environment can be crucial to carrying out the organization's mission. For example, a social worker who became the warden of a women's prison in the US implemented the new mission statement 'changing society one life at a time' by creating a number of service and environmental changes in the prison that showed keen awareness of the impact of environment on rehabilitation.

> The new organization principles were expressed in redesigned cells with attractive furniture; in on-grounds garden apartments where women could spend weekend visits with their children; in visiting areas that were made comfortable and attractive and

afforded some privacy for family visits; and in the refurnished dining room with small, comfortable seating arrangements and tables decorated with linens and flowers. (Healy *et al.* 1995, p.144)

A consideration of design can help workers in social care organizations return to the 'primary task': that is, the reason for the organization or project's existence:

What is this building for? Which needs will be met by this room or that piece of furniture? What are we trying to say to people by the way we arrange the front door and entrance? (Burton 1998, p.151)

Sometimes, the message sent at the front door and waiting areas is a negative one. Citing a 1994 *Washington Post* article by R.K. Lewis, Gibelman noted that many public welfare offices in the US are 'downright dreadful in appearance' (2003, p.110). Waiting rooms in public welfare offices often have hard seats arranged in rows where clients wait to be called (sometimes by number) by a clerk behind a window. No magazines for waiting clients or toys for their children are provided, unlike common practice in offices of private agencies or physicians. One welfare director lamented that he would love to set up a coffee pot for those waiting, but that this would be frowned upon by higher level managers. This seems to corroborate Gibelman's assertion that the physical environment of public social services offices in the US may well reflect the attitudes of citizens toward welfare workers and their clients (2003). Similar observations could be made about the reception areas of some social services departments in the UK.

In relation to residential settings, the kitchen is a focal point for its symbolic emotional value as the heart of many care homes, whether for adults or children (Whitaker, Archer and Hicks 1998), providing more than mere physical nourishment (Burton 1998). Yet, in many residential homes, kitchens are off-limits for older people (mostly women) perhaps for hygiene or safety reasons. What does this choice of space tell us about care, familiarity, risk taking and underlying gender issues? Many managers will be aware of the role that the design of their building plays in facilitating the kind of service they are trying to give. The challenge for the manager is in balancing different requirements, some of which may conflict (those of health and safety with those of naturalness, for instance) alongside the cultural needs of different individuals, staff and residents for an environment that best suits them.

Power and control

Lewis and Gunaratnam's research on hospice care discusses concern from nurses about the mourning rituals pursued by people from West Africa. These could be construed by other dying patients and their visiting friends and relatives as 'noise' that was offensive to them and invaded their own sense of privacy or quiet intimacy. There can be cultural differences in the experience of privacy. Whose need to pursue their preferred cultural behaviour should predominate when needs compete in such ways? Is there a role for staff in 'managing' these tensions?

Issues of power and control emerge in several forms here. Where different ethnic groups are involved, there may be a tendency to assume that the behaviour of those in the dominant white culture is the 'norm' and that anything different is 'other' and not to be encouraged. It is a short step from such an assumption to a racist response that fails to give appropriate care to people from ethnic minority groups. There is a need to develop culturally sensitive care practices (Lee 2004).

The manager's role in relation to diversity is explored further in Chapter 6 of this book. Here, we give examples of how important the management of diversity can become. Addley (2001) provides a disturbing example of what can happen when racial tensions are not effectively managed, describing the threat from several white residents of a care home in a multiracial area that they would 'walk out' if a 76-year-old African-Caribbean moved in. In relation to this incident, the manager expressed shock at the attitude of these residents, but the action needed should have been taken much earlier. In order to create a home that is multicultural, the underpinning values need to be made clear to people before they move in through contracts or agreements that outline equal opportunity expectations. This point was discussed in relation to individual cases and general policies by Lynne Healy and Barbara Pine in Chapter 4. Values can also be conveyed through the staff employed, their attitude, the holidays celebrated and the food served or, more commonly in the US, dual language greetings on agency answering machines.

Power relations between staff and residents are omnipresent. Physical dependency can itself imply an imbalance of power, and managers need to be alert to opportunities through staff training to consider how practice can enable residents rather than encourage dependency. The values that inform caring activities can also undermine the power of residents. Core objectives of care provision, such as control, containment or protection, may conflict with the residents' rights to territory, personal space and privacy. Burton (1998, p.48) proposes that clarifying the primary task is the first act of management at every level. This may not be straightforward – flushing out and debating competing views is part of the process, but some of the more covert objectives and values that create and reinforce dependency may not be accessed or voiced easily.

There are many practical decisions in residential care that managers need to make with their staff team on a case-by-case basis. For example, a severely disabled 17-year-old, who had no speech, could not be persuaded to sleep in the bed in her room when she came into respite care for periods (Open University 2003b). This caused much anxiety and disagreement among care staff on how the situation should be handled. The manager of the home encouraged staff to express their views at a meeting and to try to work out a cohesive response that everyone could support. They reached agreement that making the resident comfortable and helping her sleep was more important than whether she used her room or slept in a bed. A member of staff was allocated the role of 'key worker', charged with the task of observing the young woman. Her observation suggested that it was important to the resident to see what was going on, which she could not do from her room and in a bed. Over time, she was able to encourage her to use a mattress, at first in the corridor where she liked to sleep, and later just inside her room. Such practical dilemmas invariably bring with them issues of values. It is the manager's job to help the staff team to develop an approach that addresses competing perspectives on what is right.

There can be a tendency in residential care to push complexity away and to avoid recognizing the tensions (Clough 1998). Clough calls for management to create the forum in which people can recognize the complexity of the task, define the purpose and be free to air their concerns. The balance of power and issues of partnership are central to developing independent living in a range of settings. In care homes, it is the manager's job to try to ensure that residents' privacy and independence are respected. The foundation for this will be through a common understanding by care staff of the standards they work to.

Managing at a distance

So far in this chapter we have been looking at the managerial role, boundaries and the environment when people work closely together, often in an interdependent way. Although there are many situations where this is the case, frequently line managers do not work on the site where the care takes place. Instead, they may visit it. Home care managers, for instance, will probably visit a person requiring home care in order to assess the situation but they may not need to enter the service-user's home again. Managers of fieldwork teams may visit service-users only when a problem has arisen.

What are the challenges of managing or being managed when there is a spatial distance in the location of managers and managed? We look at some issues for managing at a distance through an example concerning the external management of children's homes.

Whipp and his colleagues (1998) studied 12 local authorities in England and Wales that were all large 'users' of residential group home care for children in out-of-home care. Some were also large providers themselves, with over 40 homes owned by the local authority, while others relied on placements in the voluntary and independent sectors. The researchers found a wide variation of management practices both within and between authorities. This was particularly true of the relationship between line management and the control of homes, with differences between managerial approaches.

The numbers of children's homes that a line manager had responsibility for varied greatly, affecting the amount of time available for supervision. Some had a 'hands-on' approach maintaining frequent contact. A more 'hands-off' style could be seen positively, as offering the officer in charge more autonomy, or negatively, because the home was more isolated from the rest of the organization. Line managers who had previous experience in residential care had greater credibility with the home staff. In about half the homes there was recognition that the home was becoming increasingly isolated and attempts were made to draw the officers in charge into wider decision-making processes through joint training sessions, placement meetings, project groups and strategic workshops. In some authorities, the responsibility for budgets had been delegated to the officer in charge, which gave more flexibility for spending decisions to be linked to the needs of the resident group (Whipp *et al.* 1998). (Issues relating to financing are further explored in Chapter 11.)

Issues for managing at a distance

This sketch of different management systems and styles highlights many tensions for managers and those they manage, especially those who are off-site, and we consider them in more detail. Key issues for managers are:

- practice experience
- regular contact
- recognition of the need for autonomy
- recognizing isolation
- engagement in decision-making
- devolution of budgets.

Practice experience

Managers have more credibility if they have experience of the kind of work that the people they are managing are doing. Where management of a residential home is concerned this is important. The unit is a whole system in itself and the off-site manager requires understanding of the culture of the home. What about home care workers? Do their managers need direct experience of home care work? Home care workers often face stressful and difficult situations of their own: for instance, the death of a client, high levels of dependency which require commitment and reliability, handling finances and exposure to accusations of theft (Bradley and Sutherland 1995).

Managers may have to manage people doing jobs for which as managers they lack experience of or expertise in the skills involved. This can be a source of anxiety: how can they develop as managers to provide good support and management to these people? Learning to understand the job from the workers' point of view is important, perhaps by spending time with them while they are doing the job. Consultancy from outside experts or mentors may be another resource for a person whose manager is not experienced in their field, as well as 'learning from each other' through peer support.

Regular contact

Keeping closely in touch can guard against the dangers of isolation. Burton (1998) gives an example of a service manager who spends much time in the homes he is responsible for, and acts as a conduit with senior management, explaining the needs of the residential establishments. A line manager who is 'hands-on' and keeps up regular contact and involvement in different care homes' concerns will need to be sensitive to issues of territory and boundaries. The front-line manager also has a role in sensitizing his or her line manager to the day-to-day intensity of their work so that the off-site manager does not get too detached. This approach can also be applied in day care or fieldwork settings: line managers can develop their sensitivity to the culture of the unit or their sense of the service-users and their needs. In order to do this they need some direct contact with service-users and familiarity with the setting. A midwife recalled her awareness as a trainee that some of her fellow students did not visit mothers for the required period following a birth (Open University 2003a). In her experience, she seldom saw her supervisor while on her rounds, giving her the impression that there were no real checks in the system. For those who manage at a distance, the term 'managing by travelling' might be an appropriate alternative to Peters' idea of managing by walking around (Peters and Waterman 1982).

Recognition of the need for autonomy

This might seem the obverse of a 'hands-on' approach, but people who work at a distance from their managers need clarity about what their defined roles and tasks are and what authority they have. Without a degree of autonomy to respond to situations as they arise, they can feel undermined and ineffective.

Recognizing isolation

Alongside autonomy there can be isolation in work done at a distance from managers. A study of stress experienced by home care workers considers the isolation of their work and the possibilities for staff support networks. The authors point out that this would require a clear commitment by the organization to make time available for it since work overload is also a frequently cited source of stress (Bradley and Sutherland 1995, p.329). Support through telephone contact and the use of mobile phones are other ways to help combat isolation.

Engagement in joint decision-making

This is a way of integrating front-line managers into the wider purposes of the organization, and of making sure that considerations about their work are taken into account when planning policy and strategy. Whipp *et al.* (1998) found in their study that activities that might be called 'training' are the vehicle for inclusion of the views of different stakeholders, with perhaps some involvement in strategic discussions. Such inclusion is not without problems and there are some tensions in drawing unit managers into joint decision-making. How much time do managers have for organizational meetings? Does activity of this kind draw them away from their detailed involvement in their unit's practice and give them new organizational duties? From the perspective of senior staff, the front-line manager can become too focused on practice, yet the staff within a unit may want their manager to be more involved in day-to-day practice. The advantages of such participatory management were discussed by Barbara Pine and Lynne Healy in Chapter 2.

Devolution of budgets

Bright quotes an example of a care home manager who cut back on use of incontinent pads, to the detriment of the residents who needed them, as a result of pressure from her line manager to make economies (1999, p.194). Devolution of budgets can be a mixed blessing bringing additional administrative work. However, many budget decisions are better made at the point where their impact will be felt, providing there really is some flexibility about how money will be used.

In this section we have discussed some of the tensions that distance involves for managers and those they manage. Managers who have responsibility for care services at some distance from their own workplace will need to strike a delicate balance. Too much intervention can be undermining; too little can seem like indifference. Thus, the location of managers in relation to their staff, their distance and frequency of contact, become additional elements of 'place' and 'space'.

Conclusion

We have explored the manager's role in relation to the different and complex settings in which social work and social care take place. Managers have some responsibility to facilitate the use of space, territory and privacy by different people, with different aims and preferences, interacting in any one social care environment. Although not all social care environments serve as many different purposes as residential care homes, they are all likely to be multifaceted. Environments can be affected by changes in the use of a room or a building throughout the day. We suggest that managers need to develop awareness of the different functions and meanings held by the care environment. In particular, it will be useful if they analyse the public/private and formal/informal nature of what takes place, and the implications for this of the degree of privacy and territorial ownership needed by the people using it.

Notions of territory carry the potential for competition and dispute. We have considered issues of power and control over how space is used. Values underpin the provision of care, yet these may not be openly acknowledged. The manager has a role in drawing out values more explicitly and debating those that are contested with staff and with service-users. In this way some understanding and agreement can be reached as to how people's needs for privacy, self-expression and choice can best be met. Effectively this involves the development of 'ground rules'. Such rules should include some consideration of the management and facilitation of visitors and other outsiders who need to use the care space for different purposes.

A good starting point for considering the use of design is to think about the main purpose of a building, and the environment and atmosphere that need to be created. Making places accessible for people with disabilities and considering the meaning of different kinds of building for the people using it have major implications, but not all design issues carry heavy costs. Additionally, convening a workplace environment committee, comprised of staff and users, may be helpful in generating ideas for low cost improvements.

When the territory where care is taking place is not shared by the manager, and is managed at a distance, managers need to strike a balance with those they manage that takes into account the need for autonomy, reduces feelings of isolation and fears of insufficient accountability, and engages those working at a distance to create a vision of aims and ethos that the larger organization can support without distracting them from their primary task of providing good care.

Acknowledgement

This chapter draws on material in Peace, S. and Reynolds, J. 'Managing environments', in J. Henderson and D. Atkinson (2003) *Managing Care in Context*, London: Routledge and The Open University. The authors are grateful to the publishers for being able to use this work.

Chapter 9

Active Service-User Involvement in Human Services: Lessons from Practice

Janet Seden and Trish Ross

Introduction

What's the use of asking us if you don't take any notice?

This question, posed by a service-user, invited to take a role in an advisory group committee, encapsulates the dilemmas of service-user/patient consultation, involvement, participation and control of services. Beneath the philosophies and aspirations of handing over power and recognizing people as experts about their own lives who can competently comment on services, lurk the dangers of tokenism. This may prevent them from being involved in both the design and management of services. Complex dilemmas exist when professionals try to create real partnership between people who are not equal because of social and role differences (Thoburn, Lewis and Shemmings 1995). This chapter starts by outlining the current policy mandates and drives for service-user led and controlled services. Then we examine some of the contradictions, dilemmas and challenges this presents, not least from the people who are said to be 'empowered' by such approaches to health and social care provision.

The ideological basis for health and social care services in the UK was changed by significant policy shifts in the late 1990s and early 2000s. As John Harris outlined in Chapter 1, there has been a move from the paternalism that was inherent in the way welfare services were set up after World War Two and conceptualized in the 1950s–1980s. The three governments under the premiership of Margaret Thatcher between 1979 and 1997 introduced significant changes to the way services were provided, changing public sector provision to a 'mixed economy of welfare'. This was based on arrangements that set up internal markets within welfare services for 'purchasing' and 'providing' services, a practice referred to as contracting in the US.

Such changes brought with them parallel changes in the language and thinking about welfare (Page and Silburn 1998; Waine and Henderson 2003). When the first New Labour government under Tony Blair's premiership took office in 1997, the changes of the Thatcher years were already established in practice. The new government issued a range of papers aimed at modernizing health and social services across the UK (see, for example, Department of Health 1998a, 2000a; Scottish Office 1999) to regulate the market and move from notions of consumerism to an emphasis on social inclusion, participation, citizenship and partnerships between agencies, workers and users of services.

There has been a parallel move in the US to involve service-users in planning, evaluating, and delivering the services they use. A good example is Project Head Start, an early childhood program begun in the 1960s as part of America's 'War on Poverty'. Head Start aimed at helping pre-school children from disadvantaged families get a 'head start' on elementary school through a range of health, nutrition and educational program components. Early on, the value of parent involvement was recognized and fostered. Today, Head Start parents are involved in the classroom and in policy making in local centres (Maluccio, Pine and Tracy 2002).

Service-users 'having a say' in the provision of services

There is now an awareness, both in the UK and the US, that most people at some time in their lives will need some kind of service, and will expect, when that time comes, to have a 'voice' about what services they receive and how they receive them. Alongside this notion of participation in service delivery runs the concept that service-users are actors in their own lives, whether or not social disadvantage or exclusion leads them to be people needing support to achieve their full potential. Services are viewed as a growing force for combating disadvantage and promoting citizenship and social inclusion (Department of Social Security 1998; Scottish Office 1999; Scottish Executive 2001). People are seen as citizens who have rights and entitlements. In Scotland, for example, a recent policy directive for children (Scottish Executive 2005) includes a vision from the Scottish Cabinet that all Scotland's children should be: 'safe, healthy, active, nurtured, achieving, respected and responsible and included' (p.3). The devolved Scottish Parliament believes it has an obligation to provide a range of universal and targeted services to ensure these aims are achieved for every child. As Chapter 12 outlines, similar policy initiatives have been developed in England. In the US, too, there are several national advocacy organizations such as the Children's Defense Fund, the Child Welfare League of America and the National Association of Social Workers that have similarly sought and gained, through public policy, increased rights for children.

Listening to what people say about services has become a key feature of public policy (Connelly and Seden 2003). Service-user views are seen by government as a powerful component of shaping and evaluating what services should be in place (Scottish Executive 1999; Department of Health 2000b). *A Quality Strategy for Social Care* asserts: 'We must focus on what people want from services. There is now a strong body of evidence pointing to the qualities people value in social services' (Department of Health 2000b, p.6).

There are many examples in health and social care of consultation and research into user views of services (see Henderson and Atkinson 2003). Key words which characterize the relationship of health and social care with its service-users and patients are: information, consultation, involvement, partnership, participation, ownership and control. In the National Health Service (NHS) patient involvement in clinical governance has become a critical issue (Sang and O'Neill 2001).

The idea of the service-user or patient as expert has taken hold, but it is not unproblematic. Research and literature have raised the dilemmas of practice and the complexity of making such policies work on the ground (Beresford and Croft 2003; Read 2003) Further, service-users should not just be consulted about what they want and asked to evaluate what has happened, but can more actively manage the processes and means of delivering services. And, as Beresford and Croft point out, involving service-users in service management means much more than seeing user involvement as an 'add on' to the conventional, management mix. It has implications for the whole ethos and philosophy of management, 'a real shift to "user-led" services demands a different, much more participatory approach to management' (2003, p.21). In Chapter 2, Barbara Pine and Lynne Healy discussed the participatory approach in detail and provided a case example of an agency using a team that included parents.

Taking an active approach to service-user involvement in management

As Sang and O'Neill (2001) suggest, when discussing patient involvement in clinical governance in the NHS, effective implementation means taking an active, mapping, communicating and networking approach to management activity. If the NHS is to be patient-centred or social services is to really be managed by service-users in partnership with fund holders and workers, the approaches that can deliver this will need to be learned and implementation worked out carefully. In adult services, the lead has come from services created and controlled by service-users, who have come to be known as 'survivors' of services (Read 2003) and also from personal assistance schemes where individuals directly pay care workers. Additionally such 'survivors', particularly in mental health services, have taken up paid employment in the social care field. This makes them pivotal in seeing the issues, but again there are dilemmas, as Beresford and Croft comment:

> involving service users in service management needs to be approached in a holistic and strategic way. This must be recognised if broad based and systemic involvement is to be achieved. Two components seem to be essential if people are to be able to get involved effectively and if all groups are to have equal opportunities for involvement. These prerequisites are *access* and *support*. Both are needed. (2003, p.27)

A continuum of involvement

Thus ideas about the role of service-users and patients in care services move on a continuum (Association of Metropolitan Authorities 1991) which starts from ideas about better information giving, moves through consultation and participation to user-control of service provision. It is only when users control services or manage elements of service provision that they can be said to be managing the service. For example, former users of mental health services who are working in health and social care services are now seeking to set up a user-controlled national co-ordinating scheme to support their work (James 2002).

While mental health services provide some examples of this happening, for most organizations it can be argued that service-users are taking on management functions and roles within organizations on a participatory model, but that truly user-controlled organizations and services remain rare. Nonetheless, the 'survivors' of adult services have set a lead and generated a discussion that has fed similar developments in child and family services.

It can be argued that unless the building, other resources, personnel management (e.g. staff selection) and a range of other management functions are handed over, service-users are involved but not in control. (This is an issue which is also addressed in relation to the use of space in residential care by Jill Reynolds and Sheila Peace in Chapter 8 of this book.) It is also a feature of many social work services that elements of compulsion are often thinly disguised as partnership. Furthermore, people are 'choosing' to use the service because of 'needs' arising out of social disadvantage, or a level of vulnerability. Such situations add another layer of complexity to the issues of power sharing and to how service-users might really manage services. These hurdles alone are no reason to hesitate and once such imbalances are in the open and shared, the redistribution of some power becomes more likely. In the next chapter, Myron Weiner and Peter Petrella note the important uses of technology to facilitate communication with service-users and involve them directly in the agency's work.

Users of services seldom hold the traditional management roles. Nor do they frequently have real roles in managing and supporting staff, appraisal, budgets, buildings, training objectives or complaints procedures unless they become paid staff, although there are some exceptions in the area of family centre services (Tunstill, Aldgate and Hughes 2006). It can be argued that no one should have to carry these roles unpaid or without the necessary training and support for what are complex and onerous tasks. Once service-users are in these roles, not only may they not be fully supported and protected by the organization for possible difficulties that may arise, but also there can be additional conflicts of interest, which come from their own requirements as users of the service.

For example, the allocation of scarce resources such as crèche places (child care or nursery care places in the US) is difficult enough, but more difficult perhaps when it involves competition between your own, your relatives' and neighbours' children and those from further afield. Is it feasible to expect parents of young children who have at last gained access to some much needed and scarce services to want to try and target new people, thereby increasing competition for the scarce places? Will they want to reach all children, perhaps outside the immediate area, because the social services department has a wider brief and a more strategic view? It takes some confidence and skill to argue against the paid managers and government backed large agencies. On the other hand, service-users cannot be dismissed from employment, cannot be disciplined and may have little to lose. Such an absence of sanctions may cause much anxiety for paid managers and certainly add layers of complexity to their role.

Issues and dilemmas that arise from service-users being involved in management

Many questions arise about the involvement of service-users. Are roles for service-users in managing or on management committees sustainable or do they exemplify power imbalances, such as possessing or not possessing information, giving or withholding access to resources, education and prior work experience? If service-users want services that are not in line with policy directives, how is this managed? Are service-users set up to fail by systems that claim to devolve power but do not? Such dilemmas are far from academic. For example, if service-users are running the service, it still has to be provided to the standards of the organization, but as the service-users are effectively volunteers, the quality of the performance may not be monitored in the usual way, such as through agency supervision and appraisal systems.

Writing about paid managers supervising volunteers, Charlesworth (2003a) points to a range of issues around managing people in the role that, following Willis (1992), she calls an 'exchange relationship' (p.54). Paid managers working with service-users who are giving their time freely are in a similar position. There may be legal anomalies and role tensions and without formal agreements about roles and responsibilities misunderstandings and conflicts may occur. There are complexities and ambiguities in these relationships which need to be considered.

Here, we argue that these dilemmas are as apparent in children's services as they are in adult services. We now explore some of the challenges for practice further through considering examples of service-user involvement in managing activities. This is based on the authors' experiences as children's services managers, working in a range of parent support settings. These include two family centres, both situated on outer city estates in the East Midlands, one run by a social services department and one by a voluntary childcare agency. Family centres blossomed under the Children Act 1989, as a designated family support provision. There are many types of centres, some run by local authorities and some by voluntary agencies. Some have an 'open door' policy and some only take referrals from statutory social work (see Tunstill *et al.* 2006). The authors also draw material from a Sure Start programme, established under the government's initiative for preventive targeted early years projects. The Sure Start programme we were involved with is in a town within a former coalmining area of the north Midlands. All the centres we looked at are situated in socially and economically disadvantaged areas, where residents often experience discrimination because of where they live, varying degrees of social exclusion and difficulties in accessing mainstream services.

Lessons from practice

Within all the settings there has been a commitment from agencies and staff to working within and building on the strengths of the local communities. This means there has been an expectation that parents and carers will participate in the planning, delivery and management of the services. Therefore, the examples on which the chapter draws are real and come from practice experience of working with parents, carers and community activists across the continuum of partnership, involvement and control over a period of 20 years, from the 1980s to the present day. They illustrate some of the contradictions and dilemmas discussed earlier in the chapter about decision-making, accountability, responsibility, consent, power and priorities and, we hope, also highlight some solutions and useful working practices. The views of service-users (with their knowledge and consent) have been included but some situations have been disguised to ensure anonymity where necessary. The discussion also draws from material included in user consultations undertaken for the Open University course, *Managing Care* (Henderson and Atkinson 2003; Henderson and Seden 2003b).

Service-user membership on management boards

Service-user representation on management boards or committees is frequently seen as desirable to ensure that services are credible, effective and relevant and meet the needs of the service-user group. However, as argued, there are important issues to consider in practice, both in the process of establishing the board (or in introducing users to an existing board) and in ensuring effective and genuine participation.

First, there is a need for clarity about the role and responsibilities of board members: Do service-user representatives have the same powers as other board members to make decisions about service delivery, allocation of resources and funding? How far can they be held accountable for decisions made? Are there policy directives or funding requirements that must be adhered to? It is important to address these by agreeing terms of reference generally and/or before undertaking a specific piece of work.

Misunderstandings can lead to resentment and disenchantment, such as that expressed by the service-user at the outset of the chapter. This disillusion with the kind of participation which is experienced as ineffective by service-users is frequently reported. For example a service--user at a consultation reported on being asked to participate in selecting staff in an adult residential service. She said to the researchers, 'They ask us but it's the bosses that make the decisions in the end' (Henderson and

Seden 2003b). Another person in the same consultation expressed frustration at frequently being invited as the 'token Asian service user'. She was becoming frustrated with the lack of outcomes for her time and commitment.

Service-user representation

Recruiting users to an advisory or management committee who reflect the diversity of the user group is often a major difficulty. Kubicek (2003) identified this as an issue in setting up patient forums within Primary Care Trusts (the NHS units that provide primary health services for everyone in local areas in the UK) and states that outreach is essential in recruiting more people from 'hard-to-reach' groups. This has also been an experience within Sure Start in trying to ensure that representation on Boards includes all sections of the local community. It is usually articulate, socially active members of a community who will put themselves forward; more disadvantaged residents may be suspicious or sceptical, may lack confidence or have other priorities or commitments (Beresford and Croft 2003; Connelly and Seden 2003).

Practical considerations

Practical considerations will need to be addressed, such as provision of transport, interpreters and childcare to enable participation, but the more difficult task is to persuade service-users of their own abilities, of the value of their contribution and of the genuine commitment of the programme or agency to the principle. Outreach work in developing networks, building on skills and confidence is vital. Reputation is a key factor: evidence that views of service-users have been listened to and the experiences of others involved will influence more reluctant participants. Resources in terms of both time and effort need to be made available to ensure success. Given that in the context of social care many service-users will be from socially excluded groups or will be experiencing difficulties in their lives, there is little point in espousing the principles of user management unless the resources are made available.

Empowering service-user participation

It is important to ensure that, having established service-users as members of a board, the role is more than tokenistic: that indiviuals feel able to participate fully and that their views and ideas are valued and acted upon. Practical considerations as mentioned above are vital, but issues of power group dynamics, interest groups and personal agendas, motivation and commitment are also significant. These become even more complex when a committee or board has a mix of service-users and service providers, a diversity of skills and experience and often a variety of stereotyped views of other members. There may be some service providers who are cynical about the participation of service-users. They may patronize, exclude or sideline them. Hidden agendas or conflicts between different professional or community groups may lead to misunderstandings.

Training and support

Training and support can be instrumental in creating an ethos where these issues can be addressed. It is widely accepted that service-users may need training to participate effectively in meetings (Connelly and Seden 2003). It may also be necessary for professionals, with vast experience of bureaucratic meetings within their own organizations, to learn to communicate without the use of jargon, to be open to different ideas and to be aware of their own behaviour and use of power.

An example of the impact of training comes from the experience of setting up a Sure Start programme. Two training days with an external trainer were organized prior to the establishment of a Sure Start Board to support a local programme. These days were attended by service-users, representatives from different agencies, managers and a community development worker who was to provide ongoing support to the parents on the Board. The training gave everyone an opportunity to agree ground rules and terms of reference but also to express anxieties and get to know each other. The trainer attended the first two Board meetings to monitor the balance of contributions and concluded that parents were able to participate effectively.

Parents also continued to meet with the community development worker before the Board meetings to discuss the agenda and any concerns. However, two years later, difficulties emerged that demonstrated the need for regular review. New parents had joined existing parents on the Board and agency representatives had changed. Though new parents had undertaken training, no further joint training had taken place. Attendance at meetings by parents had declined: some had family difficulties, others had gone on to training or employment (a possible positive outcome of the experience of being a Board member). Others were dissatisfied with meetings; they sometimes felt patronized, meetings were boring and action often deferred. There was some learning for parents in understanding that issues could be complex and change inevitably slow but there were greater learning needs for the whole Board. The formal nature of the meetings was not always conducive to genuine discussion and partnership. However, the challenge itself led to a less formal atmosphere, more humour and a breakdown of some of the professional barriers. It also led to a review of structures and procedures.

Service-users appointing paid staff

Agencies increasingly involve service-users in the appointment of staff. Two large UK not-for-profit agencies, Barnardo's and, in Scotland, Children 1st, always include young people on their appointment boards. There are many others. Another example, from a Sure Start programme, demonstrates how an effective partnership can be established:

> The Management Board needed to appoint to a management post within the Sure Start programme. An underlying principle of the programme was that parents/carers should be involved in decision-making and the Board discussed how this should be carried out in the recruitment and selection process. Parent representatives on the Board were clear that they had expertise in some areas, whereas others on the Board had professional expertise, and a recruitment process was devised, drawing on the different skills and knowledge of Board members.
>
> Candidates were asked to make a presentation to a group of parents, who assessed their skills in communicating, their ability to relate to members of the local community and in offering

workable solutions to problems. Representatives from education, social services and the voluntary sector and the Programme Manager formally interviewed the candidates to assess their management skills and practice knowledge. The outcome was that responsibilities were clearly defined, all felt valued for their contribution and, more importantly, the successful applicant came to the post with the support and confidence of the service-users.

Organizational issues

Organization theorists have found that organizations tend to become entrenched in their own bureaucratic procedures and that new members are expected to fit in with existing arrangements. We have found that social care meetings can become ends in themselves, with the main aim becoming how to get through the agenda as quickly as possible, rather than to foster open discussion and a problem-solving approach to providing better services. True partnership requires the commitment of all members of the group and a culture of questioning the status quo on a regular basis. There are real constraints of time and resources, and there may be conflicts of interest and need (for example, service-users may find weekend meetings more convenient, but agency representatives may have their own commitments at this time). These issues need to be recognized and worked with in order to achieve optimum participation.

Many examples of user involvement in the management and delivery of children's services have come from the voluntary sector. However, the aim of some to hand over control of a project to service-users has usually been difficult to sustain over time without continuing funding from either charitable sources or grants; fundraising in disadvantaged areas is difficult and time-consuming. Over the last two decades there has been an increasing regulation of children's services to ensure high standards of childcare, safety and probity. While this is obviously positive for children, it has meant many community initiatives have no longer been financially viable, particularly in poor neighbourhoods where parents are unable to afford the true cost of the resource.

Funding bodies will always require a degree of management control; oversight of standards will usually require professional input so that the delivery of services to children and their families will inevitably mean a partnership between funders, professionals and service-users (including both parents/carers and children themselves). Though this can be an exciting and dynamic process with positive outcomes for children, it gives rise to the potential for conflict, notably in the allocation of scarce resources and in planning services, and to many dilemmas around aims and objectives, differences in power, experiences and skills.

Differing viewpoints

Parents usually prefer universal services where there is no stigma attached to attending; there is also the advantage of prevention and the early identification of difficulties. However, when resources are scarce, decisions need to be made about who receives services, and there is an inevitable move towards targeting certain groups or setting eligibility criteria. This can lead to conflict between paid workers and service-users, or between different interest groups in an area. There are some examples of misguided practice where, for example, targeting one group discriminated against another.

In a community centre there was a great deal of anger among some white parents when a group for black children was set up, as they felt their children 'were getting a worse deal'.

A staff team had been set a target to attract more families from a certain 'rough' area where there were children living in families experiencing major social issues. Staff had tried to enlist the help of current parents to advertise the centre but had underestimated the threat newcomers would pose to parents. The response was opposition to any erosion of the status quo, 'Why do we want any more people coming? We're alright as we are and it would get crowded with any more.'

If service-users are responsible for, or are involved in, deciding how resources are allocated, it is important that they are representative of the community or user group, and they may also need training. Parents on the Sure Start Board we observed quickly learned to look at the needs of all families: 'We don't just say what we want; we try to represent all the parents' views.' Service-users often have the advantage of not having years of providing services in a certain way and can come up with more innovative solutions.

Planning services can give rise to dilemmas, as service-users often have very different ideas about what constitutes a good service. The experience of many Sure Start programmes is that parents want local services, delivered by friendly people in an informal setting. They need to be able to get there easily, at a convenient time and to have facilities for young children. Yet many agencies are streamlining resources by providing centralized services within set hours. Social work teams have moved from neighbourhoods to an area-wide service and this has sometimes been judged as effective because it has reduced referrals! Family Centres often cover a wide catchment area rather than being a community resource and referral systems can be a major barrier to accessing a service.

Quality assurance

On a more local level, service-users can often have more influence on the way services are delivered. An exercise in establishing a quality assurance system for a parent and toddler group was undertaken by a voluntary agency. The group was funded and supported by the agency but the parents attending were responsible for activities and fundraising for outings and so on, so it was felt that they should participate in the exercise. Parents were asked, 'What is important in deciding how good the group is?' They identified many indicators in common with staff, such as safety and good quality play, but also, based on their own experiences, highlighted the importance of the atmosphere in welcoming new people, and in making sure disabled children and their families were made to feel comfortable. As a result of this, parents wrote a 'welcome' handbook, and some took on responsibility for befriending new families and undertook training in listening and helping skills. They also demanded that a member of staff was always available at sessions and that regular review meetings were held.

This example demonstrates that where resources are available and aims are common to providers and users, involvement of service-users in the management of the service can be effective in ensuring it meets the needs of families. By contrast, where the provision of services involves bureaucratic organizations with specified targets and limited resources, it is perhaps more appropriate and honest to work towards user 'consultation' rather than 'management'. Issues around professional demarcation of roles, perceived threats to jobs if services are provided in a different way, the need to reduce stress for workers and safety considerations are all real concerns to workers. Such issues may be of no significance to service-users living in poverty or who are trying to protect their children from engaging in criminal activities. Such differences of perspective can create misunderstanding and conflict.

The tensions of involvement for service-users and managers

While it is seen by professionals and academics as fundamental that services should meet the needs of the service-user if they are to be effective, other considerations may take priority in planning. There is often little time to make service-users aware of all the factors and decisions may be made pragmatically by paid workers under pressure to meet deadlines, with the result that service-users do not feel consulted. It can sometimes seem that the main aim of professional workers is to fill in the forms and to ensure procedures are carried out. A young mother, referred to social services for the third time by a voluntary worker, who was concerned about her care of the children, put this acutely. She reported back after a visit from a social worker, 'They're going to do an assessment. I've had so many assessments – when are they going to *help* me?'

Child protection issues may also raise dilemmas where service-users are involved in management. Parents are usually very aware of the need for confidentiality and if they are part of a management committee will usually be bound by an agreement. However, if an investigation is taking place into alleged abuse in a family, other service-users may be concerned for the safety of their own children. Judgements and gossip may be widespread and the situation may become far more complex than the investigation into one family. In allocating resources (for example, in deciding a child has a priority need to attend a club where there is a waiting list) a family in need may be seen as receiving preferential treatment. Service-users involved in decision-making can face questioning or even abuse because of their part in it. It could be argued that it is morally unacceptable to expect service-users to handle such situations, unless a great deal of support is available.

While it is important to ensure more disadvantaged groups of service-users are represented on boards or advisory groups or in other decision-making processes, consideration needs to be given to the level of participation and responsibility. The needs of the individual and of his or her family are paramount. To set someone up for failure because she or he cannot meet the demands and constraints of a committee can have serious consequences. Power imbalances also need to be recognized by workers: a mother who has been helped to gain some control in her life and to increase her self-confidence, for example, may need further support and training to be ready to be part of an advisory or planning group. Gratitude for the help received, or fear of not being offered further support, may lead her to feel unable to refuse if invited to participate. If she subsequently feels unable to sustain her involvement, and this is not sensitively resolved, she may feel a sense of failure and her previous progress may be set back.

There are also areas of management that demand professional skills and experience, and it is vital to recognize the possible limitations of non-professional partnerships. Small voluntary organizations are often run by a management committee, comprising service-users, community representatives and interested others. There may not be anyone on the committee who can provide the supervision and professional support that the co-ordinator or manager needs to implement the changes the committee wants. Where there is no professional line management, it may be necessary to buy in external support.

Another dimension in children's services is that children and older young people are themselves users of services and it is essential to consider how they can participate in decisions and shaping services, according to their age, ability and need. Work on consulting children and ensuring they are actors in their own lives is increasingly happening in agencies and children's homes. Similar care needs to be taken to make sure that listening to children, ascertaining their wishes and making sure they participate in decision-making moves to real empowerment (Department of Health 2001a; Aldgate and McIntosh 2006).

Conclusion

In this chapter, we have explored the policy drive to make service-users more active in how services are managed. We have raised some questions, dilemmas and challenges, and illustrated them through experiences from various family support settings where attempts were made to make information, consultation and participation and user-control of service provision a reality. From this we conclude that if service-users are to be active in managing services:

- A consultative, participative, model of management, which is 'bottom-up' not just 'top-down', is essential, both within the particular setting and within other organizations to which it relates.

- Time is needed to consider roles and responsibilities carefully and to discuss and explore them.

- Support and training will be needed.

- Dilemmas and challenges are inevitable and need care, commitment and flexibility.

- The desirability of service-users being active in management is clear, but there are pitfalls caused by power imbalances that cannot be ignored or underestimated – rather they are to be acknowledged and 'worked with'.

- The danger of rhetoric without reality and tokenism is ever present and has to be constantly under review.

- Working models for service-user activity need to be robust, but subject to constant revision, there is no neat pro-forma approach.

- Communication that is open, honest and at levels where both parents and paid staff can make sense of it is the bedrock of practice. Working out a mutual sense of meaning and purpose, where understandings are frequently checked out, is needed to make partnership work.

Acknowledgement

The authors would like to thank the following for supporting the work drawn upon in this chapter: Andrea Sharp; Richard Lea; Pauline Jones; Sure Start, Ravensdale, particularly members of the Management Board; National Children's Home; Nottinghamshire Social Services; The Open University.

Chapter 10

The Impact of New Technology: Implications for Social Work and Social Care Managers

Myron E. Weiner and Peter Petrella

Introduction

Every aspect of the organization, management, and delivery of social services is experiencing the impact of modern technologies. Not only are the roles of social service professionals and employees being challenged, opportunities for clients and consumers of services to be more active participants in social service systems have increased significantly. Computers of all sizes, networked or stand-alone; telephones and telecommunication systems with multiple capabilities; cell phones with voice, text, photo, and internet capabilities; faxes; the internet; broadcast or cable TV; imbedded microprocessors; electronic surveillance and security devices; global positioning and geographic information systems; and other emerging electronic technologies are significantly changing the ways in which we organize and deliver social services. New technology offers possibilities for spanning traditional and often rigid boundaries of organizations, systems, functions, and disciplines with the potential for more productive and individual need-focused services for our clients, consumers, and communities. The challenge for everyone involved in social services is to more thoroughly understand these technologies and the opportunities they provide for increased productivity and effectiveness (Glastonbury, Lamendola and Toole 1989; Ousley *et al.* 2003) and to follow some fundamental guidelines that will permit greater exploitation of the potentialities of these technologies for improvement of the social services. A burgeoning literature on the topic during the past twenty years both attests to the growth of, and provides guidance for, the social work/social care manager seeking to capitalize on these new technologies. See for example Murphy and Pardeck (1988); Cnaan and Parsloe (1989); Downing *et al.* (1991); Geis and Viswanathan (1986); Karger and Levine (2000); and Weiner (1990).

One can view the pervasive nature of technology, particularly the new electronic environment we live in, as another wave of human inventions and tools shaping our living patterns or as the latest phase of the industrial revolution. Either way, the technologies that are having a profound impact on the way we live and work have their roots in the work of theoreticians and inventors in the UK over the past two centuries.

It is generally recognized that the world's first computer was Charles Babbage's Analytical Machine that was "programmed" by Lady Ada Lovelace during the nineteenth century. Her role as the world's first computer programmer was acknowledged by those who developed the world's first database software, which they named "ADA." The discovery of the "valve" (i.e. the vacuum tube), in 1904, by J. Ambrose Fleming became the cornerstone for modern day electronic devices from radios to computers. While Fleming gave us the critical device permitting construction of the first electronic computers, it was Alan Turing whose theoretical work on the "paper machine" provided the model that remains as the dominant foundation for the world's computers. While Turing is not a name most remember in connection with electronic technologies, more are aware of Dennis Gabor's technological breakthroughs in holography, or the writings of Charles Handy on the ultimate impact of the electronic technologies: virtual organizations. (Marcus and Marcus 1943; McCarthy 1966; Handy 1995).

Thus, these early contributions have led to the current reality: the electron has become the foundation of modern living and complex societies. Electronic devices are replacing electrical-mechanical devices as the driving force for societal processes and the electron media is replacing paper as the source for institutional and societal memory. Increasingly, we live, play, and work in an electronic environment. Although some have expressed concerns about the role of media in the surveillance of workers and clients (Lyon 2001) and, together with managerialism, in eroding professional autonomy (Harris 1998), it can also be argued that our "electronic world" now provides a range of opportunities and potentialities for enhancing the quality of life for people, both individually and collectively (Finn and Holden 2000; Schoech 1990, 1991; and Nurius and Hudson 1993). Thus, this chapter will provide information to allow social care managers to more fully understand electronic technologies for improving administration of our social service agencies, organizations, and systems.

Contrary to popular understanding of the history of the utilization of the electronic technologies in society, some of the initial and pioneering applications of the information technologies (IT) have been in the human services. In the US, aside from the defense department, the largest users of this new technology were federal, state, county, and municipal government agencies devoted to social work services and record keeping, especially provision of social security, state benefits, and Medicaid (medical benefits for the poor). While there are many social work professionals and lay people who held negative perceptions of technology use in social work, at the practical level social workers have always used any new technology—motor vehicles, telephones, typewriters—in order to deal with more clients more effectively while handling the mountains of paperwork required professionally and politically (Bates 2003). In modern times, social workers have not only turned to computers, but to the wide range of electronic technologies. Web-based services are now commonplace. Use of cell phones for communications and security is a standard artifact of the social work workplace environment. The issues involved in utilization of the electronic technologies by social work agencies are many, including:

- ensuring that application of technology is compatible with and shaped by social work values

- maintaining the focus on ways technology can improve the effectiveness of service delivery for clients

- recognizing that data generated from technology-based systems increase the knowledge base upon which professionals can clarify and strengthen the impact of services for clients and community.

At the same time, there are impediments to greater use of the technology by social work agencies. Many social work agencies are small and their market so diffuse that they do not have the critical mass to attract investments necessary for effective technology transfer. In addition, the dominant mental model for a social work agency is one that creates a culture highly devoted to strong interpersonal relationships among all stakeholders. Some consider technology as either foreign in such a culture or a threat. These impediments are challenges for social work agencies as they recognize that in today's world, technology—properly designed and used—is a requisite for the productive and effective delivery of social work services and resources.

Fully utilizing the electronic technologies for the wide range of social service purposes fully consistent with the values and culture of the profession requires:

- mastering current technology and staying attuned to changes, opportunities and risks

- acquiring and maintaining knowledge and skills to use modern technology and

- using the potentialities of technology to strengthen all aspects of social services.

In the section that follows we will explore the potential of electronic technologies for social service organizations.

The potential of electronic technologies

Forms of electronic media

Utilizing the full potentialities of the modern technologies for social services organizations begins with an understanding of the different forms of electronic media and how these technologies can be applied. A brief discussion of four forms of electronic media follows: digital, image, audio, and text. Digital data are data stored in a standard encoded form to be processed for specific purposes; a good example is the data extracted from a Section 8 housing certificate (a subsidized housing program in the US) and stored in a computer database. Whole image or video image data are static or dynamic electronic images of a person, place or thing; a "copy" of a Section 8 housing certificate or a videotape of a group dynamics workshop session are good examples of the whole/video image media form. Audio is data stored in a form that can be heard on cassettes, compact discs (CDs), or DVD disks. Telephone stored in messages voicemail or client sessions stored on voice or video cassettes are good examples of the audio media form. Finally, text data refers to electronic storage of a whole page of text such that it can be read in geographically dispersed locations: a medical specialist's review of a client's data for reviewing or confirming diagnoses is a good example.

Initially, each of the above four forms of electronic-based technologies evolved separately. Now, however, all electronic forms are being integrated resulting in a wide range of different combinations of the four electronic forms. An example is a new wave of consumer devices such as cellular telephones that connect wirelessly to the internet for email, for storing and transmitting digital photographs, as well as providing voicemail and interactive text messaging that will increase both the security and productivity of social service professionals and employees.

Different lens for viewing technologies

There are essentially two ways that social care managers can view the potential of electronic technologies. The first is their use for *specific* applications, the second to shape our lives and environment in more general ways. Neither of the two views is mutually exclusive. Examples of the former include a *high speed calculator processor printer* that helps in dealing with the overwhelming amount of paperwork and record keeping required for the continuous stream of transactions such as client scheduling and accounting, payroll processing and record keeping, document preparation, and processing transactions and checks. Another specific application is use of technology as an analytical machine, which enables us to pull together data from a large number of sources and manipulate it in different ways to analyze and better understand social problems; an example is analyzing client demographics such as the percentage of people living in poverty, teen pregnancy rates, etc. to determine program needs. Electronic technology can also serve as an information system for processing data to solve problems and acquiring new knowledge and skills to deal with and adapt to continuously changing environments. An example would be to assess effectiveness of a new social service program.

Finally, humans have always created and surrounded themselves with "artifacts" in their personal life space (e.g. tools and appliances) that make their home, work and leisure lives easier, more productive and effective. For example, an increasingly electronic work environment includes desktop or laptop computers, faxes, cell phones, voicemail, email, and user-friendly office-focused software. A broader view on the use of electronic technology includes seeing technology's applications beyond the immediate environment or need. These include the perception of electronic technologies as an extension of humans, as a "wired" global community, as an electronic brain, and as a virtual entity. These applications are illustrated below.

As an extension of humans, these are technologies and tools that permit humans to extend themselves into the lives of others beyond their immediate environment. An example might be using a telephone, cell phone or computer to communicate with clients and/or other social service and community agencies to create service opportunities for clients. Another, broader, view is that the "electronic revolution" has created a wired world or global village, an example of which is using the internet to access information to enhance client services.

The development of AI (Artificial Intelligence) to help humans expand their brainpower or assist in "brain work" views technology as an electric brain, for example, "expert systems" that monitor clients continuously and alert professionals when human intervention is necessary. Finally, the electronic technologies are based on symbols that are surrogates for the real world and thus can be configured and reconfigured to create "virtual" or "imaginary" organizations peopled by a mix of operations, professional, and administrative employees based in a number of geographically dispersed structural organizations. An example of this would be an electronic-assisted neonatal interdisciplinary response team.

All of these applications of electronic technology—narrow or broadly focused—can be very helpful in recognizing and better understanding the opportunities that the electronic technologies have for improving social service functioning. In summary, social services professionals and organizations can use information technology in the following ways:

- as a personal tool including user-friendly email, word processing, presentations and spreadsheet applications

- to facilitate data analysis for policy and program planning and for research. By using database software (such as Microsoft ACCESS) one can "warehouse" data that is "mined" to support operations, planning and management functions. Social work agencies have also begun to utilize geographic information system (GIS) technologies for their data analytical activities. These facilitate the analysis and display of social work data in geographic-spatial terms

- to facilitate use of the "web" capabilities as a tool and resource for clients/consumers/customers/community. Increasingly e-services are being provided for clients, for the general community, staff, and policy makers. With links to other websites, these services can support and strengthen self-help and mutual help groups

- as a management tool for performance and accountability reporting, scheduling and monitoring work, project management, and decision support

- for e-learning including programmed instruction for clients, staff and community, CBT (Computer Based Training), and for staff training/professional development

- to facilitate/support communications among staff and policy makers, for clients, consumers and community, for interagency networking, with funders and other service providers

- for fundraising and development based on campaign software that supports such activities as fundraising, donor tracking, and document production.

A framework for using electronic technology in the social service agency

With a better understanding of the different forms of electronic media and their potential for social service, what is the best way for social work and social care managers to apply these technologies? The following five-part model can be helpful for considering and planning for the agency's technology needs:

1. direct use by clients, consumers and community

2. extending employees' capabilities

3. automated routines

4. integrated data processing systems

5. organization support.

Each part of the model will be discussed briefly below, with additional examples provided in Box 10.1.

1. Direct use by clients, consumers, and community

When a manager begins to design the use of ET (Electronic Technologies) for the social services organization it is important to begin with, and continually maintain, the first design guideline: How can our clients, consumers and community groups directly use these technologies to improve the quality of their lives, individually and collectively? Successfully following this primary guideline has obvious payoff for everyone involved in the functioning of the human services organization. Many social service agencies now have internet web pages that provide e-services, such as making appointments, reminders of appointment, signing up for special services (e.g. respite care), processing payments automatically, providing health or nutritional advisories (or linking to websites that do so), providing "chat room" availability for clients wishing to participate in a mutual-help group, and for donors, providing opportunities for direct donations or for volunteering time and talent. There should be continuous development of innovative uses of the electronic technologies for social services organizations that provide direct technology use for clients and consumers.

2. Extending employees' capabilities

In order to extend the capabilities of operational, professional, and administrative personnel charged with organizational functions, "general purpose" workstations, "specialized" workstations, and "monitoring" systems all using comprehensive integrated technologies are a requirement for social services today. Box 10.1 provides some examples of the functions embedded in these technologies. While the cornerstone of these capabilities for extending employees' productivity and effectiveness is desktop and laptop computers, there are additional electronic technologies. They include cell phones which also have paging, voicemail, or emergency response capability and a personal digital assistant (PDA) such as a Palm Pilot. In time there will be one handheld device that will be used for all electronic forms of communication and information processing.

3. Automated routines

The electronic technologies make it possible to automate the routines of an organization, such as processing, updating, and retrieving data related to and required for client record keeping. This has become a necessity as employees and professionals are freed from data and information processes so that they can provide human-oriented services. Systems can now be designed to undertake, on an automatic systematic basis, a large amount of routine processing and retention of data which previously required a heavy investment of organizational human and material resources.

4. Integrated data processing systems

Creating and maintaining electronic databases generated from agency programs and services, interrelating them, providing user-friendly data analysis tools, and relating agency databases to data from the community are becoming automated processes in most social service organizations. Together they provide the electronic technology-based integrated data processing necessary for more productive and effective delivery of social services. Geographic-based Information Systems (GIS) is a good example of integrated data processing. It combines mapping with computer-based need or service data to enhance social service decision-making, for example facilitating a decision to place a senior center in a location where there is the greatest concentration of people aged 55 and older.

5. Organizational support

Supporting the organization is another aspect of the agency's technology utilization. It grows out of a paradox: the greater the extent of electronic technology use, the greater the level and complexity of organizational "paperwork" and transactions. Human services organizations have no choice. The only way to deal with this increased level and complexity of agency functioning is to increase use of the electronic technology primarily to support two aspects of this functioning: resource allocation/control (i.e. scheduling, routing, calendaring, accounting, monitoring) and staff development, (i.e. skill banks, e-learning, flex-benefits, virtual work units, home-based work). Computer Based

---

Box 10.1: Model social services information system

Direct use by clients, consumers and community	*Transactor:* Acquiring services interactively, processing the "paperwork."
	Scheduler: Client makes appointments directly.
	Tickler: Providing reminders to clients, consumers, or citizens.
	Resource: Helping pinpoint potential, available resources.
	Dispatcher: Arranging for normal or emergency help?
	Instructor: Providing continuous education.
	Researcher: Keeping the latest information at the fingertips of clients, consumers, community groups.
Extending employees' capabilities	*General purpose workstations:* Word processing, spreadsheets, data base management, graphic presentations, accounting, personal and agency calendaring, statistical analysis, tele-internet communications.

Special purpose workstations: Designed for specific social service environments (e.g. clinics, community agency, schools, hospital) or disciplines (e.g. behavioural health, family services, youth services, substance abuse.)

Monitoring systems: "24/7/354" has now become an expectation of broadened services capability/ availability. Professionals are expected to "stay on top" of all aspects of agency functioning at all times. A broad set of integrated information/ electronic technologies is required to meet this expectation.

Organizational support	*Resource allocation and control*

Scheduling: Client/consumer appointments; work schedules.

Routing: Home visits, bus pickups, meal deliveries.

Calendaring: Automatic ticklers for professionals: events and dates.

Community resources: Skill banks of people who are potential volunteers for service support or emergency backup.

Accounting: Continuous cost, performance, cross-classified program data.

Monitoring: Tracking supplies, vehicle maintenance, office maintenance and employee/consumer safety and security.

Staff Development

IDPs: Creating and maintaining individualized development plans for every employee in the organization to maintain an employee development focus on an employee by employee basis.

Skills bank: Creation and maintenance of an automated database of the specialized talents and skills of each employee in the agency which is available to the employees themselves to draw upon for mutual and collective professional and organizational development.

E-learning: There is a need for the capability to have a web-based learning system in place which employees utilize for their own professional development to meet learning outcomes developed mutually.

	Flex-benefits: Creating an environment of flex-benefits for employees plus flexibility in work schedules to meet the universal need to balance work and professional lives of employees.
	Virtual work units: The capability to form a "virtual" team of employees dispersed geographically who can work in an integrated fashion.
	Home-based work: The capability for employees to work from their homes.
Automated routines	The electronic technologies make it possible to automate the routines of an organization, and for that matter daily living. We have reached the point where we all depend upon them. Pick up a telephone, dial a toll-free number, order a product, have it paid for by your credit card and have it delivered within 24 hours—none of this is possible without *automated routines*. Automating the routines of an organization is a necessity as we free employees and professionals to provide the *human* agency services.
Integrated data processing	Creating and maintaining electronic databases generated from agency programs and services, interrelating them, providing user-friendly data analysis tools, and relating agency databases to data from the community, the environment, and the profession.

Training (CBT) has become an integral part of agencies to assure that all employees acquire up to date information and regulations on new programs or new policies, especially regarding complex and frequently changing public entitlements. Box 10.1 provides examples for organizational support applications.

Requisite knowledge and skills for social work and social care managers

There is a need to demystify the knowledge and skills, even the terminology and jargon, required to utilize new technology for the social services. The implementation of new systems for performing both new and familiar tasks can take time to imbed in agencies (Bates 2003; Kerslake 1998). It is true that the information and electronic technology (IT/ET) field is the source of expert information in the many dimensions and aspects of the field. At the same time, however, it has become increasingly necessary and possible for social work professionals to acquire knowledge about the state of the art developments in IT/ET hardware and software.

With a general understanding of these developments, a social work or social care manager has sufficient awareness to be able to communicate with specialists and to utilize the technology as it evolves, drawing upon the support of one or more experts as the need arises during the technology transfer process. It is important, therefore, for a social work agency to find ways for its operational, professional, and administrative employees to continually update their IT/ET knowledge in both hardware and software. Schools of social work have an obligation to introduce new technologies into their curriculum, for example ensuring, in the UK, that during their qualifying training students are equipped with the knowledge and skills for the European Driving Licence in Information Literacy and Information and Communication Technology. Social service agencies cannot escape the need to utilize the potential of these technologies and unless workers are knowledgeable and skilled, they most probably will find clients who know more than they do and will be demanding more technology use to make service delivery more efficient and effective.

Knowledge is needed about recent developments such as an awareness of hardware developments including mice, scanners, modems, network cards and configurations, CD drives, DVD players and recorders, hard drives, floppy drives, memory cards and drives, voice recognition systems. It is important to know about *central processing units*, including their speed and power as well as amount and type of random access memory; *output devices*: monitor types, video cards, sound cards, printers types (i.e. laser, ink jet, color); *storage devices* such as CD, DVD, hard disks, memory cards, off-site storage technology, file servers; and *communication devices* such as modems, routers, hubs, and wireless technologies.

Knowledge is also needed about the application software developments including general purpose applications (of which Microsoft Office is a good example, because of its extensive use) and special purpose applications that have been designed specifically for an agency or for a specific group of professionals. Most state governments in the US use MMIS (Medicaid Management Information System), a system designed to process the wide variety of Medicaid transactions. Many solo practitioner clinical psychologists use software specifically designed for their profession.

Finally, knowledge about development of systems software is critical for managers. Systems software focuses on the IT/ET system itself, improving its productivity and its effectiveness. There are several categories of systems software: operating systems (i.e. Windows, UNIX, LINUX); network software, security systems (i.e. Norton's anti-virus or firewall software); programming software (i.e. Visual Basic, Oracle, Java, C++); and specific function software, for example, web development, desktop publishing, computer aided design (CAD), voicemail management, and geographic information systems (GIS).

In addition to knowledge about technological developments, managers need skills in using them. The IT/ET explosion also had required professionals in all fields, social work included, to acquire a minimal set of skills for utilizing the latest technological developments to be more productive and effective. This is no longer a problem for the vast majority of social work professionals. In less than a generation, a new word has entered the dictionary: "user-friendly." A few decades ago, the only way to use the technology, which did not even have a typewriter keyboard or a TV-type display, was to punch some data into cards, enter the cards into the computer and have the computer print the results or message on a paper printer. In today's society, electronic technology devices are used freely in the schools, homes, at work, and on the street. Desktop and laptop computers, cell phones and multipurpose call phones, palm/pocket PCs, motor vehicle and kitchen devices are all "user-friendly." Communicating with an IT device has gone full circle—one can communicate either by voice or by a ten—key numeric pad.

In a society with ubiquitous use of wired and cell phones, TVs, DVDs, and motor vehicles, personal mastery of IT/ET devices has become second nature. Making the leap to be able to use applications specific to social work agency functioning has become much easier and personal mastery is becoming the rule, not the exception. It has become necessary in order to be part of a social work organization, and the benefit in improved functioning (as well as increased professional skills) exceeds the required investment of time and energy.

Maintaining one's skills at state of the art of the profession level is an obvious aspect of professional life today. This is true for all dimensions of a professional's skill set and requires an ability to communicate with a wide variety of specialists in one's professional field. Today, a professional must include in the array of specialists with whom they communicate those who guide the use and management of the organization's information and electronic technologies and data resources. These specialists include network and database managers, who are the key for helping a social work professional transform data into information and eventually knowledge that will increase their professional effectiveness. Being involved in decisions affecting the use of information technology for their organization is becoming a requirement for the social services professional.

The data and information in a social work organization drive the activities, services, and transactions of that agency, and creates the information upon which professional, administrative, executive, planning, and policy decisions are based. Clients and communities use these data for a wide variety of purposes, all focused on improving the quality of life for individuals and communities. These data become more meaningful when related to data and information that are generated by the sum total of all social work organizations in a society. While there is a tendency to see currency and personnel as the key assets of an organization, in today's world one needs to quickly acquire the perception of information as another vital and critical agency resource.

Managing information in a social work organization has become as important as managing money, people, and property. However, it raises a number of legal and ethical issues that the social services organization must be prepared to deal with. The Identification, Referral and Tracking system (IRT) in England is intended to provide a mechanism for pooling information. It highlighted that there are ethical issues of consent and confidentiality to be worked out in order to achieve effective information sharing (Cleaver *et al.* 2004). Guidance on information sharing has been developed to address this issue (HM Government 2006b). At the time of writing, similar issues are being addressed in Scotland with the development of a single record of assessment for all children under the *Getting it Right for Every Child* policy initiative (Scottish Executive 2005).

Acquiring and managing the technology

Understanding the potentialities of technology and how they can be utilized for social services has to be accompanied with one last area of technology application: implementation—understanding how to implement technology application. The following are some insights and suggestions for the best ways to go about acquiring and managing the technology.

The Electronic Technology (ET) Steering Group

Because the electronic technologies seem so complex, there is a tendency to turn over the acquisition and management of the technology utilization, including system design and implementation, to IT (Information Technology) specialists. This is a common mistake made by many organizations. It results in mis-utilization or less than maximum utilization of the potentialities of these new technologies. The electronic technologies are like any new organizational improvement. Their acquisition and utilization needs to be shaped and guided by the agency. This requires total involvement of the employees and agency stakeholders—at all stages in the acquisition and utilization process. The starting point is creation of an ET Steering Group. The members of this group would be representative of the social services agency's various stakeholders; most important of all, they should be familiar with all aspects and dimensions of agency operations. Since there are multiple ET technologies that will be acquired over a long period of time, it would be helpful to have an ET Steering Group that provides long-term guiding of the process, with user groups or teams set up for planning and managing *each* implementation project.

Technology resource acquisition options

There are several options available for acquiring ET/IT resources. The best option is one in which a social service organization can acquire its own staff of IT specialists, who serve as facilitators for all agency employees to participate in the system design and implementation process. IT staff can either develop systems unique to the agency's needs or purchase a system from a vendor. In either case, IT specialists help to implement these systems. Acquiring a staff of IT specialists requires resources from within the agency or from an external source invested in the organization's technological development. When hiring IT staff is not possible, there could be an opportunity for the organization to collaborate with other similar agencies to work together in the system development process. The notion of a computer utility (much like an electric or telephone utility) that serves several social services organizations is a viable option given the rapid changes in the IT field which require constant updating of any system installed and implemented.

Finally, another option would be to acquire "loaned" IT specialists (e.g. on "loan" from a company in the community.) If that is not possible, consultants should be retained to serve as facilitators for the process. Importantly, either the consultant or "loaned" specialist must be teamed with a project team in the agency, with the objective being to continually merge knowledge of the agency with knowledge of the technology. For example, the routine collection of data might be more advantageous than doing so only in response to critical audit or budgetary problems (Ousley and Barnwell 1993). The specialist can advise and work with the agency on these kinds of issues.

A system development and implementation process

A well-defined system implementation process begins with specification of Performance Outcome Requirements, selecting a systems development strategy, and involving everyone in the organization in the process. At all times, the focus should be on two design principles: comprehensive and integrated. The following is a set of guidelines for social care managers in implementing information systems.

1. DEVELOP PERFORMANCE OUTCOME REQUIREMENTS (PORS) FOR EACH ELEMENT OF AN ET UTILIZATION PLAN OR SYSTEM

PORs are functions that the organization's ET-based system will perform which result in outcomes that will meet all of the various stakeholders' requirements/needs/desires. An example for agency client admission process follows:

Does the admissions module of the proposed system provide access to any person or group in the community to enter an application for a client online and track his or her progress through the application process? In other words, focus first on user impacts: What are the outcomes and results that the system is designed to achieve once it is operational? For every element of the ET-utilization model (e.g. direct use by clients, extending employees' capabilities, organizational support, automated routines, and integrated data processing) the agency should develop a detailed list of performance outcomes requirements (PORs) that will serve as criteria for measuring the success of technology utilization.

2. DECIDE ON A SYSTEM DEVELOPMENT STRATEGY

Generally this a choice between an "in house" system development effort using the organization's own IT staff, or selecting an "off the shelf" system developed by a commercial vendor that has successfully implemented an unique system for social work agencies. For social service agencies, most probably the choice will be a combination of the two. An "off the shelf" system may be acquired but modified with the heavy involvement of agency social work and IT professionals. Another combination choice might be to contract existing IT operations, freeing up the social services organization IT staff to develop and implement a new system that takes advantage of the latest developments in the technology (Schoech 1999). Box 10.2 provides the stages that generally are followed to develop and implement an "in house" system. Box 10.3 shows stages for selecting and implementing an "off the shelf" system.

3. INVOLVE EVERYONE IN THE ORGANIZATION IN ALL OF THE PHASES OF TECHNOLOGY IMPLEMENTATION BEGINNING WITH THE DEVELOPMENT OF THE PORS

Regardless of the system development strategy selected (e.g. internal or external), it is important to restate that the total organization needs to be

Box 10.2: Systems development strategy "A", selecting and implementing an in-house system

Step 1 Steering Group formation	Appoint a group of employees representative of all units, disciplines and levels in the organization to guide and steer the process.
Step 2 Feasibility analysis	Establish the organizational and economic feasibility of technology utilization and develop long-term and short-term goals, resource requirements, and impact criteria.
Step 3 Systems analysis	Analyze the existing organizational systems; transaction process, data flows, decision, and database requirements for all levels and stakeholders in the organization.
Step 4 Systems design	Conceptualize a system that will exploit the potential of existing and evolving electronic technologies and craft a time-phased technological master plan for the organization.
Step 5 Systems development	Identify the Performance Outcome Requirements of the system or sub-system being developed and define the detailed systems specification: transactions processing, database maintenance, application and systems software, and hardware requirements.
Step 6 Systems implementation	Program the application and systems software with existing or augmented technical staff resources, acquire required hardware, test the programs using benchmark criteria, document operating procedures and interfaces with all organizational stakeholders, and convert to the new system using a methodical, time-phased plan.
Step 7 Orientation and training	At all steps in the process undertake orientation and comprehensive training for everyone in the organization and everyone interacting with the organization and its systems.
Step 8 Monitoring and evaluation	Continually monitor and evaluate the system at each phase of its development and implementation against Performance Outcome Requirements, systems' specifications, impact criteria, and organizational transformation opportunities.

Box 10.3: Systems development strategy "B", selecting and implementing an off the shelf system

Step 1 Develop specs	Develop specifications that will be used to design and implement the system with the capability for achieving the Performance Outcome Requirements (PORs). This is the equivalent of a blueprint for those who will actually build the system.
Step 2 Requirements	Specify the software and hardware requirements that can meet the systems' specifications. These are the basis for the preparation of a detailed and comprehensive document that becomes the basis for an RFP (Request for Proposals).
Step 3 Solicit proposals	Once finalized, the RFP is promulgated and circulated to secure the best vendor to provide the software and appropriate hardware, and install/implement the system along with agency personnel. The vendors identified for the solicitation are those who have designed, developed, tested, and implemented a system specific for the environment and functioning of your type of organization (e.g. social services agencies.)
Step 4 Select vendor	The proposals submitted by vendors in response to the RFP are reviewed with a uniform process and a set of criteria by a proposal selection committee representative of the total organization. The vendor selection process includes visits by user groups to locations where the vendors who are the finalists in the selection process have already implemented their systems. The process is completed once the selected proposal's vendor has drafted a contract that all groups involved in the selection process have reviewed and approved.
Step 5 Comprehensive training	From the very beginning of Step 1, undertake comprehensive continuous training focused on utilizing and exploiting the full potential of the system as it is being installed and once it is fully implemented.

involved in the planning, acquisition, implementation (including training) and management of all aspects of the ET utilization process. In other words, while a stakeholder-based ET Steering Committee is a requisite, it is just the tip of an iceberg of total organization involvement in this process. It is crucial to resist the notion that only experts or specialists in the organization, or those brought in as consultants, should design, develop and implement an IT effort. Experts and specialists obviously will be a part of any IT implementation process, but their role is facilitative and supportive, not being in charge of the effort.

4. AT ALL TIMES, FOCUS ON TWO DESIGN PRINCIPLES: COMPREHENSIVE AND INTEGRATED

Comprehensive applies to: 1. the stakeholders in the organization who will become the system users (clients/consumers, community, operation employees, professionals, clinicians, planners, administrators, executives, policy makers, researchers, other social service agencies); 2. the information, computer and telecommunication *technologies* that will be exploited/utilized such as desktop computers, laptop computers, workstations, wired and cell telephones, PDAs (e.g. palm pilots), pagers, digital cameras, faxes, the internet and the web, interagency systems, cable TV systems; and 3. to all of the different *perceptions* of the technology use. The IT/ET technology is moving in a direction that integrates *all* of the stakeholders' data, information, services, and staff operations as well as all of the technologies (e.g. cell telephones with multiple electronic information capabilities). Therefore, at every step and phase in the process, design the ET utilization process and system to be *integrated*.

Related important issues for consideration by social care managers

Social services organizations will use technology; social work professionals, therefore, face the challenge of shaping the technology, for their organization and for society, with the values of social work. This requires, at the minimum, reflecting on and dealing with a number of challenges that are the results and impacts of this particular type of technology transfer. If this were a chapter about technology transfer for most professions, the above is sufficient. But since this is written for social workers, whose fundamental value is social justice in the broadest sense of the word, there is a role and responsibility for social workers to engage with the wide variety of issues that deal with the implications and impacts of the information and electronic technologies, as described below.

Impact on work life

Technology affects work life positively and negatively, simultaneously. Norbert Wiener (1965) in his landmark book Cybernetics, called for "the human use of human beings." The fitness for purpose, therefore, of the use of information and other technologies remains the critical issue (Ousley et al. 2003). Technology has indeed taken over a large amount of automaton-type processes in an organization, freeing up the human mind to undertake activities that only human beings can perform. The issue is one of quality of work life so as to utilize the human qualities of human beings. Technology can be used successfully as a tool of productivity. Organizations, corporate and governmental, have provided opportunities for workers to "telecommute": work out of their homes in ways that improve their ability to manage both their home and work lives. But when technology is used excessively, 24 hours a day, 7 days a week, in the home or even in motor vehicles, operational employees and professionals can be exploited. Some organizations monitor worker productivity closely, including their use of the internet or telephones for non-work purposes. These are all issues that need to be recognized and understood to develop a balanced technology use policy.

Contrary to popular belief, technology is neutral; it loses that neutrality when humans use technology for purposes that degrade, not improve, the quality of life, including the quality of work life. Robotry and artificial intelligence (AI) have great potential for increasing the economic quality of life for all; being sure that this potential is channeled for the common good is an issue that requires constant attention and concern.

Maintaining a healthy work environment is another aspect of this concern. There are concerns about impacts of radiation, eye-strain, wrist-strain, and back-strain with the increased use of electronic-based workstations. A relatively new field, ergonomics, has emerged to create and maintain a safe, healthy work environment. Utilizing the best of this new field has become a requisite for managing modern social work agencies.

Security and privacy

Security has always been an issue for modern society. Until the September 2001 terrorist attacks on New York and Washington, most people in the US never had to fully deal with this issue. Technology-based systems are vulnerable, particularly as critical data and processes are increasingly electronic in nature. Maintaining the security of critical systems is of the highest priority, not only for national security. This is as true for general community systems such as national defense, air traffic control, electricity utility, or hospital systems as it is for systems used to provide social services to clients, consumers, and community. While technology can be used to make life more insecure, it also can have a positive impact on work life. Social workers who have to move about into the community, often in neighborhoods or buildings that are security risks, have greater security now because of telecommunication technologies such as cell phones. But increased security systems raise a concern for protecting the privacy of an individual or group of individuals and require consideration of who owns data and how data can be used or changed. Finding a good balance or fit between these legitimate societal concerns will require constant vigilance along with concern. Social workers will remain concerned that their values are preserved when they work in innovative ways with new media.

Equitable distribution of technology resources

As computers and telecommunication devices become more ubiquitous day by day, social workers and other human-oriented professionals have to devote time and energy to assuring that technology resources will be distributed equally to the full diversity of our populations. Along with equitable resource distribution, for at least several more generations technology literacy will be an issue of constant concern. Social workers along with others must guard against a digital divide in the population that further disadvantages a particular socioeconomic class or community. Much will depend on the extent to which new technologies are made available as community resources, particularly in disadvantaged areas (Aldridge 1995; Department of Health 2001c). In a *knowledge-based* economy, the more knowledge and skills a person acquires, the greater their possibility to acquire and maintain a good quality of life. But even this is not a fail safe. In a world-focused economy, a corporation can freely transfer work "off shore" to countries with a reservoir of "knowledge workers" whose wages are significantly lower. Can social service agencies be far behind?

Virtual organizations: from unidisciplinary to interdisciplinary service delivery

The electronic technologies have created almost a revolution in the way in which goods and services are being provided to people worldwide. Traditional, highly structural discipline and organizational boundaries can simultaneously be maintained and spanned with virtual entities that can focus a broad set of talents and skills to provide a unique set of services to each client and consumer in ways that address their specific needs for improved quality of life. The ultimate impact of the computer and telecommunications on society is a new form of organizing. A virtual entity is an organization or system of selected professions from different organizational structures located in widely dispersed geographic locations, who possess a wide array of specialized knowledge, skills, and experiences. The group is formed for a time-limited or repetitive special task to carry out a specific set of strategic and operational goals and objectives, with a set of cross-organizational, transdisciplinary processes, roles, and relationships carefully designed for effective performance and optimum achievement of its mission. The virtual organization is maintained and enhanced through the use of modern management and behavioral science knowledge and techniques, utilizing state of the art electronic computer and telecommunication technologies. What drives the expansion of virtual organizations are the demands of individuals to manage their own acquisition of goods and services that are sensitive to their unique needs, lifestyle, and definition of quality of life. Increasingly, social service organizations are recognizing the need to reshape and transform their service delivery and management approaches to include a virtual entity strategy. Optimal utilization and exploitation of the electronic technologies now provide the option of becoming a virtual agency in which client/consumer services are uniquely shaped and provided. Examples of these virtual organizations would include employee assistance programs which now permit employees to access and manage the system through telephone networks or agency websites; governmental mental health or developmental disability departments providing services designed uniquely for each client; and a community-based non-profit agency providing both direct and contract services in a number of different cross-organizational collaborations.

Technology and clients, consumers, and communities

Too often there is an image that the clients and consumers of social services are technology-deprived, either because of the lack of resources or lack of knowledge and skills. Most observers would question this conclusion, surely for developed societies and even for those we consider underdeveloped. The electron is pervasive. It has affected countries large and small, developed and developing. And, in less than two decades, we have witnessed a major transformation in the economies of the vast majority of countries because of technology-impact. As more and more current and potential clients and consumers become technology capable, social service organizations along with other public non-profit entities have to transform themselves to recognize the desire and capability of individuals to be more proactive and even manage their own acquisition of social and human services. Whether it focuses on reducing the administrative burdens for acquiring services or on searching for new information and service resources that will enhance their abilities to be more self-sufficient, the changing technology proficiency of clients will influence the way in which social service organizations provide services to the community. For years, professionals and organizations have been advocating for enhancing the resilience and self-sufficiency of clients, consumers, and communities. We now have to recognize that technology is forcing social service entities to make this a reality.

Conclusion

There is a fundamental irony when utilizing the electronic and information technologies for social work organizations. Both the computer and the telecommunication technologies require linear, logical thinking, while transferring and using these technologies for social work organizations that serve clients and community requires non-linear, holistic thinking. As social workers, we need to be proficient in both mind sets and mental processes.

This chapter has provided a framework for thinking about and implementing technology in human service agencies. We would summarize by offering a set of guidelines for social work/social care managers:

1. Use all four forms of electronic media: digital, whole image, audio, and text.

2. Think broadly about electronic technologies and better understand their potentialities for social services agencies.

3. Enhance the opportunities for harnessing the electron in social services organizations through direct use by clients, to extend implementation.

4. Master current technology and stay attuned to changes, opportunities and risks of new technology. Be open to developing new knowledge and skills.

5. Use IT to strengthen all aspects and dimensions of social work services.

6. The acquisition and utilization of the electronic technologies (ET) for a social service agency should be guided and managed by an ET Steering Group.

7. Explore the appropriate options available for IT resource acquisition.

Finally, managing information in an organization is as important as managing money, people, and property. Thus, information management is a fundamental management process for social services agencies. But the term "information management" has multiple implications and impacts. It includes continually utilizing and exploiting the full potential of all of modern electronic and telecommunication technologies that ultimately will permit new forms of human service organizations. Since these technologies will continue to evolve over the next several decades, this will be a constant challenge for social services managers for the foreseeable future. At the heart of information management is using every possible means to be able to measure the organization's success in terms of effectiveness and impacts of client/consumer services as well as the productivity, economy, and efficiency of all agency employees. At stake is more than the ability of the human service organization to focus and refocus its mission, strategic goals, and program objectives; it is the quality of life of clients and people in the community. Ensuring effectiveness and efficiency requires a wide range of comprehensive and interrelated information, and the ability to reflect on and analyze data in ways that keep the agency "on target" and even "ahead of the curve."

Since the widespread availability and use of information is a requirement and foundation for a democratic society, social workers along with other professions must be in the forefront of the ongoing effort to utilize the information and electronic technologies in ways that will protect and strengthen societal processes devoted to sustaining and strengthening democracy. Thus, we close with a final guideline:

8. Social services managers must create a climate for continual utilization and exploitation of emerging IT technologies for the broad range of agency and societal purposes all focused on improving the quality of life for clients, consumers, and community while strengthening democracy in our societies.

This challenge is formidable but exciting.

Chapter 11

Managing Diverse Sources of Funding

Mark Ezell

"Be careful what you wish for" is a saying that seems to be popular these days. Virtually all non-profit organizations, especially in the social service sector, wish for more money. This is not greed: the funds are needed in order to accomplish their goals and provide quality services to their clientele. When individuals are able to invest funds through retirement plans or otherwise, the commonly heard advice is that a diversified investment portfolio is wise because the individual is protected from downward trends of individual stocks. (Not that social workers, given their pay, will necessarily be able to do this, but they probably know of this strategy.) The wisdom of revenue diversification has been extended to non-profit and voluntary organizations and it is recognized that there are definite advantages to having multiple sources of funds, especially if some of them provide large amounts of revenue. The public relations, marketing, and fundraising activities needed to attract diverse funders are challenging and costly. Those agencies that are successful are then faced with another set of challenges.

Two more common sayings seem relevant when the wish for more and diversified funding comes true, "there's no such thing as a free lunch," and "there's no such thing as funding with no strings attached." It is a generally positive development when agencies attract diverse and increasing funding, but the management staff soon find out that they have another set of challenges to face. The purpose of this chapter is to present issues that relate to managing diverse sources of funding. Effective management of any given fund depends on several critical factors such as the source(s) of the fund, the events that lead to the acquisition of the funds, the specific restrictions on the use of the funds, if any, ethics, tax codes, and relevant law. The chapter does not focus on techniques and tactics of acquiring different types of funding, but on issues related to the types of different funds acquired and how to manage multiple funds and funders.

For the purposes of definition, funding sources are those entities such as governmental agencies, foundations, corporations, or individuals that provide revenues to an organization. *Resources* is a broader term that includes not only money but also volunteers, non-cash contributions, and even staff. A *fund* will be used in the same sense as in accounting, revenues that may only be used in a manner consistent with the guidelines of the contributor (National Health Council and the National Assembly of National Voluntary Health and Social Welfare Organization 1998). Managing diverse funds and managing diverse funding sources are somewhat distinctive but interdependent enterprises. Managing funds can be thought of as an internal management function and managing funding sources as external functions such as marketing, public relations, negotiating, and communicating. However, using funds as the contributor intended and being fiscally and programmatically accountable to the funding source will, by and large, contribute to positive relationships.

The topics discussed in this chapter are relevant to social work administrators in both the US and the UK. Government purchase of services through contracts, discussed below, is one of the primary factors driving organizations to diversify funding. Richardson and Gutch (1998) describe the rise of contracting in the US as "ad hoc," whereas in the UK, it is a "deliberate aim of government policy" (p.155). In her interview of Stuart Etherington, chief executive of the National Council for Voluntary Organisations, Harris (2000) reports Etherington's observations that services previously provided by the state have been "offloaded" to the voluntary sector (p.319) and that there is increased interest in partnerships between government programs and the voluntary sector.

While the field generally accepts the wisdom of having diverse funding sources, there is very little empirical evidence that confirms that more good things will come to the organization, its staff, and clients with more diversified funding than in organizations with little or no diversification. While it may be common sense, an empirical body of evidence on diversification is needed in order to gain a more in-depth understanding of its advantages and disadvantages. A relatively extensive literature search resulted in the discovery of only one relevant study.

Based on an exploratory study of 17 non-profit youth service bureaus, Besel and Andreescu (2003) reach interesting conclusions about which ones survived. These agencies were started in the 1970s with federal funding but this source of funds greatly declined over the years. The agencies that survived started with larger budgets and this seemed to be more important than the rate of budget growth. The ability of an agency to penetrate local fiscal streams was a primary determinant of survival (p.259) and agency directors reported that city and county governments were the most sustainable sources of revenues. Generalizing beyond these particular agencies should be done with great caution and there may be practice implications worth exploring. In this particular case, as federal funds declined and other sources of funding were attracted, securing local funding had an impact on agency survival.

Before discussing issues related to managing various funds, it is important to understand the policy and funding environments that, in general, have created pressure on social service agencies to diversify their funding base (Rubio, Birkenmaier and Berg-Weger 2000). In addition, a comprehensive description of different types of funding will be presented to enable agencies and managers to consider all possible options. Finally, the chapter includes several suggested techniques that managers can use when managing multiple funding sources.

Policy and agency environments

As Gronbjerg (1993) explains so well, the environments of non-profits are complex, filled with many other organizations, private, non-profit, and otherwise, and almost all are attempting to secure resources. These highly competitive environments are strongly impacted by policy and funding at all levels of government, and non-profits are more and more concerned about funding: "In the United States today, the new forces of privatization and devolution are affecting the relationship between non-profit and public social service agencies" (Austin 2003, p.98). This statement resonates with the UK situation as well, where not-for-profit agencies are in part, if not wholly, dependent on contracts from publicly--funded agencies and where there is often competition among these agencies to secure such funding (see, for example, Tunstill *et al.* 2006). An added factor is that to secure continuance of funding, managers have to show that their service remains the best value when compared with the alternatives. This process was introduced in the Local Government Act 1999 in England to make a real and positive difference in the services that people received from their local authority. Devolved government and changing organizational arrangements for service delivery mean that the implementation of audit which decides what is the best value for money varies, but the key principle remains the same (Gallop 2003). This external framework has had an impact on the way that contracts are both awarded and reviewed.

In this section, specific environmental forces that shape organizations' increasing pursuit of funds from alternative sources are discussed. Besides the environmental factors discussed below, there are two basic reasons why non-profits need multiple sources of funds. First, non-profits are legally prohibited from selling shares of stock to raise revenues (Weisbrod 1988). Second, the consumers of services directly pay very little, if anything, for the receipt of services. Third parties such as governments and insurance companies pay for most services, but rarely cover the full costs of service design, delivery, overhead, and depreciation. And, as noted above, in the UK there is no guarantee that funding from government, via a local authority, will continue if it appears that another organization can be more cost effective and produce better outcomes.

Privatization and contracting

Many government agencies have decided to buy programs and services from other agencies rather than build and operate programs themselves. In addition, public agencies are choosing to close many of their own programs and convert to private purchase arrangements. Depending on

the specific situation, the organizations bidding for government contracts could include local governmental agencies (when the state is the
contractor), private non-profit organizations, and private for-profit organizations. In both cases of private organizations, they might be local,
statewide, or national in scope.

Although many definitions exist, when government divests its
responsibility for the delivery and funding of services, this is referred to
as "privatization" (Gibelman and Demone 1998). Contracting is the
mechanism used to implement privatization policies and there are many
different types of contracts, payment, and accountability mechanisms. As
a result of privatization, human service organizations frequently bid
against one another for the contract to deliver specific services to identified client groups in a particular geographic area. If the bid is successful,
and after negotiations and the finalization of the contract, at some point
(usually later than sooner) funds will flow to the agency and must be
managed in a manner consistent with the contract, the law, ethics,
accepted accounting practices, unwritten rules of the funding agency
and, if applicable, policies of the agency's board of directors.

To some degree and, as most persons in the social service sector recognize, "privatization" is a misnomer: "Private market forces are not able
to address issues of the distribution of resources within our society that
are required to meet the psychosocial, economic, and employment needs
of citizens" (Gibelman and Demone 1998, p.xi). Governments, not consumers of service, continue to be the primary source of funds that fuel
this system. Governments, by and large, will also maintain responsibility
for determining the specific designs of programs and the nature and
scope of delivered services. This is far from the free market in operation
that is implied when privatization is discussed.

Kettner and Martin (1996) point out that although one might expect
the opposite, purchase of service contracting is increasing. As they
explain, leaders of non-profit agencies complain about being controlled
and under-funded by their government funders, and that funding restrictions keep them from serving the poor and oppressed. Rather than
"swearing off," these contracts as a major source of revenue and seeking
other types of funding, the non-profits continue, and increasingly so, to
stand in line for more of the same.

Inadequate funding

Another feature of agencies' environments is the unwillingness or inability of governments to provide adequate levels of social service funding, whether it is due to bad economic times, political philosophy and/or will, or numerous other reasons. This may be one of the primary motivators for agencies to seek diverse sources of funds. As certain types of programs and groups of clients fall from popularity, the agencies delivering those programs and serving those clients scramble for new and different funders. All too often in recent decades the avoidance of retrenchment has been a marker of successful management rather than program growth. In fact, privatization and contracting are frequently adopted because it is asserted to be more efficient and less costly than the "old" way. Privatization also includes tactics advertised to reduce the size of government bureaucracy, a popular platform of certain political parties.

Whether funding increases, decreases, or remains stable within the social service sector or for specific types of services, the contract environment within which agencies operate allows government to determine what are "allowable" and/or "reimbursable" expenses. Administrative costs are a good example of this. It is common for contracts to include language that sets a maximum percentage of expenses for administrative purposes. Exactly which expenses fall under this category of spending may or may not be well defined in the contract. It is very rare for the administrative costs associated with bidding for and negotiating contracts to be considered allowable expenses.

At the same time, governments are insisting on greater accountability for funds, program operations, staff credentials, and client outcomes. Administrative staff devote time to designing and overseeing these accountability systems, and direct service staff spend time inputting information into these systems. Hardware and software for information systems are expensive and need to be replaced more frequently than contract funds allow. Throw in the costs of information system consultants, and one can see that administrative costs will easily exceed contract limits. Thus, they must find and use other funds to cover these costs.

It is important to note that government, although the primary source, is not the only source of funding. Confederated fundraising and giving mechanisms such as a community chest or, in the US, the United Way, provide substantial funding to social service agencies. They, too, limit administrative costs and determine allowable expenses.

Devolution

Another policy on the rise in recent years is the devolution of policy, decision-making and, often, funding from the federal government to state governments and/or state governments to local governments (Coble 1999). An example of the impact of this is described in Ezell's (2002) agency and contract case study. In earlier years, the agency in the study had one contract with the state (i.e. the central office of the child welfare agency) whereas, after the state decentralized, the agency made a bid on contracts offered by six regional offices. The agency won contracts in all six regions, all of which had different reimbursement rates, and the agency was expected to be accountable to six regional offices instead of one state office. Smith (1998) discusses this same phenomenon in Massachusetts and for different types of services (i.e. alcohol and drug treatment) and found there to be vast differences in reimbursement rates, accountability requirements, and service features.

As clearly demonstrated above, through privatization and contracting, governments are only partially covering the costs to deliver the services for which they contract (Kettner and Martin 1996). To avoid bankruptcy, agencies must seek funding elsewhere. At the same time, governments retain the contract oversight function and this differs by nature and extent from one governmental body to the next. A related trend is government's declining interest in program evaluation and staff development. If an agency chooses to invest in either, as would be recommended as major contributors to service quality, the associated expenses frequently cannot be reimbursed with contract funds and must be paid from other coffers.

Funding mechanisms

When government agencies and employees operate programs and deliver services, their source of funds is immediately at hand whereas contracted agencies are often required to deliver the service first and then invoice the appropriate governmental agency for payment. "Up front" funding of services is rare. How and when a contractee receives payments should be articulated in the contract. Even if this is the case, there can still be delays and errors. Agencies, therefore, must have other sources of funds, even lines of credit that allow them to meet payroll and cover other expenses.

Managed care, variously defined, brought capitated rates with it. As the United HealthCare Corporation has suggested, "Capitation…denotes that a fixed amount of money has been negotiated to be paid to a provider on a regularly scheduled basis for [services] to all people covered under a contract" (Davis 1998, p.53). For example, foster care was contracted to private providers in the State of Kansas, and they received approximately $14,000 for each client they received. Some of this might be paid early in the case and the remaining amount when the case was closed. If a particular child were very healthy, for example, and only stayed two months in care, the agency's costs would be lower than the capitated rate. However, if the child remained in foster care for a long time and received extensive health and mental health services, the capitated rate would fall short of the real cost of this case. Note that this rate was also supposed to cover administrative costs. In theory, the severity of the cases and the lengths of stay should average out, and, hopefully, revenues exceed expenses. A major flaw in this system is that the agency itself does not have discretion when to end a child's stay in foster care. Whether the child is to be returned home or parental rights terminated, judges make these decisions and they have no responsibility for making agencies' budgets balance. When being financed with capitated rates, be very aware of who makes the decisions on the types and duration of services and how these decisions are made.

The more traditional funding mechanism in social services is fee-for-service, when the provider negotiates a specific rate for a defined unit of service. A unit of service could be, for example, a counseling hour, a bed-day in residential care, or a delivered hot meal. The agency will bill the government for the number of service units delivered either periodically or when a case is closed. It is very easy to see that maintaining a steady cash flow is likely to be a challenge and other unrestricted funds will need to be used to pay expenses. In some contracts, a fee is paid per hour for a particular service and the fee for the same service differs depending on the credentials of the person delivering the service. For example, a family therapist involved in face-to-face family preservation work could generate $46 per hour for the agency. The same family therapist would generate half that amount per hour for "case related travel." On the other hand, a paraprofessional either engaged in face-to-face work or case related travel generated $15 per hour for the agency (Ezell 2002). At the end of every month, the therapists spent hours (that were not reimbursable) compiling their detailed bills for each family receiving services. Supervisors subsequently reviewed all the bills before sending them to the agency's central office. Again, these hours were not reimbursable. Social work administrators may need to pay very close attention to the timing of funding and the requisite paperwork when negotiating contracts.

Another factor that strongly influences cash flow is the number and frequency of client referrals to agencies. In some cases, the government might set a minimum and a maximum number of cases the agency will receive in the contract, but Ezell's (2002) case study found that while contracts defined the nature of services to be delivered and the fees for these services, the contracts were explicit about not guaranteeing referrals. In the best case scenario, decisions on referrals will not rely on the referring caseworkers' whims, but agencies clearly become beholden to those making referrals to the point where administrators of the agency studied sadly described how the government, not the family or child in need, was now their client.

Finally, staffing patterns and staff development are greatly influenced by funding mechanisms, cash flow, and rates of referrals. Agencies have found that the unpredictability of referrals and payments has caused them to reduce the number of permanent staff and develop a cadre of contract staff who may have to pay for their own benefits. Agencies are more likely to fund staff development activities for permanent staff, if they can, than for contract staff. Even if the agency would like to provide training to contract staff, one might question the wisdom of this investment when these types of private practitioners can have contracts with multiple agencies. The bottom line here is that different types of funding mechanisms in varying types of contracts can have an impact on the quality of staff in an agency and ipso facto the quality of services.

Agency survival strategies

The environmental forces discussed above put pressure on non-profit agencies to increase and diversify their funding base. Survival strategies such as mergers and alliances (McLaughlin 1998) and involvement in entrepreneurial activities also diversify agency funding. McLaughlin explains that the best time to merge is before circumstances force consideration of this option and when two or more organizations have complementary strengths. Mergers involve changes to the legal aspects of non-profit corporations when two or more corporations become one (McLaughlin 1998), and the combination of operations is permanent (Golensky and DeRuiter 1999). Alliances and collaborations maintain separate corporations but joint programming or management, or sharing resources occurs (McLaughlin 1998). When two or more non-profits merge, the number of funding sources and therefore funds will increase. Golensky and DeRuiter (1999) documented this in their case study of a merger of five small agencies. Prior to the merger, only two of the five agencies had all of the six categories of funding the authors examined. The newly created agency had substantial amounts of funding in all six categories.

Although Kettner and Martin (1996) point out that non-profits rely less on strategies such as mergers and franchising than corporations, their survey of social service executives found that 24.4 percent had taken over another agency, 11 percent developed a for-profit subsidiary, and 8.5 percent merged with another non-profit. There is very little empirical literature on the results of mergers and take-overs. Golensky and DeRuiter (1999) conducted a case study of what they perceive to be a generally successful merger of five small human service non-profits. Besides providing a list of "lessons learned," they conclude that the new corporation became "a force in its dealings with governmental agencies" (p.151), and had the merger not occurred, one or more of the non-profits would have folded.

Since "few nonprofits even receive a substantial portion of revenues from donations" (Weisbrod 1988, p.107), many non-profits engage in one or more entrepreneurial activities separate from the types of activities for which tax exemption was granted. Weisbrod found that when governments reduce funding for human services, sales activities of non-profits increases (1988, p.111). Several agency programs might be breaking even, but the one program designed to serve the most oppressed and hard to reach clients, for example, may not. In the corporate world, money-losing products are usually taken off the market, but due to the mission and/or philosophy of non-profits, they frequently struggle tenaciously to maintain these programs. Revenues from sales and other entrepreneurial activities help balance the budgets of these programs. Another advantage of using sales to increase revenues is that these funds are usually unrestricted and can be used by different programs for various expenses (Adams and Perlmutter 1991).

One possible downside to the participation in commercial activities, or what Adams and Perlmutter (1991) call "venturing," is that non-profits may be doing the same things and be in competition with for-profits, creating what Lewis calls "sectoral ambiguity" (1998, p.135). There have also been political repercussions due to this competition (Weisbrod 1988; Ezell and Wiggs 1989; Coble 1999). In addition, Adams and Perlmutter's (1991) study indicates that some agencies—those with a strong administrative base—were better prepared to engage in commercial ventures than others. Based on their study, they also warn of negative consequences that can result from venturing, such as mission drift and the marked decrease of services provided to the poor.

Diverse sources of funds

There are dozens of sources of funds that non-profits have been using to balance their budgets and even generate surplus funds. This section of the chapter is intended to list many of those sources of funds. While the focus is on sources of cash, administrators should not forget about in-kind funds and other cost-sharing arrangements. Agencies frequently occupy donated or reduced-cost space. Volunteers or loaned staff are very valuable as is equipment that is donated or loaned. Many funders require agencies to provide match for their grants and contracts and this can range from "hard cash" match to in-kind match (also referred to as cost-sharing). For example, all or parts of the salaries and fringe benefits of existing staff can be earmarked as in-kind match, or the agency contribution to a shared project, depending on the specific rules of the funders.

Table 11.1 lists many sources of funds by categories. This list is not exhaustive and may be of help when administrators are planning to diversify their funding.

Table 11.1 Diverse sources of funds

Category	Source
Public bodies	✓ Grants
	✓ Contracts
Private bodies	✓ Corporate grants and donations
	✓ Foundation grants
	✓ Confederated giving
	✓ Church donations
	✓ Civic organizations
Individuals (non-consumer)	✓ Donations
	✓ Dues
	✓ Bequests
	✓ Endowments
	✓ Capital gifts
Consumers	✓ Fees
	✓ Co-pays
	✓ Insurance
Fundraising mechanisms	✓ Special events
	✓ Entrepreneurial activities (e.g. sales of products or services, rental income, etc.)
	✓ Investments

Certain types of funding are more desirable than others, as Gronbjerg (1993) explains in the third chapter of her book. Clearly, the ideas offered here should be interpreted in the specific context of an agency and be treated as broad, yet relative, guidance. It almost goes without saying that funders who provide larger amounts and who require a relatively low investment on the agency's part to acquire the funds, are a better target than the converse.

Funding sources that are prevalent in an agency's particular service arena have well-known and established procedures for acquiring and being accountable for the funds whereas funders new to a particular service arena may bring unknown complexities. Funders who are predictable and ensure continuity of funding are desirable. Gronbjerg (1998) gives the example that many fundraising special events are held outdoors and the unpredictability of the weather can impact the amount of revenue produced. On the other hand, continued funding from United Way has, in the past, been more predictable (p.57). While funding diversification is thought to be desirable, it also increases management and accountability complexity, and increases the number of exchange relationships to be maintained.

Funds with few or no restrictions are more desirable than highly and narrowly restricted funds. For example, when an agency sells products or services, or collects rental income and generates revenue, there are few strings attached. The same is true if surplus funds or an endowment has been invested and interest is being earned. Individual donors may, however, attach many restrictions to the use of their donations up to a point where agencies would be well advised to look to other sources. As funders increasingly proscribe specific program activities, types of clients to be served, the qualifications of staff, information to be collected, and performance expectations, just to name a few, the greater the cost and complexity of management.

Management implications

This chapter has already given managers numerous general issues to think about when considering the diversification of their agency's funding base. In this section, more specific management and accounting practices that are helpful when dealing with diverse sources of funds are discussed. In every case, these are practices that are needed once funding has been accepted from a particular source.

Management practices

First, managers should become thoroughly familiar with all programmatic and fiscal accountability requirements and deadlines for reporting, as well as the amount of managerial discretion permitted by specific funders. For example, it is very common for funders to approve a budget prior to providing funds and give management the discretion to move a certain percentage (usually 10 percent) from one budget category to another without prior approval.

Second, the agency should convert all annual budgets to monthly budgets (at least) and determine how much cash needs to be on hand throughout the year so that payroll and other expenses can be covered. We'll call this "agency expense flow" and these projections should project expenses liberally. This will be of little use if the method used is simply to divide amounts in the annual budget by twelve. This may be accurate for items such as rent and full-time staff salaries, but other expenditures require closer analysis to determine when they will occur. Also a timetable needs to be developed of when and how much cash should be expected from every source of revenue. Cash flow projections should be made in a conservative manner. Expense flow should be compared to cash flow carefully noting when cash flow will fall below expense flow. Specific contingency plans for extra cash need to be made to cover those situations such as securing a line of credit from a local bank and/or clarifying board policies on when loans can be taken from the endowment. Likewise, plans should be made either to reduce or reschedule specific expenditures.

Third, managers should develop and use expense and revenue monitoring systems that will provide management with the earliest warning possible that expenses and/or revenue are deviating from anticipated amounts. To do so generally requires a computerized system with a good financial software package. Ezell (2000) discusses in great detail the characteristics of a good monitoring system. The quality of the monitoring system depends heavily on the quality of planning and analysis invested in developing the cash flow and expense flow plans discussed above. The information in these plans becomes benchmarks against which actual expenditures and collection of revenues will be compared. Revenue shortfalls and unanticipated expenditures are never good news, but it is much better to get the news sooner than later. If caught early, managers have many more degrees of freedom to make adjustments. When identified late in the fiscal year, drastic corrections must happen quickly.

Finally, managers should endeavor to maintain the clarity and centrality of the agency's mission and invest in staff and other mechanisms that scan the environment for funding opportunities. These two management activities, while seemingly separate, must operate interdependently. A clear mission influences fund-scanning, in that sources of funds that might take the agency away from its mission are ignored. (This is not meant to rule out creativity and innovation.) Egger sums up the idea when he says: "In today's competitive fund-raising climate, too many nonprofits are chasing the money, not their mission. They're begging for money when they need to realize what they need to be doing is begging for change" (Egger and Yoon 2004, p.xvii).

Agencies whose missions are not central to their organizational culture will change personalities based on the highest bidder. Agencies invest heavily in staff and they generally develop expertise in somewhat defined fields of practice and practice methods. Staff cannot quickly learn different methods and client groups. As Peters and Waterman (1982) so strongly advised in their very popular book, *In Search of Excellence*, "Stick to your knitting." By this, they meant that organizations should know what they do best and stick with it.

Chetkovich and Frumkin (2003) studied the divisions, regional centers, and local chapters of the American Red Cross (ARC) to explore the impact of fundraising strategies on an organization's ability to serve their organizational mission. One division of ARC, Biomedical Services, sells its products in a very competitive market through 47 regional centers. This division operates off sales revenue. The other division provides disaster relief and other humanitarian services through 1,300 local chapters. The activities of these chapters are largely funded from donations. The authors conclude that non-profits will find it easier to stay close to their mission when seeking different kinds of donated revenues as opposed to competition for revenues from fees.

Modern accounting practices

Accounting concepts and techniques provide tools for the management of different sources of funding. McKinney (1995) suggests that nonprofits have been using fund accounting systems for many years, although the language has recently been changed. "A Fund is a separate accounting entity with a self-balancing set of accounts for recording assets, liabilities, fund balance and changes in fund balance. The distinctive characteristics of Funds are that they are established to reflect the wishes and restrictions of contributors, or the intentions of the organization's governing board" (National Health Council and the National Assembly of National Voluntary Health and Social Welfare Organizations 1998, p.11). Funds are sets of assets such as contracts, grants, donations, and gifts. Non-profits are required to classify funds in a manner such that they are used only for the purposes intended by the giver or agency.

When an agency receives a public contract to provide services, the revenue generated from that contract constitutes a fund and it is restricted in that the money can only be used for the agreed-upon program or services. If every program operated by an agency has a specific source of restricted funds, the budget summary would look like Example A in Table 11.2. On the horizontal axis are the different sources of revenue separated into the two categories of restricted and unrestricted funds. Unrestricted funds could be general donations made to the agency where the donor has not designated a specific use for their donation.

As is frequently the case, the contract for a program does not cover all the costs an agency incurs while delivering the agreed-upon service and funding has to be supplemented. The contract may have low allowances for the percentage of funds that can be used for administrative costs, for example. Example B demonstrates what a hypothetical budget would look like in these circumstances. Program 4 uses revenues from restricted Fund A and unrestricted Fund X. Programs 5 and 6 have similar patterns. The unrestricted funds might be revenues from rental income, and/or client fees, for example. The major point being demonstrated here is that practices associated with fund accounting are useful tools to manage diverse sources of funding.

Other accounting practices suggest that expenses be reported in functional classifications (National Health Council and the National Assembly of National Voluntary Health and Social Welfare Organizations 1998). The two major classifications usually used are *program services* and *supporting services*. The National Health Council asserts: "Functional reporting of expenses...requires that organizations combine the

Table 11.2 Sample budgets with restricted and unrestricted funds

	Revenues					
	Restricted funds			Unrestricted funds		
	Fund A	Fund B	Fund C	Fund X	Fund Y	Fund Z
Expenses						
A Example of agency with multiple programs each with a restricted source of revenue						
Program 1	xxx,xxx	0	0	–	–	–
Program 2	0	xxx,xxx	0	–	–	–
Program 3	0	0	xxx,xxx	–	–	–
B Example of agency with multiple programs that use restricted and unrestricted revenues						
Program 4	xxx,xxx	0	0	xx,xxx	0	0
Program 5	0	xxx,xxx	0	x,xxx	x,xxx	x,xxx
Program 6	0	0	xxx,xxx	0	xx,xxx	0
C Example of agency using restricted and unrestricted funds and functional reporting of expenses						
Program services						
Program 7	xxx,xxx	–	–	–	–	–
Program 8	–	xx,xxx	–	–	–	–
Program 9	–	–	x,xxx,xxx	–	–	–
Support services						
Management and general	xx,xxx	–	–		xx,xxx	–
Fundraising	–	–	–	xx,xxx	–	xx,xxx

expenses of particular activities according to the essential purposes—i.e. program, management and general, and fundraising" (p.66). Again, because different sources of revenue may have policies that limit their funds to program services only, for example, other sources of revenue will have to be used to pay for fundraising and management and general.

Example C in Table 11.2 shows an example of a budget that uses both fund accounting (horizontal axis) and functional reporting of expenses (vertical axis). In this hypothetical example, restricted Fund A allows funds to be used for Program 7 and some management expenses, but those have to be supplemented by unrestricted fund Y. The funders providing revenues in Fund B and C disallow any management or fundraising expenses and those are paid from revenues in unrestricted Funds X, Y, and Z.

Conclusion

Non-profit agencies' need for fund diversification is practically a rule in today's policy and funding environment. Effective non-profit managers have in-depth knowledge of this environment and stay highly attuned to shifts and trends so they can position their agency to collect revenues from a variety of sources as they seek the achievement of their missions. Great skill is required to assess the relative desirability of funding sources so that the costs needed to acquire, utilize, and be accountable for the funds do not exceed the value of the revenues for the organization.

When agencies are operating with diverse funds, this chapter has suggested several specific management practices that are necessary to stay out of trouble and on mission. These include developing and comparing expense flow to cash flow, the use of an expense and revenue monitoring system that can provide early warnings and, finally, the combination of fund scanning while staying on mission. The helpful accounting practices of fund accounting and functional reporting of expenses were also discussed.

As Gronbjerg so aptly reminds us:

> Each individual funding source presents nonprofit service organizations with an ongoing series of strategic opportunities and contingencies. Nonprofit administrators—if their organizations are to continue to operate—must manage these opportunities and contingencies with some degree of effectiveness and must understand how they combine and interact. (1993, p.23)

Chapter 12

From Policy Visions to Practice Realities: The Pivotal Role of Service Managers in Implementation

Wendy Rose, Jane Aldgate and Julie Barnes

Introduction

> Our intention is to bring about radical reform of the public services.

> Our aim is to improve the lives of children, young people and their families in this country.

> Our vision is that every child and young person is able to fulfil their full potential.

These and similar statements are familiar pronouncements from contemporary government leaders. Such statements often have a high level of public support and even cross-party political agreement. Achieving the changes required to realize these ambitions, however, is more difficult. Evidence of successful implementation of new policy initiatives or programmes makes an important contribution to a government's record of achievement but is sometimes hard to find, however strong the consensus has been about the policy direction. The question of what supports or hinders the translation of policy vision into practical reality becomes critical not just to politicians and policy makers but to the citizens who are intended to benefit from the proposed changes and to the confidence of the wider public in governmental effectiveness.

This chapter explores some of the ideas which underpin policy makers' perspectives on policy implementation and then examines what happens in the process of translation to service delivery. A case study from the UK illustrates the experience of moving from policy to practice in a local child welfare authority and the factors which influenced the process. The chapter concludes that the pivotal role of first-line and middle managers has been seriously underestimated, and their greater involvement in both the development and implementation of policy change is essential to bring about desired welfare service improvements.

The rational bureaucratic view from the top

> We now need to translate our common vision and commitment to change into real delivery on the ground. (HM Government 2004, p.2)

These ringing words from the 16 Ministers who held responsibility for co-ordinating the delivery of services for children, young people and families in England, introduced a national framework for local change programmes following legislative reforms in the Children Act 2004, under the policy banner of Every Child Matters. This ambitious, whole system reform programme has as its aim the improvement of outcomes for all children in England and 'to narrow the gap in outcomes between those who do well and those who do not' (HM Government 2004, p.4). The five key outcomes are identified as 'being healthy, staying safe, enjoying and achieving, making a positive contribution and achieving economic well-being' (p.4). As suggested in Chapter 9, these outcomes are similar to those in Scotland, put forward by the Scottish Cabinet (Scottish Executive 2005).

Delivery of these policy aims by service agencies is now the name of the game in both countries of the UK. Such a perspective exemplifies the rational bureaucratic view of policy change adopted by governments in the UK and the US for moving from 'intent to action' (Rein 1983). This approach has often been characterized from the policy makers' perspective as ideally a unified, ordered, seamless process of translation from central government down to front-line service deliverers, thereby bringing about the desired improvements.

The process is, of course, not all one way even when there is broad public and professional agreement about the policy goals and objectives. Local politicians and senior managers in public service organizations, charged with responsibility for putting new policy directives into operation, certainly do not see themselves as passive implementers. They seek to influence policy administrators to ensure the requirements are workable, feasible and adequately funded, and that their organizational perspectives from a position nearer the point of delivery are taken into account, feeding reality into the directives. They do this by representation through a variety of means, for instance by lobbying through professional associations, by feedback during consultation phases and in resource negotiations. As a result, there is likely to be some tension for senior managers or social administrators if policy directives are perceived as 'weak', with policy goals and strategies for pursuing them lacking in clarity or specificity (Gummer 1990). Similarly, conflicts may arise for senior managers if they have doubts about the viability or timescales of proposed changes, particularly when they carry responsibilities for ensuring compliance by the practitioner workforce. Such dissonance is given an added dimension with the importance attached by contemporary governments to performance management and the publication of local performance ratings (see also Chapter 3).

It is possible, therefore, to see how a rational top-down view continues to permeate policy makers' thinking in some parts of government about how to bring about desired improvements in welfare services following legislative change. However, since the mid-1980s a more sophisticated understanding of the difficulties of introducing change in public service agencies can be detected among parts of the policy making community responsible for child welfare reform in the UK. In reaching agreement about the problems to be addressed and the policy changes to be introduced, policy design in the different countries of the UK has drawn on the views of research and practice communities and the experience of children and families. Implementation has been integrated into the policy development process, addressing the need for careful planning, preparation and resources. In a new departure for the time, when Royal Assent to the Children Act 1989 was granted in November 1989, it was announced that a Joint Action for Implementation Group (JAFIG) would be established, a national committee of government and external stakeholders set up to plan and oversee the implementation of the new legislation over the following two years.

Such attention to implementation from government administrators was evident in subsequent initiatives and programmes in England, such as Looking After Children: Good Parenting, Good Outcomes in 1995, aimed at improving outcomes for children in out-of-home care, and the introduction of a national Assessment Framework for children in need and their families in 2000, discussed later in the chapter (Ward 1995; Jones et al. 1998; Rose 2002; Cleaver, Walker and Meadows 2004). Evaluation of these programmes has acknowledged the complexity of the policy challenges being addressed, the 'wicked issues' (Clarke and Stewart 2003), the turbulence of the environment in which change is required and the difficulties of changing working cultures and practices (referred to by a senior manager in the case study as being 'like moving a cruise liner – you can't just turn it round'). A more collaborative and negotiated model begins to emerge, although essentially still top-down. The case study later in this chapter provides more detailed exploration of the processes involved once policy requirements reach the service deliverers, including the unexpected twists and turns, and the implications of this for policy development.

Reality is a messy business

What happens when pristine policy, clear in its objectives and proposals for delivery and fully supported by all relevant stakeholders, leaves the hands of central government policy makers and becomes the responsibility of local government authorities or service providing agencies, such as health? Often huge disappointment is expressed as reforming policy makers are left surprised and bemused by the apparent failure of others to deliver the best of intentions. Explanations are sought in terms of 'faulty translations' (Rein 1983, p.69), resistance to change, insufficient local management commitment, practitioner incompetence and so forth. It is argued that the policy was sound but the problem it was meant to address did not go away; the required change did not happen or not at the desired rate; there was not the anticipated level of improvement and better outcomes were not achieved. It is not surprising that the classic text on implementation is subtitled:

> *How Great Expectations in Washington are Dashed in Oakland: Or, Why It's Amazing that Federal Programs Work at All. This Being a Saga of the Economic Development Administration as Told by Two Sympathetic Observers Who Seek to Build Morals on a Foundation of Ruined Hopes.* (Pressman and Wildavsky 1973)

Yet desired change and improvement does occur, even when the problems seem most intractable, or the pattern of service provision appears entrenched, or the resources to fund legislative intent are found to be inadequate. The proportion of children growing up in residential out-of-home care has declined dramatically over the last 50 years in England and alternative family care has developed as the placement of choice in most circumstances where children are unable to grow up in their own homes, in all four UK countries. This is one example of significant change in the field of child welfare which has been supported, although perhaps not consistently driven, by various policy initiatives since the Children Act 1948. In the US, there are also examples of change driven by policy. Fears about the adequacy of funding for an important piece of federal legislation (the Adoption Assistance and Child Welfare Act 1980) did not impede the philosophy and methodology of permanency planning having a significant impact on service delivery in the US (Maluccio, Fein and Olmstead 1986).

A further example from the UK, where there has been a clear policy drive, is the extent of child and parental participation in key child welfare decision processes affecting children's lives, enshrining a principle at the heart of the Children Act 1989 in England and Wales, the Children (Scotland) Act 1995 and the Children (Northern Ireland) Order 1995 (see Hill and Aldgate 1996). The English and Welsh experience, recorded by Aldgate and Statham in their review of 24 research studies on the implementation of the Children Act 1989 in England and Wales, showed significant improvement in child and parental participation, even though much remained to be achieved (Department of Health 2001a).

This begs the question why some policy initiatives are successful and others are not or produce quite unintended consequences. Exploring the processes involved in how such policy intentions are translated into practice becomes critically important in providing some of the answers both for policy makers and for public service organizations charged with implementation and judged on their performance.

The policy process

Policy analysts from both sides of the Atlantic have been influential in developing theory and knowledge about the policy process. From their work, Sabatier and Mazmanian (1979) concluded there were a number of conditions which must be satisfied for implementation to be effective. Policy has to have clear objectives, be well founded, properly planned with skilled managerial leadership in the agencies, fully supported and not undermined by conflicting priorities. However, even if these conditions are almost entirely satisfied, they assume 'that those responsible for administering policy are in a position of total and "rational" control, that implementation takes place in a static environment and in a politics-free world' (Barrett and Fudge 1981, p.18). The real world of public welfare agencies is much more messy and unpredictable.

Case studies allow us, Hill suggests (cited by Barrett and Fudge 1981, p.viii), to examine the interactions between factors in the dynamics of the policy process and the characteristics and impact of environments. Pinkerton and colleagues emphasize the importance of 'charting and analysing these interactions' (Pinkerton, Higgins and Devine 2000, p.17). Since the New Labour government came into power in the UK in 1997, there has been an unprecedented plethora of public policy activity, agendas and initiatives. Government in England has commissioned national research studies to evaluate the effectiveness of new programmes such as Quality Protects and Sure Start (see discussion by Coote, Allen and Woodhead 2004 and Tunstill *et al.* 2005), and more recently Children's Trusts, Extended Schools and Children's Centres. However, there have been few case studies of contemporary policy implementation in child welfare, although this has been an area of intense activity and ambitious aspirations.

The influence of service managers on policy implementation

Consideration of the part which service managers play in influencing the success or otherwise of policy implementation is often rolled up into discussion about 'managing change' and the importance of effective leadership in achieving modernisation and improvement (see, for example, Carnochan and Austin 2002; Martin 2003a; Rogers and Reynolds 2003b; Schmid 2004). Martin (2003a, p.248) observes that 'management of change is a core role for managers in the public services' as the result of policy changes reflecting public opinion and perceived need, and also changes initiated from direct experiences of practice or service-users' evaluation. Rogers and Reynolds (2003b, p.85) confirm that as a consequence, 'managers and workers are always operating on several levels at the same time' in endeavouring to make the different types of changes required of them and, agreeing with Schmid (2004), they need to be both active and reactive in influencing the introduction of change.

Managers' perspectives on implementation

Two studies offer some important insights into the implementation process from the perspective of children's services managers. Brown and her colleagues (1998) undertook a study of structure and culture in nine children's residential homes in England and Wales, in order to identify the essential features of a 'good' home and to clarify the benefits to the children. The model was also then applied by Bazemore and Gorsuch in two residential homes in Florida (see Brown *et al.* 1998).

The research in the UK pinpointed the significance of concordance between three types of objectives or goals. *Societal goals* were those implied by legislation (in this case, the Children Act 1989). *Formal goals* were adaptations of societal goals by children's services managers into local decisions, processes and procedures. *Belief goals* were the reflection of the underlying values of managers and their staff.

The degree of concordance between these three was strongly associated with a positive response of children's homes to change and the likelihood of continuing improvement. This was exemplified by the extent to which managers developed local procedures in accordance with legislation, regulations and guidance, and then demonstrated, through their own behaviour and communication, their commitment to the spirit and detail of those national and local objectives. A high level of concordance created a healthy staff culture supportive of the aims and objectives of the home which, in turn, had a positive impact on the children's culture and the quality of the home. Where there was a level of discord, this produced the opposite effect.

This study provides a useful framework for examining the process of policy translation and for understanding the critical role of managers. It echoes ideas expressed elsewhere in the literature on change management (see, for example, Jones, Aguirre and Calderone 2004) that successful transformation of companies requires the alignment of a company's culture, values, people and behaviours as well as the best designed strategic plan. This conceptual framework was also discussed earlier in this book by Lynne Healy and Barbara Pine in Chapter 4, in relation to ethical social work management.

A second important study by Cleaver and her colleagues (2004) explored the early implementation of the English and Welsh Assessment Framework, referred to earlier in the chapter and the subject of the case study by the authors. Cleaver and colleagues looked at the introduction of the new requirements in 24 local authorities in England to find some measure of the impact of the Assessment Framework on practice in assessing children in need and their families. The study was also replicated in Wales. The study reveals a very mixed picture of general welcome for the new approach, underestimation of the scale of change involved and inconsistency in the early stages in the development of practice. Cleaver *et al.* comment on the impact of the prevailing environment in which these changes were being introduced but conclude on a cautiously optimistic note:

> At the time of the study most councils were characterised by major problems of recruitment and retention of staff, innumerable organisational changes, and low levels of IT

provision, and were having to respond to the demands of the Government's performance agenda… In spite of this backdrop some councils were able to make considerable progress in implementing the Assessment Framework. (2004, pp.265–266)

From their research findings, Cleaver *et al.* (2004, pp.266–268) suggest several essential features for successful implementation. These include some important observations in relation to the role of managers in the process:

- Senior management commitment is required at an agency and interagency level from the outset and strong leadership is essential.

- Recognition is required by senior management of how implementation fits within the local children's services strategy.

- An interagency implementation group of staff should be established of sufficient level of seniority and influence.

- There should be an appointment of a dedicated project manager to plan, co-ordinate and promote the implementation process.

- Managers and practitioners will have different levels of knowledge, skills and competence in relation to the new requirements for which responsive and iterative training provision should be made.

- Managers and mentors need to be trained before practitioners in order to have the knowledge and confidence to support practitioners in adopting a new approach.

- Acknowledgement of and application of resources is required in critical parts of the practice system such as recording and IT infrastructure, as well as to training, monitoring and providing practice guidance.

The identification of critical ingredients for successful implementation (which echo those suggested by Sabatier and Mazmanian, 1979) is relevant to the experience of the local authority in the case study and will be returned to later in the chapter.

A national framework for assessing children in need and their families

In parallel with the study by Cleaver *et al.* (2004), two of this chapter's authors, Rose and Barnes, undertook a close examination of the process of implementing the Assessment Framework in one local authority over a period of two years, starting in 2000. At that stage, national policy development had been underway for almost two years. In April 2000, the government in England and Wales issued national guidance for their countries about the assessment of children in need and their families, requiring local implementation from 2001 by the 150 English local authorities with child welfare responsibilities (Department of Health *et al.* 2000). The Welsh authorities followed a year later.

The purpose of the guidance was to achieve a more consistent and structured approach to assessing the needs of vulnerable children, and to ensure an effective and timely response from child welfare services, as set out in the *Government's Objectives for Children's Social Services* (Department of Health 1999). A conceptual framework for use in assessing children in need and their families was outlined, a distinction was made between different types and levels of assessment, and timescales for their completion were laid down (Rose 2001). At the same time, a set of recording forms was issued as exemplars for agencies to use in the development and improvement of their own recording systems (Department of Health and Cleaver 2000). The guidance recognized that implementation of the Assessment Framework would require major review and revision of local children's services' policies, procedures and practices, and interagency protocols (see Department of Health *et al.* 2000). Existing organizational arrangements for responding to referrals and undertaking assessments of need were likely to require overhaul, and compliance with the new timescales for response would be subject to regular monitoring under the government's performance management agenda for social care services.

The policy context of the Assessment Framework

The introduction of the Assessment Framework was not taking place in a policy vacuum. It had its roots in more than two decades of policy attention, under different governments, to improving services to vulnerable children, which had produced the Children Act 1989, referred to earlier in the chapter. At the time, the Lord Chancellor had described the legislation as representing 'the most comprehensive and far reaching reform of child care law which has come before Parliament in living memory' (Hansard 1988). Translating the intentions of the Children Act 1989 into operational practice continued throughout the 1990s.

The Assessment Framework, which built on the principles of the Children Act 1989, was a significant contribution to that process. Adopting a developmental/ecological approach to assessment was seen as particularly important in addressing growing political and professional concerns that too many children were being funnelled through the child protection system, and vulnerable children and families were not being offered services early enough when they needed them, which had not been the intentions of the legislators (Rose 2002). Practitioners, wherever they were working with children and families, were being asked in the new guidance in 2000 to gather information and analyse what was happening to a child by assessing:

- the child's developmental needs

- the parents' or carers' capacity to respond to the child's needs

- the impact of the wider family, including family history, and environmental factors on the both the child and the parents/carers.

Improved assessment, policy makers believed, would provide a better foundation for effective planning and intervention in circumstances where children's development would otherwise be impaired without the provision of services to them and/or their families. Similar discussions were also taking place at the same time in the US (see the Framework of Needs and Resources for Family and Child Well-Being in Maluccio *et al.* 2002, p.8).

There were several unusual features about the development of the Assessment Framework. It was marked from the start by a high degree of collaborative involvement in government-led working groups of representatives from professional and service organizations on an interagency basis and from the academic community. National consultation was conducted in a spirit of genuine enquiry and the responses influenced significant changes to the final guidance. Careful thought was given to implementation and its implications for local authorities throughout the development phase. Extensive resource and training materials were commissioned for national use, dissemination events held across the country and support provided to local authorities by regional development workers. A chapter was also included on Organisational Arrangements to Support Effective Assessment of Children in Need in the formal government guidance (Department of Health *et al.* 2000) which addressed implementation issues to assist authorities in their preparation for the Assessment Framework's introduction in a year's time. While the requirements were fairly stringent and compliance would be carefully monitored, the programme for implementation was a transparent process and there was a considerable level of support for the policy initiative from across child welfare organizations. The critical question was how they would translate the policy intentions into practice with children and families at a local level.

Browning Forest: a case study

Browning Forest is a small authority with social services responsibilities, which at the time of the study was still relatively new, formed out of a larger county authority following the reorganization of local government in England in 1997. Since two of the authors (Rose and Aldgate) had had a significant role in the conceptual development of the Assessment Framework, they wanted the opportunity to study in detail what happened during the implementation process. A case study approach was chosen because it allowed questions of 'how' and 'why' to be explored in circumstances where the contextual conditions were likely to be highly relevant to the process and outcome and where the developments that occurred were of interest in themselves (Cheetham *et al.* 1992; Yin 1994; Naumes and Naumes 1999).

Senior children's services managers of Browning Forest welcomed the researchers' (Rose and Barnes) interest and generously gave access to staff at all levels in the organization, made documentation and case records available, and connected them with staff in other agencies such as health and the voluntary sector. Between 2000 and 2002, three significant periods were spent in Browning Forest interviewing staff, reading material and observing children's services at work, using a similar methodology to the case study of a multi-agency child care network by Wigfall and Moss (2001). These visits allowed immersion in the organization and a degree of trust to be built up between staff and the researchers. It meant treading a careful path between becoming a sounding-board for staff offloading in stressful situations, avoiding over-identification with managers who were champions for change and maintaining a dispassionate perspective in the analysis of data collected, while providing some feedback to the agency on their progress (see Bosk 1979 for exploration of these dilemmas).

The environmental factors influencing Browning Forest's state of readiness to start implementing the new guidance on the Assessment Framework in 2000 were rich and complex. Browning Forest was still a new authority in 2000. The transfer of responsibilities from the county to Browning Forest three years before had been far from smooth, there had been political tensions, and the inheritance of resources and services by the infant authority was seen as miserly and poor quality. Ahead of its time, the former social services were split organizationally at this point between adults and children, and the latter were located and managed with education and other children and family services in a new directorate. New senior managers were appointed to run the Children's Services. They knew they were taking over an area which had previously been perceived by many as the 'problem child' of the county and they regarded it as an exciting and challenging opportunity.

Some of the legacy from the former county authority soon became apparent to the senior managers. At a time when the government had been urging councils to refocus their children and family services and invest more in family support, the county's social services continued with what was described as 'a culture of high tariff interventions applied at relatively low thresholds of risk'. Children's social care services operated in a 'punitive culture'. As a result, in its first year (1997/98), Browning Forest had a level of statutory intervention to protect children far above the national average in England. The rate per 1,000 of children on the child protection register was 4.61 compared with a national figure of 2.9. The rate per 10,000 of children looked after in out-of-home care from the local population was 62 compared with the national average of 47, and the percentage of those subject to statutory care orders was 79 per cent compared with the national average of 65 per cent. The new authority was a statistical outlier on many fronts.

There were further trends that were of concern to local politicians and managers, including the high number of cases unallocated to a named social worker among those children on the child protection register or who were looked after in out-of-home care. In addition, a large percentage of children looked after were placed outside the local geographical area either in residential or in independent (as opposed to local authority) foster placements. This was not only undesirable in terms of the best interests of the children but also expensive and placing great pressure on the children's services budget. At the same time, an active lobby of parents whose children were subject to care proceedings in the courts was seeking better treatment for them and their children from the authority. Combined with the underdevelopment of community resources to support children and families, these factors locked the authority into a spiral of increasing budgetary overspend and statutory intervention.

The management team endorsed a major strategy in 1998/99 to break into this spiral by stimulating the development of local family placements, bringing children back, where appropriate, from expensive placements to live locally and to maintain their family links, and to refocus services towards family support using redirected resources. The professional culture and practice of the organization would be tackled on a number of fronts as part of the strategy through:

- restructuring the social work teams to reflect the changing focus

- management changes in personnel in key posts

- new policies and procedures relating to referral and assessment.

The latter would focus on the better management of risk of harm, achieving more consistency in professional practice and developing partnership with parents. The announcement in 1998 that there would be a new national framework for assessing vulnerable children and their families was, therefore, particularly timely and pertinent for Browning Forest. A member of the senior management team was invited by Department of Health policy makers to join a national working group as one of the expert professionals developing the new framework, and Browning Forest managers hoped they would be able to implement the Assessment Framework a year earlier than the national timetable.

During this period, which could be described as fire fighting by senior managers in Browning Forest, there were also a number of council-wide initiatives underway to improve services for children and families. Multi-agency cooperation was a strong feature of the new authority, although it was recognized that it worked well at the high risk levels but less well at the level of prevention and early intervention for vulnerable families, where provision across agencies was described as 'patchy and uncoordinated'. The authority's multi-agency network recommended that agencies should commit themselves to shifting their focus from rescue to prevention, without losing sight of the need to continue to provide services for those families who fell through the net at a higher level.

The interplay of these contextual factors was to play an important part in the process of implementing the Assessment Framework from 2000.

Waiting for Godot: March 2000

In early 2000, there was an atmosphere of excitement, interest and optimism about the Assessment Framework throughout Children's Services in Browning Forest. Some restructuring of social work teams had already taken place to reflect the changing focus in assessing children's needs and supporting families, and new assessment procedures had been introduced which reflected some of the early thinking about the national Assessment Framework. Two implementation groups had been set up: one internally in Children's Services incorporating a wide range of agency responsibilities including administrative and financial personnel (although no social workers as they were represented by two of the team managers) to agree how the assessment process would work in practice, to develop a plan and to get the building blocks in place; the second implementation group was multi-agency, to develop interagency protocols and training strategies, as well as to produce appropriate information for parents and carers across the agencies. A training strategy had been drawn up in September 1999, to familiarize the staff with the Assessment Framework, its intentions and operation. It was notable as the first coherent programme of training for Children's Services since the authority had been set up, and was carried out between January and March 2000 within and across agencies. Thus the essential ingredients for successful implementation identified by Cleaver *et al.* (2004) were in place.

Staff had been stimulated by the introductory training they had received and spoke of a new enthusiasm about their professional practice, with comments such as the following from a team manager:

> The training was excellent. I enjoyed the chance to reflect on practice rather than looking at forms and procedures.

They were hopeful that the Assessment Framework would be of real benefit to families and children. Staff views ranged from those who thought it would bring about far reaching change and required a different approach to practice, to those who saw it as nothing new and those who saw it as integrating old, new and different approaches:

> It's not just a checklist but a new way of thinking about assessment (team manager).

> This is a sea change – we are on the brink of something for better partnership rather than just collaboration. We can look for strengths in families (senior nurse).

> The Assessment Framework is not new – it's just a different way of recording – recording under a different framework (social worker).

> I do like the Assessment Framework. It's what we do anyway and I feel it will take us further. The newest areas will be emotional and behavioural development and the environmental and social integration aspects. We will need time to observe and consider

areas such as emotional warmth, guidance, and boundaries and stimulation (social worker).

Their main fears were about the practicalities of Browning Forest's ability to implement it smoothly, how they would be involved in the planning and whether resources would be invested in preparing staff for change. Senior managers reported frustration that their early positive start might be endangered by delay in the Department of Health producing the final guidance and accompanying materials. They had identified the following risk areas in the Implementation Plan of November 1999:

- staff shortages
- possibility of changes in the draft government guidance in its final form
- late delivery of Department of Health documents
- lack of clarity about eligibility for core assessments
- applying the process to children with disabilities
- implementation of new IT systems creating pressure for managers and staff.

A new computerized information system was being developed to support the use of new procedures and tools, including a multi-agency referral form, but there was concern that this could not be finalized until the government guidance was issued. The changeover from the old system was taking place and already having an impact on workloads.

In March 2000, the authority was also facing a series of reviews and changes (either planned or imposed). In Children's Services the list seemed demanding while the Directorate generally was preoccupied in another direction with a forthcoming Office for Standards in Education (OFSTED) inspection of local education services. Children's Services also had to manage the plethora of initiatives and other demands coming from government, such as the Children in Need Census and preparation of a Quality Protects Management Action Plan, which had tight deadlines for completion and return. Managers were also concerned at this time about a range of staffing issues, including significant vacancies and long-term sickness levels, coupled with difficulty in recruiting staff. It was putting pressure on staff and had had a major impact on the social work teams, although ideas were being developed about more creative use of staff with other backgrounds and qualifications. Thus, what had been viewed by service managers as a useful period of consolidation (since the implementation plan had been developed the previous year) was now experienced as 'being in limbo' when little progress could be made, and they were in danger of losing the early gains of staff enthusiasm, as well as facing heavy demands from other directions.

Stormy weather: January 2001

Nine months later, team managers' and practitioners' enthusiasm for the Assessment Framework had visibly waned following a turbulent period for Children's Services. Staff were still recovering from the 'tremors through the whole service' (a senior manager) caused by a £1million budget overspend in the previous financial year. The experience had thrown into sharp relief the continuing need to refocus services and change the direction of policy and practice away from high cost 'intrusive intervention' towards community-based family support services. After a summer of reviews and action planning, the politicians of the local council had finally signed off the budget overspend at the end of 2000, and senior managers were feeling more optimistic about progress in Children's Services. The crisis had had unexpected benefits. The senior managers had taken the opportunity to examine what was happening 'under every stone in the organization' and thought it was unlikely there would be any further surprises.

The subsequent action taken had included a major reorganization of children's services team structures, processes, procedures and systems aimed at reflecting the increased focus on family support, preparing for introduction of the Assessment Framework, creating new energy to revive 'ailing front line services' (a senior manager) and demonstrating commitment to change. Creative solutions to problems had been employed such as setting up a dedicated temporary taskforce to deal with the backlog of cases in the duty system, while new arrangements came into operation. Described by one team manager as 'a stroke of genius', everyone spoke positively about the taskforce. It had enabled the new assessment and referral team to make a fresh start, had signalled the importance of the change to the authority, and had demonstrated a real investment by senior managers in helping staff to manage the change.

With the launch of the Assessment Framework in Browning Forest planned for February 2001, staff had been piloting some of the government guidance, procedures and records. There had been a heavy investment in team managers' training which recognized their crucial role in achieving change in organizational culture and practice, in addition to further training for all managers and practitioners on the Assessment Framework. Further interagency training was about to start and there was a sense of wary anticipation among front-line staff and their managers. Despite the early preparation and training over the previous year, some practitioners reported that they had still not found time to read all the material and to be clear about the implications for their practice (a feature not peculiar to Browning Forest despite the widespread national distribution of accessible guidance and other practice materials). Confusion as well as anxiety could be detected among front-line staff and the messages being received were not always as managers intended, so that some social workers said: 'We don't do child protection anymore' and 'Managers won't let us use child protection procedures'; and that they experienced the changes as 'deskilling and disempowering', and were 'uncomfortable at being pulled in all directions during the transition period'.

Piloting the new assessment processes and records was taking place which had produced a range of responses. There were generally positive reactions to the underpinning principles and ideas although some staff had found the timescales difficult, the format of records 'daunting and cumbersome', 'very repetitive, too bitty' and the process was 'intimidating for clients and difficult to share with the family'. The experience of one social worker completing a record of a comprehensive (core) assessment had become folklore throughout Children's Services as she had written 60 pages and given up in the end. There was discussion in social work teams of these early experiences, which staff seemed to find 'alarming', i.e. the work was difficult. At the same time, the experience was reassuring, i.e. knowing everyone was in the same position.

At this stage, senior managers acknowledged that the latest changes were being driven on a top-down approach. They recognized the advantages of greater front-line staff involvement and participation, but judged that their approach had been the most appropriate for achieving the changes required in the circumstances. They had identified that their priorities were to get the team managers on board, ensure children and families needing children's services were allocated a named worker and to pick up any blocks to implementation where they existed. Team managers were seen as playing a critical role in making connections with the broader national policy developments and in modelling change and commitment to their staff. Senior managers recognized that success depended on integrating change at every level 'so that it is part of what people do, rather than just being about forms or imposed procedures'.

Making it happen: May 2002

Fifteen months later, the atmosphere in Browning Forest Children's Services was altogether different. The change in attitude among staff was palpable and there was a general feeling of optimism about the work to support families. The Assessment Framework was becoming integrated into practice and trainers said they no longer had to convince staff about it. The argument had been won. Issues were emerging about the practicalities of using the Assessment Framework that required resolution (which reflected national experience and was not particular to Browning Forest). Multi-agency practice probably showed least development, despite earlier investment in the cross-agency implementation planning group, and was still heavily reliant on personal relationships in the field. The progress that had been made in Children's Services (and which had been validated nationally by an external review) was being achieved in a context of increasing pressure from staff shortages. The national recruitment and retention crisis in social work was biting deeply in Browning Forest, and staff felt under pressure from the level of vacancies and the number of permanent posts filled by agency staff on a temporary basis (reflecting the findings of Cleaver *et al.* 2004). However, there was evidence of steady improvement in Children's Services despite these threats.

By May 2002, the authority's performance against national targets reflected these local improvements. The number of children for whom there was a child protection plan (and whose names were therefore on the local Child Protection Register) had fallen steadily and there were now fewer than 60, compared with 273 in 1998. The rate per 10,000 children of those looked after had fallen below the national average; 222 children were now being looked after in out of home care, compared with 360 in 1999, a reduction of 32 per cent. The number who were in placements outside the authority had come down to 40, with the expectation that only 17 or 18 children would continue to require such care in the long term. More children had returned home, were in kinship care, local foster care, had been adopted or would be living in local group care facilities. The external review, with a reputation of being thorough and challenging, had commended Browning Forest on the progress it had made, including the greater partnership with families and the higher levels of family support.

These changes had been accompanied by streamlining operational management in the senior team, more delegation of decision-making about transition of cases and allocation of resources to team managers, and the reintroduction of senior practitioners into the teams. Issues of speedier provision of services, quality assurance and monitoring of safeguarding practice, partnerships with local voluntary (not-for-profit) agencies to extend family support services, and IT infrastructure development were all being addressed with energy. Senior managers acknowledged that the impact of these changes on collaboration with other agencies such as health, education and probation required more attention.

At the level of front-line practice, implementing the Assessment Framework was also making headway. There was clear evidence of the integration of the Assessment Framework into processes and practice. Practitioners demonstrated that they had absorbed the language and principles into their everyday thinking about work with children and families. Inevitably, there were varying degrees of enthusiasm, confidence and expertise. Some aspects were causing confusion and anxiety, such as the constraints of the timescales, reconciling undertaking more comprehensive assessments with strict child protection procedures, and the challenge of developing practice in using questionnaires and scales with families to gain more detailed understanding of difficulties. Focusing on the needs of each child as opposed to whole family assessment and recording was found to require a change in practice. Overall, there were indications that practice was evolving and becoming more innovative as confidence grew. Social workers commented:

> The quality of our initial assessments is generally good but we can't complete them within the timescales.

> The first core assessment is very hard but I'm feeling more confident about doing the second one.

> Not everyone understands the holistic vision of the assessment framework and some are still using separate systems.

However, implementation was producing some unintended practice consequences as well. For example, a new category of assessment, in addition to *initial* and *core*, had emerged called a *partial assessment*. This could be seen as a rational adaptation by practitioners and clerical administrators (in their role as street-level bureaucrats described by Lipsky 1980) in order to accommodate cases which were opened and closed on the same day, with no further action required, or immediate referral onwards because of complexity or seriousness, or referral for services to the rapid response team. Another explanation given, however, was that the category was introduced because some initial assessments were too detailed, taking too long and some never completed within the timescale laid down.

A second example of confusion had arisen about case responsibility when the needs of children and families were being assessed on a shared basis by Browning Forest practitioners together with voluntary organizations. Who carried accountability? In terms of the electronic recording system, when was the case deemed as closed or still carried by Children's Services, and what implications did this have for practice and management?

A final example emerged from the inadvertent reversal in the order on the core assessment record of children's developmental needs with that of parenting capacity. The research team was interested to find out whether this led to more focus in practice on parents' needs rather than the children's. Review of five core assessments suggested this did indeed happen, with a minimal amount recorded on the child's needs which did not accord with the circumstances, although whether the order on the record was the main or only reason for this could not be determined. Concern about such level of detail – how records are completed and the order in which information is gathered – may seem a long way from the policy makers' vision of ensuring a more differentiated and responsive service to children in need and their families, but it can be argued that it is only when change occurs at the level of individual staff behaviours and performance that implementation will have been successfully achieved. Some changes may not be in accordance with the policy intentions.

Serving children and families well: November 2002

A postscript to this case study came six months later in 2002, with the report by the Government's Social Services Inspectorate on its inspection of Browning Forest's Children's Services in November that year. It was overwhelmingly positive and, relevant to the case study, it noted that referral, assessment and care planning systems worked well and that performance management and off-line review had led to improvements and better outcomes for children. It had found that most parents whom inspectors had consulted were pleased with the help they received from Children's Services, and the concept of working in partnership with families was well embedded in social work practice. The managers' record of achieving change and improving services was reflected in the performance indicators, new services, stable financial management and good staff morale. Interestingly, the inspectors were impressed by the high level of awareness of managers about their services and their performance. They commented: 'Front-line staff were less aware of the detail, but understood what Children's Services were trying to achieve.' The report concluded that it had found Browning Forest was serving most people well and that prospects were excellent.

Discussion

A critical interplay of factors

The case study of Browning Forest shows that new policy does not arrive in a vacuum, and that, with a reforming government, a new policy directive is quite likely to be one of many policies at different stages on the implementation route, and that the local context for implementation may well be complicated by other urgent matters demanding the attention of senior managers. There may be a critical interplay of factors which either reinforce the process of policy implementation or work against it. In the case of the Assessment Framework, it was part of a wider context of national change aimed at refocusing children's services towards supporting families by ensuring more effective assessment of children's needs and improving the delivery of appropriate services. In Browning Forest, it was fortuitous that these policy aims were inextricably linked, and the Assessment Framework was seen as a catalyst for change, an essential element in its refocusing agenda. The national requirement to introduce the Assessment Framework provided both a focus and a driver for the direction in which senior managers were already intending to take the organization. This may not always be the case.

High level involvement of service managers

It was evident that considerable investment had been made by the senior management team in the careful and detailed design of its strategic and tactical plans for implementing the Assessment Framework, the scope of which covered all the features described by Cleaver *et al.* (2004) as essential for successful implementation. There was a high level of involvement of service managers but also representatives from other functional responsibilities in the organization, who were therefore engaged in the enterprise from the start and able to influence events. The role of team and middle managers was perceived as critical by senior managers, and they were the conduit to the practitioners. There was less involvement of front-line workers for pragmatic reasons, which may with hindsight have limited their sense of ownership of the changes underway. Even so, as was seen in Browning Forest, however sound the strategic plan and however well risks to the plan have been assessed, unexpected crises from within or without the organization may force the implementation process temporarily or permanently off course or bring about delay. It takes skilled and determined leadership to steer the cruise liner back on course.

The multiple steps to implementing policy

The study illustrates the multiple steps through which a policy vision is mediated and transmitted on its journey to implementation in practice. As in the UK children's party game of 'Chinese Whispers' or, in its transatlantic version, 'the old parlor game of "telephone"' (Gummer 1990), the vision and intentions are vulnerable to modification at each stage of the process. Front-line practitioners in the public services are, therefore, critically dependent on their team managers, and on their managers above them, to communicate the new policy effectively and have the knowledge and expertise to translate it into workable local processes and procedures. However, they are also directly influenced by the values and attitudes of their team managers, and the commitment they have to the changes being introduced, as found by Brown and her colleagues (1998). The attitudes of practitioners in anticipation of the introduction of the Assessment Framework in Browning Forest, whether they were optimistic or negative, could be seen to reflect those of their team managers. The social workers with more sceptical or disillusioned team managers expressed far more anxiety, lack of confidence and cynicism about the forthcoming change than their counterparts with positive team managers.

The leadership role of senior management

The senior managers understood how crucial the team managers were to achieving the required changes in practice. As a result their role in day-to-day decision-making was enhanced, both by increasing delegation down to team manager level and by making them more responsible for oversight of front-line workers' practice, for instance by their direct involvement in signing off assessments on the electronic records. There was a risk in this approach that practitioners would see the scope of their professional judgement being undermined and their practice under greater scrutiny. However, the gain was that team managers would have a more positive sense of their accountability for successfully translating the policy intentions into process and practice, which is what happened. Information about performance began to be fed back regularly on a team basis. The new emphasis placed on performance monitoring at team level meant that team managers could appreciate better the link between practice in their teams and their overall performance against national requirements.

The challenges of moving away from old ways of working

In the end, it was through the attitudes and behaviours of individual practitioners in the detail of their work with children and families that the new approach was translated into reality. Hardiker and Barker observe that 'social work in statutory agencies has always been concerned with implementation of legislation, and therefore bureaucratically based' (1999, p.422). It was not, therefore, a new role for practitioners in Browning Forest. However, there were obvious risks as well as benefits for them in moving away from the old ways of working and adopting a more structured, prescribed but broader based and inclusive approach.

The role of service managers in mediating change

The modifications and adaptations practitioners made, some individually and others which rapidly became 'custom and practice' across the wider group, could be interpreted not as deliberate corruption or avoidance but as a way of coping with a lack of fit between the new requirements and the demands of the job as they experienced it. (The scope of discretionary space available to front-line staff is helpfully discussed in relation to implementing needs assessment reforms in adult community care by Ellis *et al.* 1999.)

Service managers at all levels in the agency have a critical mediation role in this respect between the policy designers and the true policy implementers, the practitioners. Gummer concludes that in order to manage the implementation process effectively, the manager should therefore be 'a policy advocate, a negotiator of organizational linkages, and a manager of worker discretion' (1990, p.107).

Conclusion

As Lindblom observed nearly half a century ago 'Making policy is at best a very rough process' (1959, p.86). By following the journey of one policy initiative through its various stages from political vision to reality in practice, the complexity of the process is revealed. Even where there is a strong measure of policy coherence, where policy makers have incorporated implementation into their policy design, and the policy intentions accord with local strategic plans and timescales, it can be a messy business and certainly not seamless and without interruption. It also reinforces the understanding that successful implementation in the human services is reflected in the attitudes and behaviours of front-line practitioners. Their team and middle managers are, therefore, pivotal in the process. They need to be 'aligned and committed to the direction of change, understand the culture and behaviours the changes intend to introduce, and can model those changes themselves' (Jones *et al.* 2004, p.2). They also have a critical role in transmitting the consequences of policy implementation through to policy makers. As Rein identified, policy implementation is a circular not a linear process (1983, p.124). Lindblom concluded that 'A wise policy-maker consequently expects that his policies will achieve only part of what he hopes and at the same time will produce unanticipated consequences he would have preferred to avoid' (1959, p.86). It could be added that wise policy makers must involve service managers in drawing up their plans and must continue to do so throughout the implementation process. Without this involvement, effective implementation which produces real benefits for vulnerable citizens will never be achieved.

The authors would like to thank the staff of Browning Forest Children's Services, and representatives of other organizations, for their help and support in undertaking the case study.

References

Aberbach, J.D. and Christensen, T. (2005) 'Citizens and consumers: an NPM dilemma.' *Public Management Review 7*, 2, 225–246.

Adams, C. and Perlmutter, F. (1991) 'Commercial venturing and the transformation of America's voluntary social welfare agencies.' *Nonprofit and Voluntary Sector Quarterly 20*, 1, 25–38.

Adams, R. (1996) *Empowerment and Social Work*, 2nd edn. New York: Macmillan.

Addley, E. (2001) 'Pensioners spark race row at home.' *Guardian*, 5 May, 10.

Aldgate, J. (2006) 'Ordinary children in extraordinary circumstances.' In D. Iwaniec (ed.) *The Child's Journey Through Care: Placement Stability, Planning and Achieving Permanence*. Chichester: John Wiley and Sons.

Aldgate, J. and McIntosh, M. (2006) *Time Well Spent – A Study of Wellbeing and Children's Daily Activities*. Edinburgh: Astron.

Aldridge, S. (1995) 'Implementing an Information Strategy at Local Level.' In R. Sheaff and V. Peel (eds) *Managing Health Service Information Systems: An Introduction*. Buckingham, UK: Open University Press.

Alimo-Metcalfe, B. (1998) *Effective Leadership*. Local Government Management Board.

Allen, M.B. (1995) 'The ethics audit: A tool whose time has come.' *Nonprofit World 13*, 6, 51–55.

Altman, I. (1975) *The Environment and Social Behaviour*. Monterey, CA: Brooks/Cole.

Alter, C. and Egan, M. (1997) 'Logic modelling: a tool for teaching critical thinking in social work practice.' *Journal of Social Work Education 33*, 1, 85–102.

Appreciative Inquiry Commons 2006. Online at http://appreciative inquiry. case.edu, accessed 23 November 2006.

Arnold, J., Cooper, C.L. and Robertson, I.T. (1998) *Work Psychology: Understanding Human Behaviour in the Workplace*, 3rd edn. London: Financial Times and Pitman.

Arnstein, S.R. (1969) 'A ladder of citizen participation.' *Journal of the American Institute of Planners 35*, 4, 216–224.

Arredondo, P. (1996) *Successful Diversity Management Initiatives: A Blueprint for Planning and Implementation*. London: Sage.

Asamoah, Y. (1995) 'Managing in the New Multicultural Workplace.' In R.W. Weinbach (2003) *The Social Work as Manager: A Practical Guide to Success*, 4th edn. Boston: Allyn & Bacon.

Ascension Health (2004) *Healthcare Ethics – Cases – Karen Ann Quinlan*. Online at www.ascensionhealth.org/ethics/public/cases/case21.asp, accessed 15 March 2004.

Ashton, D. and Sung, J. (2002) *Supporting Workplace Learning from High Performance Working*. Geneva: International Labour Office.

Association of Metropolitan Authorities (1991) *Quality and Contracts in the Personal Social Services*. London: Association of Metropolitan Authorities.

Audit Commission (2002a) *A Force for Change: Central Government Intervention in Failing Local Government Services*. London: Audit Commission.

Audit Commission (2002b) *Report on Comprehensive Performance Assessment*. London: Audit Commission.

Audit Commission (2005) *CPA: The Harder Test*. London: Audit Commission.

Aufiero, J., DeBrito, V., Ferguson, M., Minott, A. and Thompson, S. (2002) *Celebrate Diversity: Cultural Diversity Training*. Hartford, CT: Connecticut Department of Children and Families (DCF) Training Academy.

Austin, D.M. (2002) *Human Services Management: Organizational Leadership in Social Work Practice*. New York: Columbia University Press.

Austin, M.J. (2003) 'The changing relationship between nonprofit organizations and public social service agencies in the era of welfare reform.' *Nonprofit and Voluntary Sector Quarterly 32*, 1, 97–114.

Austin, M.J. and Kruzich, J.M. (2004) 'Assessing recent textbooks and casebooks in human service administration: implications and future directions.' *Administration in Social Work 28*, 1, 115–129.

Baines, D. (2002) 'Storylines in racialized times: racism and anti-racism in Toronto's social services.' *British Journal of Social Work 32*, 185–199.

Balgobin, R. and Pandit, N. (2001) 'Stages in the turnaround process: the case of IBM UK.' *European Management Journal 19*, 3, 301–316.

Banks, S. (2001) *Ethics and Values in Social Work* (2nd edn). Basingstoke: Palgrave.

Banks, S. (2004) *Ethics, Accountability and the Social Professions*. Basingstoke: Palgrave/ Macmillan.

Barker, V.L. and Mone, M.A. (1998) 'The mechanistic structure shift and strategic reorientation in declining firms attempting turnarounds.' *Human Relations 51*, 10, 1227–8.

Barnes, J. (2004) 'Waving or drowning? Tracking performance in local authority social services.' In Social Services Research Group: *Research Policy and Planning 22*, 3, 61–69.

Barnes, J. and Gurney, G. (2004) *Supporting Improvements in Social Care Services: Reviewing the Lessons from the Work of Performance Action Teams with Councils with Social Services Responsibilities*. London: Department of Health.

Barr, H. (2002) *Interprofessional Education Today, Yesterday and Tomorrow*. London: The Learning and Teaching Subject Network for Health Sciences and Practice, King's College.

Barrett, F.J. (1995) 'Creating appreciative learning cultures.' *Organisational Dynamics 24*, 1, 36–49.

Barrett, S. and Fudge, C. (eds) (1981) *Policy and Action. Essays on the Implementation of Public Policy*. London: Methuen.

Barry, B. (2002) 'Culture and equality: an egalitarian critique of multiculturalism.' In A. Shachar (ed.), 'Two critiques of multiculturalism.' *Cardozo Law Review, 23*, 1, 253–97.

Bass, B.M. (1985) *Leadership and Performance Beyond Expectations*. New York: The Free Press.

Bass, B.M. (1990) 'From transactional to transformational leadership: learning to share the vision.' *Organizational Dynamics 18*, 3, 19–31.

BASW (2002) *The Code of Ethics for Social Work*. Birmingham: British Association of Social Workers.

Bates, J. (2003) 'An Evaluation of the Use of Information Technology in Child Care Services and its Implications for the Education and Training of Social Workers.' In J. Reynolds, J. Henderson, J. Seden, J. Charlesworth and A. Bullman (eds) *The Managing Care Reader*. London: Routledge and The Open University.

Bauman, D. (2005) 'Toughest boss in America offers advice on management methods.' *University of Connecticut Advance*, 24 October, 3.

Bauman, Z. (1993) *Postmodern Ethics*. Oxford: Blackwell.

Beauchamp, T. and Childress, J. (2001) *Principles of Biomedical Ethics* (5th edn). Oxford: Oxford University Press.

Beckett, J.O. and Dungee-Anderson, D. (1996) 'A framework for agency-based multicultural training and supervision.' *Journal of Multicultural Social Work 17*, 2, 27–48.

Beresford, P. and Croft, S. (2003) 'Involving Service Users in Management: Citizenship, Access and Support.' In J. Reynolds, J. Henderson, J. Seden, J. Charlesworth and A. Bullman (eds) *The Managing Care Reader*. London: Routledge and The Open University.

Berlin, S. (1990) 'Dichotomous and complex thinking.' *Social Service Review 64*, 1, 46–59.

Berquist, W. (2001) 'Postmodern Thought in a Nutshell: Where Art and Science Come Together.' In J.M. Shafritz and J.S. Ott (eds) *Classics of Organization Theory*, 5th edn. New York: Harcourt.

Besel, K. and Andreescu, V. (2003) 'The role of county-based funders in sustaining nonprofits within rural and urbanized counties.' *Nonprofit Management & Leadership 13*, 3, 253–266.

Bibeault, D.B. (1982) *Corporate Turnaround.* New York: McGraw-Hill.

Black's Law Dictionary (1983) 5th edn. St Paul, MN: West.

Blake, R.R. and Mouton, J.S. (1964) *The Managerial Grid.* Houston, TX: Gulf Publishing.

Bohm, D. (1994) *Thought as a System.* London: Routledge.

Borden, L.M. and Perkins, D.F. (1999) 'Assessing your collaboration: a self evaluation tool.' *Journal of Extension 37,* 2. Online at http://joe.org/joe/1999tt.1.html, accessed 15 April 2002.

Bosk, C.L. (1979) *Forgive and Remember: Managing Medical Failure.* Chicago: The University of Chicago Press.

Boyett, J. and Boyett, J. (1998) *The Guru Guide: The Best Ideas of Top Management Thinkers.* New York: John Wiley and Sons.

Bradley, J. and Sutherland, V. (1995) 'Occupational stress in social services: a comparison of social workers and home help staff.' *British Journal of Social Work 25,* 313–331.

Bright, L. (1999) 'The Abuse of Older People in Institutional Settings: Residents' and Carers' Stories.' In N. Stanley, J. Manthorpe and B. Penhale (eds) *Institutional Abuse: Perspectives Across the Life Course.* London: Routledge.

British Studies (2003) *Population of Great Britain.* Online at http://eltbritcoun.org/index.html, accessed 30 January 2005.

Brody, R. (1993) *Effectively Managing Human Service Organizations.* London, Sage.

Brown, E., Bullock, R., Hobson, C. and Little, M. (1998) *Making Residential Care Work: Structure and Culture in Children's Homes.* Aldershot: Ashgate.

Brown, H. and Seden, J. (2003) 'Managing to Protect.' In J. Seden and J. Reynolds (eds) *Managing Care in Practice.* London: Routledge and The Open University.

Bryant, S. and Peters, J. (2005) 'Five Habits: for Cross-cultural Lawyering.' In K.H. Barrett and W. Geaorge (eds) *Race, Culture, Psychology, & Law.* Thousand Oaks: Sage.

Buchholz, R. (1992) *Business Environment and Public Policy.* Englewood Cliffs, NJ: Prentice Hall.

Bureau of the Census (2000) *U.S. Department of Commerce Economics and Statistics Administration, U.S. Census 2000.* Washington, DC: Bureau of the Census.

Burton, J. (1998) *Managing Residential Care.* London: Routledge.

Butera, A.C. (2001) 'Assimilation, pluralism and multiculturalism: the policy of racial/ethnic identity in America.' *Buffalo Human Rights Law Review 1.* Online at www.nexis.com/research, accessed 3 November 2006.

Cahn, K. and Richardson, G. (1993) 'Managing for diversity in public human services.' Paper presented at the Council on Social Work Education, APM #158, 17 February.

Capps, R., Passel, J.S., Periz-Lopez, D. and Fix, M. (2003) *The New Neighbors, a User's Guide to Data on Immigrants in US Communities.* Washington, DC: The Urban Institute. Center for Mental Health Services (1998) *Cultural Competence Standards in Managed Care Mental Health Services for Four Underserved/Underrepresented Racial/Ethnic Groups.* Rockville, MD: Center for Mental Health Services.

Carnochan, J.D. and Austin, M.J. (2002) 'Implementing welfare reform and guiding organizational change.' *Administration in Social Work 26,* 1, 61–77.

Casey Family Services (2005) *Foundations of Supervision (A Training Curriculum).* New Haven, CT: Casey Family Services.

Chandler, J.A. (2000) 'Conclusion: Globalisation and Public Administration.' In J.A. Chandler (ed.) *Comparative Public Administration.* London: Routledge.

Chapman, J. (2002) *System Failure: Why Governments Must Learn to Think Differently.* London: Demos.

Charlesworth, J. (2003a) 'Managing Unpaid Workers'. In J. Reynolds, J. Henderson, J. Seden, J. Charlesworth and A. Bullman (eds) *The Managing Care Reader.* London: Routledge and The Open University.

Charlesworth, J. (2003b) 'Managing across Professional and Agency Boundaries.' In J. Seden and J. Reynolds (eds) *Managing Care in Practice.* London: Routledge and The Open University.

Cheetham, J., Fuller, R., McIvor, G. and Petch, A. (1992) *Evaluating Social Work Effectiveness.* Buckingham: Open University Press.

Chemers, M.M. (1997) *An Integrative Theory of Leadership.* Mahwah, NJ: Laurence Erlbaum.

Chernesky, R. and Bombyk, M. (1988) 'Ways and Effective Management.' In R.W. Weinbach (ed.) (2003) *The Social Worker As Manager: A Practical Guide to Success,* 4th edn. Boston, MA: Allyn & Bacon.

Chetkovich, C. and Frumkin, P. (2003) 'Balancing margin and mission: nonprofit competition in charitable versus fee-based programs.' *Administration & Society 35,* 5, 564–596.

Chief Inspector Letter and Guidance (2002), Department of Health Performance Assessment Framework. Online at http://www.dh.gov.uk, accessed 23 November 2006.

Chief Inspector of Social Services (2001) Modern Social Services, a Commitment to Deliver. 10th Annual Report of the Chief Inspector of Social Services, 2000-2001. London: Department of Health.

Child Welfare League of America (1993) *Cultural Competence Self-assessment Instrument.* Washington, DC: Child Welfare League of America.

Children Act (1989) London: Her Majesty's Stationery Office.

Children Act (2004) London: The Stationery Office.

The Children (Northern Ireland) Order (1995) Belfast: Her Majesty's Stationery Office.

Children (Scotland) Act (1995) Edinburgh: Her Majesty's Stationery Office.

Clarke, A., Hollands, J. and Smith, J. (1996) *Windows to a Damaged World: Good Practice in Communicating with People with Dementia in Homes.* London: Counsel and Care.

Clarke, J. (2004) *Changing Welfare, Changing States: New Directions in Social Policy.* London: Sage.

Clarke, M. and Stewart, J. (2003) 'Handling the Wicked Issues'. In J. Reynolds, J. Henderson, J. Seden, J. Charlesworth and A. Bullman (eds) *The Managing Care Reader.* London: Routledge and The Open University.

Cleaver, H., Barnes, J., Bliss, D. and Cleaver, D. (2004) *Developing Identification, Referral and Tracking Systems: An Evaluation of the Process Undertaken by Trailblazer Authorities – Interim Report.* London: Royal Holloway, University of London and Department for Education and Skills.

Cleaver H., and Walker S. with Meadows P. (2004) *Assessing Children's Needs and Circumstances: The Impact of the Assessment Framework.* London: Jessica Kingsley Publishers.

Clough, R. (1998) 'Social services.' In M. Laffin (ed.) *Beyond Bureaucracy? The Professions in the Contemporary Public Sector.* Aldershot: Ashgate.

Cm 4169 (1998) *Modernising Social Services: Promoting Independence, Improving Protection, Raising Standards.* London: The Stationery Office.

Cmnd 5730 (2003) *The Victoria Climbié Inquiry.* London: The Stationery Office.

Cnaan, R.A. and Parsloe, P. (eds) (1989) *The Impact of Information Technology on Social Work Practice.* Binghamton, NY: The Haworth Press.

Coble, R. (1999) 'The nonprofit sector and state governments: public policy issues facing nonprofits in North Carolina and other states.' *Nonprofit Management & Leadership 9,* 3, 293–313.

Cohen, B.J. and Austin, M.J. (1997) 'Transforming human services organizations through empowerment of staff.' *Journal of Community Practice 4,* 2, 35–50.

Cohen, R. and Cohen, J. (2000) *Chiseled in Sand: Perspectives on Change in Human Services Organizations.* Belmont, CA: Wadsworth.

Colbert, C.R. and Wofford, J.G. (1993) 'Sexual orientation in the workplace: the strategic challenge.' *Compensation & Benefits Management,* Summer, 1–18.

Colorado Association of Nonprofit Organizations (1994) *Conducting an Ethics Audit: A Checklist for Nonprofits.* Denver, CO: Colorado Association of Nonprofit Organizations.

Committee on Racial Equality (2001) *General Duty to Promote Racial Equality: Guidance for Public Authorities on their Obligations under the Race Relations Amendment Act 2000.* London: Committee on Racial Equality.

Common, R. (1998) 'The New Public Management and Policy Transfer: The Role of International Organizations.' In M. Minogue, C. Polidano and D. Hulme (eds) *Beyond the New Public Management: Changing Ideas and Practices in Governance*. Cheltenham: Edward Elgar.

Congress, E. (1997) 'Is the Code of Ethics as Applicable to Agency Executives as it is to Direct Service Practitioners? Yes.' In E. Gambrill and R. Pruger (eds) *Controversial Issues in Social Work Ethics, Values and Obligations*. Boston: Allyn & Bacon.

Connelly, N. and Seden, J. (2003) 'What Service Users Say about Managers: The Implications for Services.' In J. Henderson and D. Atkinson (eds) *Managing Care in Context*. London: Routledge.

Cooperrider, D.L., Sorensen, J., Yaeger, T.F. and Whitney, D. (2001) *Appreciative Inquiry: An Emerging Direction For Organisation Development*. Illinois: Stipes Publishing.

Coote, A., Allen, J. and Woodhead, D. (2004) *Finding Out What Works*. London: King's Fund.

Coulshed, V. and Mullender, A. (2001) *Management in Social Work*, 2nd edn. Basingstoke: Palgrave.

Cousins, M. (2005) *European Welfare States: Comparative Perspectives*. London: Sage.

Council on Social Work Education (2001) *The Educational Policy and Accreditation Standards 2001*. Alexandria, VA: Council on Social Work Education.

Cox, T. Jr (1994) *Cultural Diversity in Organizations: Theory, Research, and Practice*. San Francisco, CA: Berrett-Koehler.

Cummings, T.G. and Worley, C.G. (1997) *Organisational Development and Change*, 6th edn. Stamford, CT: South Western College Publishing.

Cutler, T. and Waine, B. (2000) 'Managerialism reformed? New Labour and public sector management.' *Social Policy and Administration 34*, 318–332.

Data Protection Act (1998) London: The Stationery Office.

Davis, K. (1998) 'Care, Mental Illness, and African Americans: A Prospective Analysis of Managed Care Policy in the United States.' In G. Schamess and A. Lightburn (eds) *Human Managed Care?* Washington, DC: National Association of Social Workers.

Dawson, A, and Butler, B. (2003) 'The Morally Active Manager.' In J. Henderson and D. Atkinson (eds) *Managing Care in Context*. London: Routledge.

Dawson, P. (2003) *Understanding Organizational Change: The Contemporary Experience of People at Work*. London: Sage.

Deacon, B., Hulse, M. and Stubbs, P. (1997) *Global Social Policy: International Organizations and the Future of Welfare*. London: Sage.

DeCoste, F.C. (2001)'Faith and Political Philosophy in the Canadian Academy.' In R. Beiner and W. Norman (eds) *Canadian Political Philosophy: Contemporary Reflections*. Don Mills, Ontario: Oxford University Press.

Department for the Environment, Transport and the Regions (1998) *Modern Local Government: In Touch with the People*. London: The Stationery Office.

Department of Health (1998b) *Modernising Social Services, National Priorities Guidance*. London: Department of Health.

Department of Health (1999) *The Government's Objectives for Children's Social Services*. London: Department of Health.

Department of Health (2000a) *The National Health Service Plan 2000: A Plan for Investment, a Plan for Reform*. London: The Stationery Office.

Department of Health (2000b) *A Quality Strategy for Social Care*. London: The Stationery Office.

Department of Health (2000c) *Guidance on Health Act Section 31 Partnership Arrangements*. London: Department of Health.

Department of Health (2001a) *The Children Act Now: Messages from Research*. London: The Stationery Office.

Department of Health (2001b) *Working Together, Learning Together: A Framework for Lifelong Learning for the NHS*. London: Department of Health.

Department of Health (2001c) *Making It Happen – the Key Areas for Action.* London: Department of Health.

Department of Health (2002) *HR in the NHS Plan.* A document produced by the National Workforce Taskforce and HR Directorate for consultation. Online at http://www.doh.gov.uk/assettroot/04/08/42/14/04/04084214.pdf, accessed 16 November 2006.

Department of Health (2003a) *Amended National Minimum Standards for Care Homes.* Press release reference 2003/0070.

Department of Health (2003b) *Turning Around 'Failing' Organizations – Literature Review,* by J. Barnes for the Department of Health. London: Department of Health.

Department of Health (2003c) *Care Homes for Older People: National Minimum Standards,* 3rd edn. London: The Stationery Office.

Department of Health and Cleaver, H. (2000) *Assessment Recording Forms.* London: The Stationery Office.

Department of Health, Department for Education and Employment, and Home Office (2000) *Framework for the Assessment of Children in Need and their Families.* London: The Stationery Office.

Department of Health and Department for the Environment (1997) *Housing and Community Care: Establishing a Strategic Framework.* London: Department of Health.

Department of Health and Department for the Environment, Transport and the Regions (1999) *Better Care, Higher Standards: A Charter for Long Term Care.* London: Department of Health, Department for the Environment, Transport and the Regions.

Department of Social Security (1998) *Opportunities for All: Tackling Poverty and Social Exclusion.* London: The Stationery Office.

Disability Discrimination Act (1995) London: The Stationery Office.

Disability Rights Commission Act (1999) London: The Stationery Office.

Disability Rights Commission (2002) *Disability Discrimination Act 1995* (c.50). London: The Stationery Office.

Doherty, T.L. and Horne, T. (2005) *Managing Public Services: Implementing Changes – A Thoughtful Approach.* London: Routledge.

Dominelli, L. (1998) 'Multiculturalism, Antiracism and Social Work in Europe.' In C. Williams (ed.) *Social Work and Minorities.* New York: Routledge.

Douglas, A. (2005) 'Leadership for leaders.' Presentation at the SIEFF Conference, Windsor, UK, 8 September.

Downing, J., Fasano, R., Friedland, P. A., McCullough, M. F., Mizrahi, T. and Shapiro, J.J. (1991) (eds) *Computers for Social Change and Community Organizing.* Binghamton, NY: The Haworth Press.

Duffy, T. (2004) 'Worker vulnerability, the shadow of power in work with court mandated groups.' Council on Social Work Education, Annual Program Meeting, Anaheim, CA, 28 February.

Dunleavy, P. and Hood, C. (1994) 'From old public administration to new public management.' *Public Money and Management 14,* 3, 9–16.

Edwards, N., Fulop, N., Meara, R. and Protopsaltis, G. (undated) *Turning Around Failing Hospitals.* Unpublished paper, The NHS Confederation.

Edwards, R.L. and Gummer, B. (1988) 'Management of Social Services: Current Perspectives and Future Trends.' In P. Keys and L. Ginsberg (eds) *New Management in the Human Services.* Silver Spring, MD: National Association of Social Workers Press.

Edwards, R.R. and Austin, D.M. (1991) 'Managing Effectively in an Environment of Competing Values.' In R.L. Edwards and J.A. Yankey (eds) *Skills for Effective Human Services Management.* Silver Spring, MD: National Association of Social Workers Press.

Egger, R. with Yoon, H. (2004) *Begging for Change: The Dollars and Sense of Making Nonprofits Responsive, Efficient, and Rewarding for All.* New York: HarperCollins.

Elkin, A.J. and Rosch, P.J. (1990) 'Promoting mental health at the workplace: the prevention side of stress management.' *Occupational Medicine: State of the Art Review 5,* 4,739–754.

Ellis, K., Davis, A. and Rummary, K. (1999) 'Needs assessment, street-level bureaucracy and the new community care.' *Social Policy and Administration 33*, 262–280.

Epstein, I. (1992) 'Foreword.' In M. Fabricant and S. Burghardt (1992) *The Welfare State Crisis and the Transformation of Social Service Work.* New York: Sharpe.

Equity Institute (1990) 'Renewing commitment to diversity in the 90s.' Paper presented at the Sixteenth Annual Nonprofit Management Conference, June, Cleveland, OH.

Europe Information Service (2003) 'Anti-discrimination: diversity is good for business.' European Report, 13 November, 351. Online at www.stop-discrimination.info, accessed 23 June 2005.

Esping-Andersen, G. (1990) *The Three Worlds of Welfare Capitalism.* Cambridge: Polity Press.

Esping-Andersen, G. (1998) *Welfare States in Transition: National Adaptations in Global Economies.* London: Sage.

Ezell, M. (2000) 'Financial Management.' In R.J. Patti (ed.) *Handbook of Social Welfare Management.* Thousand Oaks, CA: Sage.

Ezell, M. (2002) 'A case study of an agency's three family preservation contracts.' *Family Preservation Journal 6*, 1, 31–50.

Ezell, M. and Wiggs, M. (1989) 'Surviving the threats from small business advocates.' *Child and Youth Care Administrator 2*, 1, 47–53.

Fabricant, M. and Burghardt, S. (1992) *The Welfare State Crisis and the Transformation of Social Service Work.* New York: Sharpe.

Fabricant, M. and Fisher, R. (2002) *Settlement Houses Under Siege.* New York: Columbia University Press.

Ferguson, I., Lavalette, M. and Whitmore, E. (eds) (2005) *Globalisation, Global Justice and Social Work.* London: Routledge.

Ferlie, E., Ashbourner, L., Fitzgerald, L. and Pettigrew, A. (1996) *The New Public Management in Action.* Oxford: Oxford University Press.

Fernandez, J.P. (1991) *Managing Diverse Workforce: Regaining the Competitive Edge.* Lexington, MA: D.C. Heath & Company.

Finn, J. and Holden, G. (eds) (2000) *Human Services Online: A New Arena for Service Delivery.* Binghamton, NY: Haworth Press.

Fisher, R. and Karger, H.J. (1997) *Social Work and Community in a Private World: Getting Out in Public.* New York: Longman.

Flannery, R., Penk, W. and Corrigan, M. (1999) 'The assaulted staff action program (ASAP) and declines in the prevalence of assaults: community-based replication.' *International Journal of Emergency Mental Health 1*, 19–21.

Fleishman, E.A. (1973) 'Twenty Years of Consideration and Structure.' In E.A. Fleishman and J.G. Hunt (eds) *Current Developments in the Study of Leadership.* Carbondale, IL: University of Illinois Press.

Flynn, N. (2000) 'Managerialism and Public Services: Some International Trends.' In J. Clarke, S. Gewirtz and E. McLaughlin (eds) *New Managerialism, New Welfare?* London: Sage.

Flynn, N. (2002) *Public Sector Management.* Essex: Pearson Education/Prentice Hall.

Flynn, N. and Strehl, F. (eds) (1996) *Public Sector Management in Europe.* Hemel Hempstead: Prentice Hall.

Flynn, R. (1999) 'Managerialism, Professionalism and Quasi-markets.' In M. Hexworthy and S. Halford (eds) *Professionalism and the New Managerialism in the Public Sector.* Buckingham: Open University Press.

Fong, R. and Furuto, S. (eds) (2001) *Culturally Competent Practice: Skills, Interventions and Evaluations.* Boston, MA: Allyn & Bacon.

Freeden, M. (1999) 'The ideology of New Labour.' *Political Quarterly 70*, 42–51.

French, W.L. and Bell, C.H. (1999) *Organization Development: Behavioral Science Intervention for Organization Improvement*, 6th edn. Upper Saddle River, NJ: Prentice Hall.

Gallop. L. (2003) 'Managing budgets and giving best value.' In J. Seden and J. Reynolds (eds) *Managing Care in Practice*. London: Routledge.

Gardner, J.R. (1965) 'How to prevent organisational dry rot.' *Harpers Magazine*, October.

Garvin, D. (1993) 'Building a learning organisation.' *Harvard Business School Review*, July–August.

Geiss, G. R. and Viswanathan, N. (1986) (eds) *The Human Edge: Information Technology and Helping People*. Binghamton, NY: The Haworth Press.

Gibbs, J. (1999) 'The California crucible: Toward a new paradigm of race and ethnic relations.' *Journal of Multicultural Social Work* 7, 1/2, 1–18.

Gibelman, M. (2000) 'Affirmative action at a crossroads: a social justice perspective.' *Journal of Sociology and Social Welfare* 27, 1, 153–74.

Gibelman, M. (2003) *Navigating Human Service Organizations*. Chicago: Lyceum Books.

Gibelman, M. and Demone, H.W. Jr (eds) (1998) *The Privatization of Human Services: Policy and Practice Issues*, vol. 1. New York: Springer.

Ginn, J. and Fisher, M. 'Gender and Career Progression.' In M. Fisher, S. Balloch and J. McLean (eds) *Social Services: Working Under Pressure*. Bristol: Policy Press.

Ginsberg, L. and Keys, P. (eds) (1994) *New Management in Human Services*, 2nd edn. Washington, DC: National Association of Social Workers Press.

Ginsberg, L.H. (2001) *Social Work Evaluation – Principles and Methods*. Boston: Allyn & Bacon.

Glastonbury, B., Lamendola, W. and Toole, S. (1989) *A Casebook of Computer Applications in the Social and Human Services*. Binghamton, NY: Haworth Press.

Glendenning, C., Powell, M. and Rummery, K. (eds) (2002) *Partnerships, New Labour and the Governance of Welfare*. Bristol: Policy Press.

Goffman, E. (1961) *Encounters: Two Studies in the Sociology of Interaction*. Indianapolis: Bobbs-Merrill.

Goffman, E. (1969) *The Presentation of the Self in Everyday Life*. London: Penguin.

Golensky, M. and DeRuiter. G.L. (1999) 'Merger as a strategic response to government contracting pressures: a case study.' *Nonprofit Management & Leadership* 10, 2, 137–152.

Gortner, H. (1991) 'How Public Managers View Their Environment: Balancing Organizational Demands, Political Realities and Personal Values.' In J.S. Bowman (ed.) *Ethical Frontiers in Public Management*. San Francisco: Jossey-Bass.

Graham, M. (2002) 'The African-centered worldview: developing a paradigm for social work.' *British Journal of Social Work* 29, 2, 252–67.

Green, J.W. (1998) *Cultural Awareness in the Human Services: A Multiethnic Approach*, 3rd edn. Boston: Allyn & Bacon.

Grey, C. and Antonacopoulou, E. (2004) 'Introduction.' In C. Grey and E. Antonacopoulou (eds) *Essential Readings in Management Learning*. London: Sage.

Griffin, W.V. (1997) 'Staff safety in human services agencies.' *Protecting Children 12*, 4–7.

Gronbjerg, K.A. (1993) *Understanding Nonprofit Funding: Managing Revenues in Social Services and Community Development Organizations*. San Francisco: Jossey-Bass.

Guba, E.G. and Lincoln, Y.S. (1994) 'Competing Paradigms in Qualitative Research'. In N.K. Denzin and Y.S. Lincoln (eds) *Handbook of Qualitative Research*. Thousand Oaks, CA: Sage.

Guest, D.E. (1999) 'Human resources management – the workers' verdict.' *Human Resource Management Journal 9*, 3, 5–25.

Gummer, B. (1990) 'The Politics of Program Implementation.' In B. Gummer (ed.) *The Politics of Social Administration*. Englewood Cliffs, NJ: Prentice Hall, 92–114.

Gummer, B. (1998) 'Current perspectives on diversity in the workforce: how diverse is diverse?' *Administration in Social Work 21*, 1, 73–90.

Haley-Banez, L., Brown, S. and Molina, B. (2003) *Codes of Ethics for the Helping Professions*. Pacific Grove, CA: Brooks/Cole.

Handy, C. (1995) *Beyond Certainty: The Changing Worlds of Organizations*. London: Hutchinson/ Random House.

Hansard (1988) House of Lords 2nd reading, 6 December, Col. 288.

Hardiker, P. and Barker, M. (1999) 'Early steps in implementing the new community care: the role of social work practice.' *Health and Social Care in the Community 7*, 6, 417–426.

Harper, C.L. and Leicht, K.T. (2002) *Exploring Social Change: America and the World*, 4th edn. Englewood Cliffs, NJ: Prentice Hall.

Harris, J. (1998) 'Scientific management, bureau-professionalism, new managerialism and the labour process of state social work.' *British Journal of Social Work 28*, 6, 822–862.

Harris, J. (2003) *The Social Work Business*. London: Routledge.

Harris, J. and Kelly, D. (1992) *Management Skills in Social Care: A Handbook for Social Care Managers*. Aldershot: Ashgate.

Harris, J. and McDonald, C. (2000) 'Post-Fordism, the welfare state and the personal social services. A comparison of Australia and Britain.' *British Journal of Social Work 30*, 51–70.

Harris, M. (2000) 'The changing challenges of management and leadership in the UK voluntary sector: an interview with Stuart Etherington.' *Nonprofit Management and Leadership 10*, 3, 319–324.

Harrison, M., Mann, G., Murphy, M., Taylor, A. and Thompson, N. (2003) *Partnership Made Painless*. Lyme Regis: Russell House.

Hartley, J. and Allison, M. (2000) 'The role of leadership in the modernization and improvement of public services.' *Public Money and Management*, April–June.

Hartman, A. (1991) 'Words create worlds.' *Social Work 36*, 4, 275–276.

Hasenfeld, Y. (1983) *Human Services Organizations*. Englewood Cliffs, NJ: Prentice Hall.

Hatton, K. (2001) 'Social work in Europe: radical traditions, radical futures?' *Social Work in Europe 8*, 32–42.

Havens, C.M. and Healy, L.M. (1991) 'Do women make a difference?' *Journal of State Government 64*, 2, 63–67.

Hawkins, L., Fook, J. and Ryan, M. (2001) 'Social workers' use of the language of social justice.' *British Journal of Social Work 31*, 1–13.

Hawkins, P. and Shohet, R. (2000) *Supervision in the Helping Professions*. Buckingham: Open University Press.

Health Act (1999) London: The Stationery Office.

Healy, L.M. (1996) 'International dimensions of diversity issues for the social agency workplace.' *Journal of Multicultural Social Work 4*, 4, 97–116.

Healy, L.M. (2001) *International Social Work: Professional Action in an Interdependent World*. New York: Oxford University Press.

Healy, L.M. (2004) 'Strengthening the Link: Social Work with Immigrants and Refugees and International Social Work.' In D. Drachman and A. Paulino (eds) *Immigrants and Social Work: Thinking Beyond the Borders of the United States*. Binghamton, New York: Haworth Press.

Healy, L.M., Havens, C.M. and Pine, B.A. (1995) 'Women and Social Work Management.' In P. Keys and L. Ginsberg (eds) *New Management in the Human Services*. Washington, DC: National Association of Social Workers Press.

Hegar, R.L. and Hunzeker, J.M. (1988) 'Moving toward empowerment-based practice in public child welfare.' *Social Work 33*, 6, 499–502.

Henderson, J. and Atkinson, D. (2003) *Managing Care in Context*. London: Routledge and The Open University.

Henderson, J. and Seden. J (2003a) *Appendix*. In J. Henderson and D. Atkinson (eds) *Managing Care in Context*. London: Routledge and The Open University.

Henderson, J. and Seden. J. (2003b) 'What Do We Want from Social Care Managers? Aspirations and Realities.' In J. Reynolds, J. Henderson, J. Seden, J. Charlesworth and A. Bullman (eds) *The Managing Care Reader*. London: Routledge and The Open University.

Henderson, J. and Seden, J. (2004) 'What Do We Want from Social Care Managers?' In M. Dent, J. Chandler and J. Barry (eds) *Questioning the New Public Management.* Aldershot: Ashgate.

Hersey, P. and Blanchard, K.H. (1983) 'An Introduction to Situational Leadership.' In W.R. Lassey and M. Sashkin (eds) *Leadership and Social Change.* San Diego, CA: University Associates.

Hersey, P. and Blanchard, K.H. (1988) *Management of Organizational Behavior Utilizing Human Resources,* 5th edn. Englewood Cliffs, NJ: Prentice Hall.

Hill, M. and Aldgate, J. (eds) (1996) *Child Welfare Services: Developments in Law, Policy and Practice.* London: Jessica Kingsley Publishers.

Hing, B. (2002) 'Answering challenges of the new immigrant- driven diversity: considering integration strategies.' University of Louisville, Immigration Symposium, 40. *Brandeis Law Review 861, LexisNexis,* accessed 26 February 2005.

HM Government (2004) *Every Child Matters: Change for Children.* London: Department for Education and Skills.

HM Government (2005) *Children's Workforce Strategy.* London: Department for Education and Skills.

HM Government (2006a) *Working Together to Safeguard Children.* London: The Stationery Office.

HM Government (2006b) *Information Sharing: Practitioners Guide.* London: Department for Education and Skills.

Hogan-Garcia, M. (2003) *The Four Skills of Cultural Diversity Competence: A Process for Understanding and Practice,* 2nd edn. Pacific Grove, CA: Thomson, Brooks/Cole.

Hood, C. (1991) 'A public management for all seasons.' *Public Administration 69,* 1, 3–19.

Horwath, J. and Morrison, T. (eds) (1999) *Effective Staff Training in Social Care.* London: Routledge.

Howe, E. and Kaufman, J. (1979) 'The ethics of contemporary American planners.' *Journal of the American Planning Association 45,* 3, 243–255.

Hudson, W.W. (1988) 'Measuring clinical outcomes and their use for managers.' *Administration in Social Work 12,* 59–71.

Human Rights Watch (1990) Human Rights World Report. Online at www.hrw.org/hrwworldreport99/intro/index.html, accessed 25 January 2005.

Humphries, B. (2004) 'An unacceptable role for social work: implementing immigration policy.' *British Journal of Social Work 34,* 1, 93–108.

Hunter, J.E. and Love, C.C. (1996) 'Total quality management and the reduction of in-patient violence and costs in a forensic psychiatric hospital.' *Psychiatry Service 47,* 751–754.

Hutton, J. (2005) 'Making public services serve the public.' Speech to the Social Market Foundation, 24 August. Online at www.cabinetoffice.gov.uk/about_the_cabinet_ office/speeches/hutton/html/smf.asp, accessed 28 July 2006.

Ife, J. (2001) *Human Rights and Social Work: Towards Rights-Based Practice.* Cambridge: Cambridge University Press.

Iglehart, A. (2000) 'Managing for Diversity and Empowerment in Social Services.' In R.J. Patti (ed.) *The Handbook of Social Welfare Management.* Thousand Oaks, CA: Sage.

Issacharoff, S. and Karlan, P. (2003) 'Groups, politics, and the Equal Protection Clause.' *Issues in Legal Scholarship, the Origins and Fate of Anti-Subordination Theory:* Article 19. Online at http://www.bepress.com/ils/iss2/art19, accessed 30 October 2006.

James, A. (2002) 'Survivors seek unity.' *Guardian,* 11 December, p.4.

Jansson, B.S. (2001) *The Reluctant Welfare State,* 4th edn. Belmont, CA: Wadsworth.

Jarvis, P. (1987) *Adult Learning in the Social Context.* London: Croom Helm.

Joint Review Team (2000) *People Need People: Releasing the Potential of People Working in Social Services.* London: Social Services Inspectorate/Audit Commission.

Joint Review Team (2002) *Tracking the Changes in Social Services in England: Joint Review Team Sixth Annual Report 2001/2.* London: Social Services Inspectorate/Audit Commission.

Jones, H., Clark, R., Kufeldt, K. and Norman, M. (1998) 'Looking after children: assessing outcomes in child care. The experience of implementation.' *Children and Society 12,* 212–222.

Jones, J., Aguirre, D. and Calderone, M. (2004) '10 principles of change management. Resilience report.' *Strategy+Business Magazine* 15 April.

Joseph, M.V. (1983) 'The ethics of organizations: shifting values and ethical dilemmas.' *Administration in Social Work 7*, 3/4, 47–57.

Kadushin, A. (1995) *Supervision in Social Work.* New York: Columbia University Press.

Kagle, J.D. (1991) *Social Work Records*, 2nd edn. Belmont, CA: Wadsworth.

Kanter, R.M. (1989) 'Foreword.' In L.J. Spencer (ed.) *Winning Through Participation: Meeting the Challenge of Corporate Change with the Technology of Participation.* Dubuque, IA: Kendall/Hunt.

Karger, H. J. and Levine, J. (2000) *The Internet and Technology for the Human Services.* Reading, MA: Addison, Wesley, Longman.

Karger, H.J. and Stoesz, D. (2006) *American Social Welfare Policy: A Pluralist Approach*, 5th edn. Boston: Allyn & Bacon.

Katan, J. and Prager, E. (1986) 'Consumer and worker participation in agency-level decision making: some considerations of their linkages.' *Administration in Social Work 10*, 1, 79–88.

Keane, J. (1988) *Democracy and Civil Society.* London: Verso.

Kerslake, A. (1998) 'Computerisation and the looked after children records: isues of implementation.' *Children and Society 12*, 236–237.

Kettner, P.M. (2002) *Achieving Excellence in the Management of Human Service Organizations.* Boston: Allyn & Bacon.

Kettner, P.M. and Martin, L.L. (1996) 'The impact of declining resources and purchase of service contracting on private, nonprofit agencies.' *Administration in Social Work 20*, 3, 21–38.

Kettner, P., Moroney, R. and Martin, L. (1999) *Designing and Managing Programs: An Effectiveness-based Approach*, 2nd edn. Newbury Park, CA: Sage.

Keys, P.R. and Ginsberg, L.H (eds) (1988) *New Management in the Human Services.* Silver Spring, MD: National Association of Social Workers Press.

Kirkpatrick, I., Ackroyd, S. and Walker, R. (2005) *The New Managerialism and Public Service Professions: Change in Health, Social Services and Housing.* Basingstoke: Palgrave Macmillan.

Knauft, E.B., Berger, R.A. and Gray, S.T. (1991) *Profiles of Excellence: Achieving Success in the Non Profit Sector.* San Francisco: Jossey-Bass.

Knights, D. and McCabe, D. (2003) *Organization and Innovation: Guru Schemes and American Dreams.* Maidenhead: Open University Press.

Kouzes, J. and Mico, P. (1979) 'Domain theory: an introduction to organizational behavior in human service organizations.' *Journal of Applied Behavioral Science 15*, 1, 449–469.

Kubicek, M. (2003) 'Society.' *Guardian*, 15 January.

Kurz, B., Malcolm, B.P. and Cournoyer, D. (2005) 'In the shadow of race: Immigrant status and mental health.' *Affilia Journal of Women and Social Work 20*, 4, 434 –437.

Kymlicka, W. (1998) *Finding Our Way: Rethinking Ethnocultural Relations in Canada.* Toronto: Oxford University Press.

Lago, C. and Thompson, J. (1996) *Race, Culture and Counselling.* Buckingham: Open University Press.

Leach S., Stewart J. and Walsh K. (1994) *The Changing Organisation and Management of Local Government.* Basingstoke: Macmillan.

Leather, P. (ed.) (1998) *Work-related Violence: Assessment and Intervention.* London: Routledge.

Lee, T.F.D. (2004) 'The goal of culturally sensitive gerontological care.' *Journal of Advanced Nursing 47*, 351–358.

Leigh, J.W. (2002) *Communicating for Cultural Competence.* Illinois: Waveland Press.

Levy, C.S. (1982) *Guide to Ethical Decisions and Actions for Social Service Administrators: A Handbook for Managerial Personnel.* New York: Haworth Press.

Lewis, D. (1998) 'Nongovernmental organizations, business and the management of ambiguity.' *Nonprofit Management & Leadership 9*, 2, 135–151.

Lewis, G. and Gunaratnam, Y. (2000), 'Negotiating "race" and "space": spatial practices, identity and power in the narratives of health and social welfare professionals.' Paper presented to the Social Policy Association Conference, Roehampton, 19 July.

Lewis, J.A., Lewis, M.D., Packard, T. and Souflee, F., Jr (2001) *Management of Human Services.* Belmont, CA: Wadsworth/Thomson Learning.

Lindblom, C. (1959) 'The science of "Muddling Through".' *Public Administration 19,* 79–88.

Lipsky, M. (1980) *Street-level Bureaucracy: The Dilemmas of Individuals in Public Service.* New York: Russell Sage Foundation.

Liptak, A. (2003) 'In Florida right to die case, legislation puts the constitution at issue.' *New York Times,* 23 October. Online at www.dwd.org/fss/news/nyt.10.23.03.asp, accessed 15 March 2004.

Loden, M. and Rosenor, J.B. (1991) *Workforce America: Managing Employee Diversity as a Vital Resource.* Irwin, IL: Homewood.

Loewenberg, F.M. Dolgoff, R. and Harrington, D. (2000) *Ethical Decisions for Social Work Practice,* 6th edn. Itasca, IL: Peacock.

Luke, J.S. (1991) ' New Leadership Requirements for Public Administrators: from Managerial to Policy Ethics.' In J.S. Bowmand (ed.) *Ethical Frontiers in Public Management.* San Francisco: Jossey-Bass.

Lum, D. (2003) 'A Framework for Cultural Competence.' In D. Lum (ed.) *Culturally Competent Practice: A Framework for Understanding Diverse Groups and Justice Issues,* 2nd edn. Pacific Grove, CA: Thomson Brooks/Cole.

Lymbery, M. (2001) 'Social work at the crossroads.' *British Journal of Social Work 31,* 369–384.

Lyon, D. (2001) 'Virtual citizens, speed, distance and moral selves.' Paper presented to New Technologies and Social Welfare Conference, University of Nottingham, 17 December.

Madden, R.G. (2000) 'Legal content in social work education: preparing students for interprofessional practice.' *Journal of Teaching in Social Work 20,* 3–17.

Madden, R.G. (2003) *Essential Law for Social Workers.* New York: Columbia.

Madden, R.G. and Wayne, R. (2003) 'Social work and the law: a therapeutic jurisprudence perspective.' *Social Work 48,* 338–347.

Malka, S. (1989) 'Managerial behavior, participation and effectiveness in social welfare organizations.' *Administration in Social Work 13,* 2, 47–65.

Maluccio, A.N., Fein, E. and Olmstead, K.A. (1986) *Permanency Planning for Children. Concepts and Methods.* London and New York: Tavistock Publications.

Maluccio, A.N., Pine, B.A. and Tracy, E.M. (2002) *Social Work Practice with Families and Children.* New York: Columbia University Press.

Manning, N. (2001) 'The legacy of the new public management in developing countries.' *International Review of Administrative Sciences 67,* 297–312.

Manning, S.S. (2003) *Ethical Leadership in Human Services: A Multi-Dimensional Approach.* Boston: Allyn & Bacon.

Marcus, A. and Marcus, W. (1944) *Elements of Radio.* New York: Prentice Hall.

Marshall, T.H. (1963) 'Citizenship and social class.' In T.H. Marshall *Sociology at the Crossroads.* London: Heinemann.

Martin, L. (1993) *Total Quality Management in Human Service Organizations.* Newbury Park, CA: Sage.

Martin, V. (2002) *Managing Projects in Health and Social Care.* London: Routledge.

Martin, V. (2003a) 'Contributing as a Manager.' In J. Reynolds, J. Henderson, J. Seden, J. Charlesworth and A. Bullman (eds) *The Managing Care Reader.* London: Routledge and The Open University.

Martin, V. (2003b) *Leading Change in Health and Social Care.* London: Routledge.

Martin, V. and Henderson, E. (2001a) 'Values and Vision.' In V. Martin and E. Henderson (eds) *Managing in Health and Social Care.* London: Routledge.

Martin, V. and Henderson, E. (2001b) *Managing in Health and Social Care.* London: Routledge.

Mary, N.L. (2005) 'Transformational leadership in human service organizations.' *Administration in Social Work 29*, 2, 105–118.

Maslow, A.H. (1943) 'A theory of human motivation.' *Psychological Review 50*, 370–378.

McCarthy, J. (1966) 'Information.' In J. McCarthy *A Comprehensive Review of the Extraordinary New Technology of Information.* San Francisco: W.H. Freeman and Company.

McCourt, W. and Minogue, M. (eds) (2001) *The Internationalization of Public Management: Reinventing the Third World State.* Cheltenham: Edward Elgar.

McDonald, A. and Henderson, J. (2003) 'Managers and the Law.' In J. Henderson and D. Atkinson (eds) *Managing Care in Context.* London: Routledge and The Open University.

McDonald, C., Harris, J. and Wintersteen, R. (2003) 'Contingent on context? Social work and the state in Australia, Britain and the USA.' *British Journal of Social Work 33*, 191–208.

McGregor, D. (1960) *The Human Side of Enterprise.* New York: McGraw Hill.

McKinney, J.B. (1995) *Effective Financial Management in Public and Nonprofit Agencies: A Practical and Integrative Approach*, 2nd edn. Westport, CN: Quorum Books.

McLaughlin, T.A. (1998) *Nonprofit Mergers and Alliances: A Strategic Planning Guide.* New York: John Wiley and Sons.

Meyer, M.W. and Zucker, L.G. (1989) *Permanently Failing Organizations.* London: Sage.

Mezirow, J. (1991) *Transformative Dimensions of Adult Knowledge.* San Francisco: Jossey-Bass.

Mika, K. (1996) *Program Outcome Evaluation.* Milwaukee, WI: Families International.

Miller, C.J., Aguilar, C. R., Maslowski, L., McDaniel, D. and Mantel, M.J. (2004) *The Nonprofits' Guide to the Power of Appreciative Inquiry.* Denver: Community Development Institute.

Miller, D.T. and Nowak, M. (1977) *The Fifties: The Way We Really Were.* Garden City, New York: Doubleday.

Milner, E. and Joyce, P. (2005) *Lessons in Leadership; Meeting the Challenges of Public Services Management.* London: Routledge.

Minogue, M. (1998) 'Changing the State: Concepts and Practice in the Reform of the Public Sector.' In M. Minogue, C. Polidano and D. Hulme (eds) *Beyond the New Public Management: Changing Ideas and Practices in Governance.* Cheltenham: Edward Elgar.

Minogue, M., Polidano, C. and Hulme, D. (eds) (1998) *Beyond the New Public Management: Changing Ideas and Practices in Governance.* Cheltenham: Edward Elgar.

Mishra, R. (1999) *Globalization and the Welfare State.* Northampton, MA: Edward Elgar.

Mizrahi, T. and Rosenthal, B.B. (2001) 'Complexities of coalition building: leaders' successes, strategies, struggles, and solutions.' *Social Work 46*, 1, 63–78.

Mohr, B.J. (2001) 'Appreciative Inquiry: igniting transformative action.' *The Systems Thinker 12*, 1, 1–5.

Moore, M.H. (2002) *Creating Public Value: Strategic Management in Government.* Boston: Harvard University Press.

Mosher, F.C. (1987) 'The Professional State.' In D.L. Yarwood (ed.) *Public Administration: Politics and the People.* New York: Longman.

Mullen, E.J. and Magnabosco, J.L. (1997) *Outcomes Measurement in the Human Services: Cross-Cutting Issues and Methods.* Washington, D.C.: National Association of Social Workers Press.

Murphy, J.W. and Pardeck, J.T. (1986) 'The burnout syndrome and management style.' *Clinical Supervisor 4*, 4, 35–44.

Murphy, J.W. and Pardeck, J.T. (eds) (1988) *Technology and Human Service Delivery: Challenges and a Critical Perspective.* New York: Haworth Press.

Murphy, M. (1993) *Working Together in Child Protection: An Exploration of the Multi-disciplinary Task and System.* Aldershot: Ashgate/Arena.

NASW (1996) *Code of Ethics.* Washington, DC: National Association of Social Workers.

NASW (1998) *Code of Ethics for Social Workers.* Washington, DC: National Association of Social Workers.

NASW (2001) *NASW Standards for Cultural Competence in Social Work.* Washington, DC: National Association of Social Workers.

Natiello, P. (2001) *The Person-Centred Approach: A Passionate Presence.* Hereford: PCCS Books.

National Health Council and the National Assembly of National Voluntary Health and Social Welfare Organizations (1998) *Standards of Accounting and Financial Reporting for Voluntary Health and Welfare Organizations,* 4th edn. Dubuque, IA: Kendall/Hunt Publishing Company.

Naumes, W. and Naumes, M.J. (1999) *The Art and Craft of Case Writing.* Thousand Oaks, CA: Sage.

Newhill, C.E. (2004) *Client Violence in Social Work Practice.* New York: Guilford.

Newman, J. (2005) *Modernising Governance: New Labour, Policy and Society.* London: Sage.

Nixon, R. and Spearmon, M. (1991) 'Building a Pluralistic Workplace.' In R.L. Edwards and J.A. Yankey (eds) *Skills for Effective Human Services Management,* 155–170. Silver Springs, MD: National Association of Social Workers.

Nolan, Lord (1996) *First Report of the Committee on Standards in Public Life.* London: House of Commons.

Northouse, P. (2000) 'Leadership ethics.' In P.G. Northouse *Leadership: Theory and Practice,* 2nd edn. Thousand Oaks, CA: Sage.

Northouse, P.G. (2001) *Leadership Theory and Practice.* Thousand Oaks, CA: Sage.

Nurius, P.S. and Hudson, W.W. (1993) *Human Services Practice, Evaluation and Computers.* Pacific Grove, California: Wadsworth.

O'Hagan, K. (2001) *Cultural Competence in the Caring Professions.* London: Jessica Kingsley Publishers.

O'Hare, T. (2005) *Evidence-Based Practices for Social Workers: An Interdisciplinary Approach.* Chicago: Lyceum.

Obholzer, A. (2003) 'Managing Social Anxieties in Public Sector Organizations.' In J. Reynolds, J. Henderson, J. Seden, J. Charlesworth and A. Bullman (eds) *The Managing Care Reader.* London: Routledge and The Open University.

Office for Standards in Education (1997) *From Failure to Success: How Special Measures are Helping Schools Improve.* London: Publications.

Office for Standards in Education (1999) *Lessons Learned from Special Measures.* London: OFSTED.

Open University (2003a) *K303 Managing Care, Unit 6, Managing Environments.* Milton Keynes: The Open University.

Open University (2003b) *K303 Managing Care, Resources Section 1, 7.* Milton Keynes: The Open University.

Orlin, M. (1995) 'The Americans with Disabilities Act: implications for social services.' *Social Work 40,* 2, 233–239.

Osborne, D. and Gaebler T. (1992) *Reinventing Government: How the Entrepreneurial Spirit is Transforming the Public Sector.* Reading, MA: Addison Wesley.

Ousley, M. and Barnwell. M. (1993) 'Reviewing fostering services.' *Local Government Policy Making 20,* 328–337.

Ousley, M., Rowlands, J. and Seden, J. (2003) 'Managing Information and Using New Technologies.' In J. Seden and J. Reynolds (eds) *Managing Care in Practice.* London: Routledge and The Open University.

Owen, H. (2000) *The Power of Spirit: How Organizations Transform.* San Francisco: Berrett Koehler Publishers

Page, R. and Silburn, R. (eds) (1999) *British Social Welfare in the Twentieth Century.* Basingstoke: Macmillan.

Parekh, B. (2000) 'Preface.' *Report of the Commission on the Future of Multi-Ethnic Britain.* Online at www.runnymedetrust.org.uk/meb/the Report.htm, accessed 26 February 2005.

Patti, R. (2000) 'The Landscape of Social Welfare Management.' In R.J. Patti (ed.) *The Handbook of Social Welfare Management.* Thousand Oaks, CA: Sage.

Peace, S. (1998), 'Caring in Place.' In A. Brechin, J. Walmsley, J. Katz and S. Peace (eds) *Care Matters.* London: Sage.

Peace, S., Kellaher, L. and Willcocks, D. (1997) *Re-evaluating Residential Care.* Buckingham: Open University Press.

Peace, S. and Reynolds, J. (2003), 'Managing Environments.' In J. Henderson and D. Atkinson (eds) *Managing Care in Context.* London: Routledge and The Open University.

Pease, B. (2002) 'Rethinking empowerment: a postmodern reappraisal for emancipatory practice.' *British Journal of Social Work 32*, 135–147.

Pedlar, M., Burgoyne, J. and Boydell, T. (eds) (1998) *Applying Self-development in Organisations.* London: Prentice Hall.

Peters, T.J. and Waterman, R.H. (1982) *In Search of Excellence: Lessons from America's Best-Run Companies.* New York: Harper and Row.

Perlmutter, F.D., Bailey D. and Netting, F.E. (2001) *Managing Human Resources in the Human Services: Supervising Challenges.* New York: Oxford University Press.

Peters, T.J. and Waterman, R.H. (1982) *In Search of Excellence: Lessons from America's Best Run Companies.* New York: Harper and Row.

Pine, B.A., Healy, L.M. and Maluccio, A.N. (2002) 'Developing Measurable Program Objectives: A Key to Evaluation of Family Reunification Programs.' In T. Vecchiato, A.N. Maluccio and C. Canali (eds) *Client and Program Perspectives on Outcome Evaluation in Child and Family Services: A Cross-National View.* New York: Aldine de Gruyter.

Pine, B.A., Warsh, R. and Maluccio, A.N. (1998) 'Participatory management in a public child welfare agency: a key to effective change.' *Administration in Social Work 21*, 1, 19–32.

Pinkerton, J., Higgins, K. and Devine, P. (2000) *Family Support – Linking Project Evaluation to Policy Analysis.* Aldershot: Ashgate.

Polidano, C., Hulme, D. and Minogue M. (1998) 'Conclusions: Looking Beyond the New Public Management.' In M. Minogue, C. Polidano and D. Hulme, D. (eds) *Beyond the New Public Management: Changing Ideas and Practices in Governance.* Cheltenham: Edward Elgar.

P.L. 96–272 The Adoption Assistance and Child Welfare Act of 1980. Online at www.info@ask.eeoc.gov, accessed 3 November 2006.

P.L. 101–336 The Americans with Disabilities Act of 1990. Online at www.info@ask.eeoc.gov, accessed 3 November 2006.

P.L. 104–191 Health Insurance Portability and Accountability Act (HIPAA) of 1996. Online at www/nhs/gov/ocr/combinedregtext.pdf, accessed 3 November 2006.

Pollitt, C. (1993) *Managerialism and the Public Services,* 2nd edn. Oxford: Basil Blackwell.

Pollitt, C. (2003) *The Essential Public Manager.* Maidenhead: Open University Press.

Pollitt, C. and Bouckaert, G. (1995) *Quality Improvement in European Public Services: Concepts, Cases and Commentary.* London: Sage.

Pollitt, C. and Bouckaert, G. (2000) *Public Management Reform: A Comparative Analysis.* Oxford: Oxford University Press.

Postman, N. (1992) *Technology.* New York: Vintage.

Power, C. and Dickey, C. (2003) 'Generation M: Muslims asserting themselves in European countries.' *Newsweek International 48*, 1 December, 26–27.

Pressman, J.L. and Wildavsky, A. (1973) *Implementation.* Los Angeles: University of California Press.

Preston-Shoot, M., Roberts, G. and Vernon, S. (1998a) 'Social work law: from interaction to integration.' *Journal of Social Welfare and Family Law 20*, 65–80.

Preston-Shoot, M., Roberts, G. and Vernon, S. (1998b) 'Working together in social work law.' *Journal of Social Welfare and Family Law 20*, 137–150.

Prevatt-Goldstein, B. (2002) 'Catch 22: Black workers' role in equal opportunities for black service users.' *British Journal of Social Work 32*, 765–778.

Pslek, P.E. and Greenhalgh, T. (2001) 'The challenge of complexity in health care.' *British Medical Journal 323*, 15 September, 625.

Quinn, R.E. (1984) 'Applying the Competing Values Approach to Leadership: Toward an Integrative Framework.' In J.G. Hunt, D. Hosking, C. Schreisheim and R. Stewart (eds) *Leaders and Managers International Perspectives on Managerial Behavior and Leadership.* Elmsford, NY: Pergamon.

Race Relations Act 1976. London: Her Majesty's Stationery Office.

Radford, A. (2004) Online at http://www.aradford.co.uk, accessed 23 September 2006

Raisbeck, B.B. (1977) *Law and the Social Worker.* London: Macmillan.

Read, J. (2003) 'Mental Health Service Users as Managers.' In J. Reynolds, J. Henderson, J. Seden, J. Charlesworth and A. Bullman, (eds) *The Managing Care Reader.* London: Routledge and The Open University.

Reamer, F.G. (1987) 'Ethics committees in social work.' *Social Work*, May–June, 188–192.

Reamer, F.G. (2000) 'Administrative Ethics.' In R. Patti (ed.) *The Handbook of Social Welfare Management.* Thousand Oaks, CA: Sage.

Reamer, F.G. (2001) *The Social Work Ethics Audit: A Risk Management Tool.* Washington, DC: National Association of Social Workers Press.

Reed Business Information (2003) 'An affirmative action: food for thought: Michel Landel wins Diversity Best Practices CEO Leadership Award.' *Restaurants & Institutions*, 15 November.

Rein, M. (1983) *From Policy to Practice.* London: Macmillan.

Reisman, B. (1986) 'Management theory and agency management: a new compatibility.' *Social Casework: The Journal of Contemporary Social Work 67*, 7, 387–393.

Richardson, J. and Gutch, R. (1998) 'Fears Betrayed: Initial Impression of Contracting for United Kingdom Social Services.' In M. Gibelman and H.W. Demone Jr (eds) *The Privatization of Human Services: Policy and Practice Issues.* New York: Springer.

Robbins, S.P., Chatterjee, P. and Canda, E.R. (1998) *Contemporary Human Behavior Theory: A Critical Perspective.* Boston: Allyn & Bacon.

Robson, J. and Gomph, K. (1994) 'Management by objecting to tradition.' *Journal of Child and Youth Care 9*, 3, 27–32.

Roche, M. (1987) 'Citizenship, social theory and social change.' *Theory and Society 16*, 363–399.

Rogers, A. and Reynolds J. (2003a) 'Leadership and Vision.' In J. Seden and J. Reynolds (eds) *Managing Care in Practice.* London: Routledge and The Open University.

Rogers, A. and Reynolds, J. (2003b) 'Managing Change.' In J. Seden and J. Reynolds (eds) *Managing Care in Practice.* London: Routledge and The Open University.

Rose, W. (2001) 'Assessing Children in Need and Their Families: An Overview of the Framework.' In J. Horwarth (ed.) *The Child's World.* London: Jessica Kingsley Publishers.

Rose, W. (2002) 'Achieving Better Outcomes for Children and Families by Improving Assessment of Need.' In T. Vecchiato, A.N. Maluccio and C. Canali (eds) *Evaluation in Child and Family Services.* New York: Aldine de Gruyter.

Rubin, H. (2002) *Collaborative Leadership Developing Effective Partnerships in Communities and School.* Thousand Oaks: Corwin Press.

Rubio, D.M., Birkenmaier, J. and Berg-Weger, M. (2000) 'Social welfare policy changes and social work practice.' *Advances in Social Work 1*, 2, 177–186.

Sabatier, P. and Mazmanian, D. (1979) 'The conditions of effective implementation: a guide to accomplishing policy objectives.' *Policy Analysis 5*, Fall, 481–504. San Francisco: Berrett-Koehler.

Sands, R. and Nuccio, K. (1992) 'Postmodern feminist theory and social work.' *Social Work 37*, 6, 489–494.

Sang, B. and O'Neill, S. (2001) 'Patient involvement in clinical governance.' *British Journal of Health Care Management 7*, 7, 278–281.

Scalera, N.R. (1995) 'The critical need for specialized health and safety measures for child welfare workers.' *Child Welfare 74*, 337–350.

Scapp, R. (2004) 'U.S. values and education: a dialogue.' *The Key Reporter: Newsletter of the Phi Beta Kappa Society 69*, 2, 5, 7 and 13.

Schein, E.H. (1992) *Organizational Culture and Leadership*. San Francisco: Jossey-Bass.

Schmid, H. (2004) 'Organization-environment relationships: theory for management practice in human service organizations.' *Administration in Social Work 28*, 1, 97–113.

Schoech, D. (1990) *Human Services Computing: Concepts and Applications*. Binghamton, NY: The Haworth Press.

Schoech, D. (1999) *Human Services Technology: Understanding, Designing, and Implementing Computer and Internet Applications in the Social Services*. Binghamton, NY: The Haworth Press.

Scottish Executive (2001) *For Scotland's Children*. Edinburgh: The Stationery Office.

Scottish Executive (2005) *Getting it Right for Every Child*. Edinburgh: Scottish Executive.

Scottish Office (1999) *Aiming for Excellence, Modernising Social Work Services in Scotland*. Edinburgh: The Stationery Office.

Seden, J. (2003) 'Managers and Their Organisations.' In J. Henderson and D. Atkinson (eds) *Managing Care in Context*. London: Routledge and The Open University.

Seden, J. and Katz, J. (2003) 'Managing Significant Life Events.' In J. Seden and J. Reynolds (eds) *Managing Care in Practice*. London: Routledge and The Open University.

Seligman, D. (1973) 'How equal opportunity turned into employment quotas.' *Fortune 162*, March.

Senge, P.M. (1990) *The Fifth Discipline: the Art and Practice of the Learning Organization*. New York: Currency Doubleday.

Sex Discrimination Act (1975) London: Her Majesty's Stationery Office.

Shachar, A. (2001) 'Two critiques of multiculturalism.' *Cardozo Law Review 253*.

Shardlow, S.M., Davis, C., Johnson, M., Murphy, M., Long, T. and Race, D. (2004) *Education and Training for Inter-Agency Working: New Standards*. Salford: Salford Centre for Social Work Research.

Shera, W. (1995) 'Organizational empowerment.' Paper presented at the annual program meeting of the Council on Social Work Education, San Diego, CA, 2 March.

Sims, H.P. Jr and Lorenzi, P. (1992) *The New Leadership Paradigm: Social Learning and Cognition in Organizations*. Newberry Park, CA: Sage.

Skelcher, C. (2003) *Learning from the Experience of Recovery: A Theoretical Framework for Understanding Poor Performance and Recovery in Local Government*. Birmingham: University of Birmingham, Inlogov.

Smith, S.R. (1998) 'Contracting for Alcohol and Drug Treatment: Implications for Public Management.' In M. Gibelman and H.W. Demone Jr (eds) *The Privatization of Human Services: Policy and Practice Issues*. New York: Springer.

Smith, S.R. and Lipsky, M. (1993) *Nonprofits for Hire: The Welfare State in the Age of Contracting*. Cambridge, MA: Harvard University Press.

Sommer, R. (1969) *Personal Space: the Behavioral Basis of Design*. Upper Saddle River: Prentice-Hall.

Spath, R. and Pine, B.A. (2004) 'Using the case study approach for improved program evaluations.' *Child and Family Social Work 9*, 1, 57–63.

Spencer, P.C. and Munch, S. (2003) 'Client violence toward social workers: the role of management in community mental health programs.' *Social Work 48*, 532–544.

Strom-Gottfried, K. (2003) 'Understanding adjudication: origins, targets and outcomes of ethics complaints.' *Social Work 48*, 1, 85–94.

Tang, K. (2003) 'Combating racial discrimination: the effectiveness of an international legal regime.' *British Journal of Social Work 33*, 17–29.

Taylor, G. (1993) 'Challenges from the margin.' In M. Lymberg (2001) 'Social work at a crossroads.' *British Journal of Social Work 31*, 369-84.

Taylor, I. (ed.) (1990) *The Social Effects of Free Market Policies: An International Text*. Hemel Hempstead: Harvester Wheatsheaf.

Thoburn, J., Lewis, A. and Shemmings, D. (1995) *Paternalism or Partnership? Family Involvement in the Child Protection Process.* London: The Stationery Office.

Thomas, E. (2005) 'People and politics.' Online at www.bbcnews.org, accessed 4 March 2005.

Thompson, N. (2002) 'Social movements, social justice and social work.' *British Journal of Social Work* 32, 711–722.

TOPSS (Training Organisation for the Personal Social Services) (1999) Modernising the Social Care Workforce: the First National Training Strategy for England, A Consultation Document. Online at www.topss.org.uk, accessed March 2002.

Tunstill, J., Aldgate, J. and Hughes, M. (2006) *Improving Children's Services Networks: Lessons from Family Centres.* London: Jessica Kingsley Publishers.

Tunstill, J., Allnock, D., Akhurst, S. and Garbers, C. (2005) 'Sure Start local programmes: implications of case study data from the national evaluation of Sure Start.' *Children and Society 19*, 158–171.

Tyler, T.R. (1992) 'The psychological consequences of judicial procedures: implications for civil commitment hearings.' *Southern Methodist University Law Review 46*, 433–445.

United Nations (1998) *Racism, Racial Discrimination, Xenophobia and Related Intolerance.* Report by Gele-Ahanhanzo, special rapporteur on contemporary forms of racism, racial discrimination, xenophobia and related intolerance. New York: United Nations.

US Census Bureau (2006) *American Fact Finder. 2004 American Community Survey Data Profile Highlights.* Online at http://factfinder.census.gov/, accessed 4 April 2006.

US Department of Health and Human Services (2003) 'Protecting the privacy of patients' health information,' HHS HIPAA Fact Sheet issued April 14, 2003. Online at www.hhs.gov/ocr/hipaa/ (accessed 21 June 2006).

US Department of Health and Human Services (2004) *Surgeon General's Report, 1999.* Washington, DC: Government Printing Office.

US Department of Justice (1997). 'Commonly asked questions about child care centers and the Americans with Disabilities Act' Civil Rights Division. Online at www.usdoj.gov/crt/ada/childq%26a.htm (accessed 20 June 2006).

Vaill, P.B. (1997) 'The learning challenges of leadership.' In *The Balance of Leadership and Fellowship: Leadership and Fellowship Focus Group.* College Park, MD: Kellogg Leadership Studies Project.

Vandervelde, M. (1979) 'The semantics of participation.' *Administration in Social Work 3*, 1, 65–77.

Van Vlissingen, R.F. (1993) 'Beyond democracy, beyond consensus.' *At Work: Stories of Tomorrow's Workplace 2*, 3, 11–13.

Veitch, R. and Arkkelin, D. (1995) *Environmental Psychology: An Interdisciplinary Perspective.* London: Prentice Hall.

Vernon, S. (1993) *Social Work and the Law.* London: Butterworths.

Vernon, S. (2005) *Social Work and the Law,* 3rd edn. Oxford: Oxford University Press.

Vinokur-Kaplan, D., Jayaratne, S. and Chess, W.A. (1994) 'Job satisfaction and retention of social workers in public agencies, non-profit agencies and private practice: the impact of workplace conditions and motivators.' *Administration in Social Work 18*, 3, 93–121.

Wahl, M. (1993) *Evaluation Outcomes for Family Service Programs.* Milwaukee, WI: Family Service America.

Waine, D. and Henderson, J. (2003) 'Managers, Managing and Managerialism.' In J. Henderson and D. Atkinson (eds) *Managing Care in Context.* London: Routledge and The Open University.

Ward, A. (2003) 'Managing the Team.' In J. Seden and J. Reynolds (eds) *Managing Care in Practice.* London: Routledge.

Ward, H. (ed.) (1995) *Looking After Children: Research into Practice.* London: The Stationery Office.

Warsh, R., Pine, B.A. and Maluccio, A.N. (1996) *Reuniting Families: A Guide to Strengthening Family Reunification.* Washington DC: Child Welfare League of America.

Watkins, J.M. and Mohr, B.J. (2001) *Appreciative Inquiry: Change at the Speed of Imagination.* San Fransisco: Jossey-Bass Pfeiffer.

Webster's Dictionary (1996), New York: Random House.

Weil, M. and Sanchez, E. (1983) 'The impact of the Tarasoff decision on clinical social work practice.' *Social Service Review 57*, 112–124.

Weinbach, R.W. (2003) *The Social Worker as Manager: A Practical Guide to Success*, 4th edn. Boston: Allyn & Bacon.

Weiner, M.E. (1990) 'Managing Computers and Information'. In W.E. Weiner *Human Services Management: Analysis and Applications*, 2nd edn. Belmont, CA: Wadsworth.

Weisbord, M.R. (1987) *Productive Workplaces: Organizing and Managing for Dignity, Meaning, and Community*. San Francisco: Jossey-Bass.

Weisbrod, B.A. (1988) *The Nonprofit Economy*. Cambridge, MA: Harvard University Press.

Wexler, D.B. (1990) *Therapeutic Jurisprudence: The Law as a Therapeutic Agent*. Durham, NC: Carolina Academic Press.

Wheatley, M. and Kellner-Rogers, M. (1998) 'Turning to One Another.' In *Y2K Citizens Action Guide*. Minneapolis: Lens Publishing Company.

Whipp, R., Kirkpatrick, I., Kitchener, M. and Owen, D. (1998) 'The External Management of Children's Homes by Local Authorities.' In Department of Health, *Caring for Children Away from Home: Messages from Research*. Chichester: John Wiley and Sons.

Whitaker, D., Archer, L. and Hicks, L. (1998) *Working in Children's Homes, Challenges and Complexities*. Chichester: John Wiley and Sons.

White, V. and Harris, J. (eds) (2001) *Developing Good Practice in Community Care*. London: Jessica Kingsley Publishers.

White, V. and Harris, J. (eds) (2004) *Developing Good Practice in Children's Services*. London: Jessica Kingsley Publishers.

Wiener, N. (1965) *Cybernetics: Or Control and Communication in the Animal and the Machine*. Cambridge, MA: MIT Press.

Wigfall, V. and Moss, P. (2001) *More than the Sum of its Parts? A Study of a Multi-agency Child Care Network*. London: National Children's Bureau and Joseph Rowntree Foundation.

Willcocks, D., Peace, S. and Kellaher, L. (1987) *Private Lives in Public Places*. London: Tavistock.

Williams, F. (1996) 'Postmodernism, Feminism and Difference.' In N. Parton (ed.) *Social Theory, Social Change and Social Work*. London: Routledge.

Willis, E. (1992) 'Managing Volunteers.' In J. Batsleer, C. Cornforth and R. Paton (eds) *Issues in Voluntary and Non-profit Management*. PLACE: Addison Wesley.

Wodarski, J.S. and Palmer, A. (1985) 'Management application of behavioral science knowledge.' *Social Casework: The Journal of Contemporary Social Work*, May.

Wolfe, C. (2001) 'Good cause found to be no excuse in ethics case.' Associated Press Story, 2 June. Online at www.enquirer.com/editions/2001/0102/loc_good_cause_found_to.html (assessed 15 March 2004).

Wood, S., de Menezes, L. and Lasaosa, A. (2001) 'High involvement management and performance.' Paper given at seminar at the Center for Labour Market Studies, University of Leicester, May.

Yin, R.K. (1994) *Case Study Research*, 2nd edn. Thousand Oaks, CA: Sage.

Yukl, G.A. (1989) 'Managerial leadership: a review of theory and research.' *Yearly Review of Management 15*, 251–289.

Contributors

Jane Aldgate is Professor of Social Care in the Faculty of Health and Social Care at The Open University.

Julie Barnes is an Independent Social Care Consultant.

Mark Ezell is Professor at the University of Kansas School of Social Welfare.

John Harris is Professor in the School of Health and Social Studies at the University of Warwick.

Lynne M. Healy is Professor at the University of Connecticut School of Social Work.

Robert G. Madden is Professor of Social Work at Saint Joseph College.

Barris P. Malcolm is Associate Professor at the University of Connecticut School of Social Work.

Vivien Martin is Principal Lecturer in Management Development in the Business School at the University of Brighton.

Sheila Peace is Professor of Social Gerontology and Associate Dean for Research in the Faculty of Health and Social Care at The Open University.

Peter Petrella is Program Director of Organizational and Skill Development of the University of Connecticut School of Social Work's training contract at the Connecticut Department of Social Services.

Barbara A. Pine is Professor Emerita at the University of Connecticut School of Social Work, West Hartford, Connecticut, USA.

Jill Reynolds is Senior Lecturer in The Faculty of Health and Social Care at The Open University.

Wendy Rose is Senior Research Fellow in the Faculty of Health and Social Care at The Open University.

Trish Ross is Sure Start Children's Centre Manager, Nottinghamshire County Council.

Janet Seden is Senior Lecturer in the Faculty of Health and Social Care at The Open University.

Myron E. Weiner is Professor Emeritus at the University of Connecticut School of Social Work.

Subject Index

Author Index